The Morrison Government

DR BRENDAN MCCAFFRIE is a senior lecturer in the Faculty of Business, Government and Law, University of Canberra.

MICHELLE GRATTAN is a professorial fellow at the University of Canberra and chief political correspondent for *The Conversation*.

DR CHRIS WALLACE is a professor in the Faculty of Business, Government and Law, University of Canberra. She is the author of *How to Win an Election* and *Political Lives: Australian prime ministers and their biographers*.

The Morrison Government

Governing through crisis, 2019–2022

Australian Commonwealth Administration series

Edited by Brendan McCaffrie,
Michelle Grattan and Chris Wallace

UNSW PRESS

A UNSW Press book

Published by
NewSouth Publishing
University of New South Wales Press Ltd
University of New South Wales
Sydney NSW 2052
AUSTRALIA
https://unsw.press/

A catalogue record for this book is available from the National Library of Australia

ISBN   9781742237886 (paperback)
        9781742238715 (ebook)
        9781742239651 (ePDF)

Internal design Josephine Pajor-Markus
Cover design Luke Causby, Blue Cork
Cover image Australian Prime Minister Scott Morrison speaks during a press conference at Parliament House, Canberra, Thursday, January 6, 2022. AAP Image/Lukas Coch

UNSW
SYDNEY

CONTENTS

Leadership

ACKNOWLEDGMENTS

This is the 14th volume in the *Australian Commonwealth Administration* series, which commenced with the end of the first Hawke Government in 1984, and has analysed each federal government administration over the past 38 years. The editors wish to thank the University of Canberra, and its Vice Chancellor Paddy Nixon, for supporting this project.

We also wish to acknowledge and thank Professor Lain Dare, for helping to keep the project running while Brendan was absent on parental leave, and Renée Otmar and Jocelyn Hungerford for their detailed and precise copy-editing work at different stages of the project.

We have been delighted to partner with NewSouth Publishing for this volume. Emma Hutchinson and the team at NewSouth have been professional, efficient and responsive throughout the project, which has made the process so enjoyable for us as editors, and has ensured an excellent final publication.

Naturally, the book is only possible thanks to the wonderful efforts of the contributing authors. We were thrilled to have assembled such expert contributors, and we would like to thank each author for being collaborative, responsive and easy to work with throughout the process.

We wish to acknowledge the Traditional Owners of the lands where the authors and editors of this book live and work. We pay our respect to all Aboriginal and Torres Strait Islander people as the First Peoples of Australia.

1

THE MORRISON GOVERNMENT, 2019–2022: A STORY OF CRISIS AND CHARACTER

Michelle Grattan

The term of the Morrison Government between the 2019 and 2022 elections was dominated by the management of the COVID-19 pandemic: a crisis of massive scale. The pandemic was all-consuming, demanding complex responses in both health and economic policies. At least for the duration, it transformed how Australia's federation operated, albeit without any rewriting of the formal distribution of power.

'Governance has increasingly become a matter of crisis management. Crises provide real-world "stress tests" to the resilience of political systems and the crisis management capacities of leaders. They play out against a backdrop of public expectations [...] that can be very challenging to meet' (Boin et al, 2017). In the early days of the COVID-19 pandemic, Australia's political leaders struggled in semi-ignorance, unclear precisely what they were confronting and how the situation would unfold. They, and the public, watched with alarm as the virus cut swathes through populations abroad.

The Morrison Government, and its state counterparts, relied heavily on the advice of experts. Health officials appeared beside their leaders, becoming household names and trusted figures, although some later found themselves political targets when controversy deepened around restrictions or specific advice. On the economic front, the Coalition Government was forced to abandon its years of railing against 'debt and deficits'. It introduced an expensive wage-subsidy scheme, and presided over a deficit that reached $134.2 billion in 2020–21. The pandemic shaped politics as well as administration, and for a time narrowed the scope for the opposition. But crises vary in form, and the pandemic was not the only one Prime Minister Scott Morrison faced in the term. The 2019–20 bushfires, and later extensive floods in New South Wales and Queensland, tested the responses of the federal government and its leader. A crisis of a totally different kind developed from the fallout of two separate rape allegations. This opened the issue of Morrison's 'woman problem' and exposed the limits of his ability to handle issues requiring high levels of sensitivity and emotional intelligence.

That brings us to the other overarching story of this term, which was how, by the end of it, Morrison had lost the confidence of the Australian public. Debate about his 'character' undermined the government, before and at the election. Morrison's unpopularity was so high in some traditional Liberal seats – subsequently lost to a new breed of 'teal' independents – that he was unable to campaign in them.

The election on 21 May 2022 saw not just a Labor victory (albeit a narrow one, with 77 seats of 151 in the House of Representatives) but also a transformed federal parliamentary landscape. As the Australian Election Study observed, people walked away from the major parties in droves, with the combined major party vote (just over 68 per cent) the lowest since the 1930s (Cameron et al, 2022). The House crossbench expanded from seven to 16. This included four Greens (previously there had only ever been one), six newly elected 'teal' independents (all women), plus one other new female independent. The teals had run on issues of climate change, integrity and equity for women. They stood for better standards in politics, tapping into the deep disillusionment many Australians had increasingly come to feel about how the political system was operating. While trust in institutions and leaders generally rose during the pandemic, by 2022 public cynicism had reasserted itself, certainly in attitudes towards the Morrison Government. The pandemic had protected governments in 2020–21, with incumbents returned in the Northern Territory, Australian Capital Territory, Queensland and Western Australia. But in 2022, the wheel turned. The South Australian Liberal Government was defeated, shortly before the demise of the Morrison Government.

When Morrison, against expectations, secured his 'miracle' victory on 18 May 2019, a result he attributed to the 'quiet Australians', some

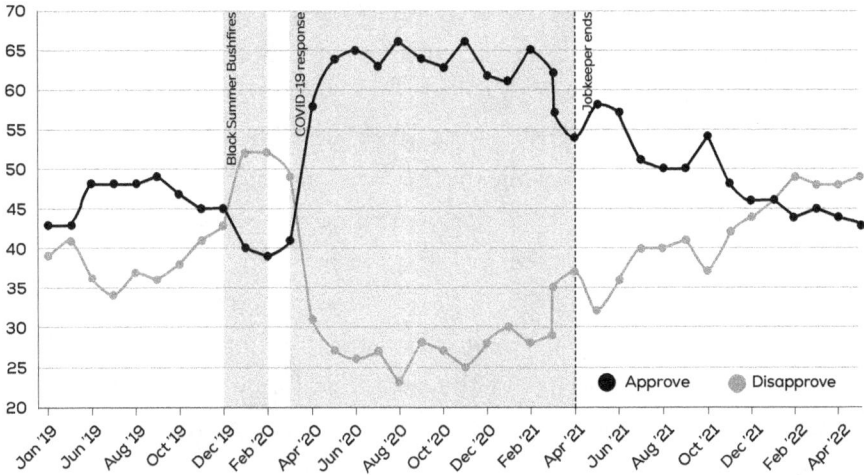

Figure 1.1
Scott Morrison's popularity
Total approve vs disapprove to the question: "Do you approve or disapprove of
the job Scott Morrison is doing as Prime Minister?", January 2019 to May 2022.

SOURCE Essential polling

commentators speculated he would be unbeatable next time. But, in retrospect, the 2019 result was in part misread. While Morrison was rightly seen as a strong campaigner in that election, Labor's over-heavy policy agenda, which would inevitably have created some 'losers' among citizens directly affected, and the unpopularity of leader Bill Shorten, were keys to why the Coalition prevailed.

Missing when it mattered

The first indications of the voter anger that would later help undo Morrison came early in the new term, when large tracts of Australia were consumed by bushfires. These catastrophic fires, with smoke reaching Sydney, Canberra and other centres, highlighted the issue of climate change. For well over a decade the 'climate wars' had produced a policy paralysis in the Coalition – although the issue had also provided it with an attack point against Labor. During the 2019–20 bushfire crisis, former fire and emergency chiefs accused the Morrison Government of ignoring their advice and said they had not been able to get a meeting with the prime minister for months.

The criticism of Morrison was turbo-charged by his December 2019 family holiday in Hawai'i, while the fires were raging. The Prime Minister's Office (PMO) attempted to keep secret that he was out of the country, and thus lied to the media. Faced with the bad publicity, Morrison returned home marginally early, but he had stoked the criticism when, defending himself, he said in a Sydney radio interview from Hawai'i: 'I don't hold a hose, mate'. Over the rest of the term, this line would be invoked to attack him over a range of issues; it became shorthand for his reluctance to take responsibility. Morrison made things worse when he later visited fire-devastated areas: the TV footage showed a hostile reception as he tried to shake people's hands.

The virus that changed everything

The fires were still burning themselves out as the COVID-19 crisis loomed. During 2020 and 2021, it would test not only Australia's health and economic responses, but also its governmental institutions. The pandemic highlighted how much authority the states possessed – especially in relation to their borders, despite the Constitution's section 92 providing for 'absolutely free' trade and intercourse between states. And assertive premiers were very willing to muscle up. In the past, there had been many strains in federal–state relations, and periodic attempts at reform, often with little success – and the pandemic raised fresh, urgent questions about whether the federation was fit for purpose.

Morrison had been frustrated during the bushfires by the limits on Commonwealth power. He anticipated similar issues as the pandemic began to unfold. His early answer was to create a National Cabinet in March 2020 to co-ordinate responses to COVID-19. He subsequently formalised this as a replacement to the Council of Australian Governments (COAG), using the argument that COAG had become too bureaucratic. The National Cabinet was, on balance, a positive innovation. But federal–state tensions were frequently on show during the crisis. Premiers shut borders to protect their own citizens and went their own ways when they had differences with the Commonwealth.

In general, Morrison and his government wanted to keep things as open as possible, including schools, over which Canberra did not have power, while the states were more cautious. But his government did make the early, and crucial, call to shut the national border, first to arrivals from China and then more generally. Australian citizens and permanent residents were exempted, but the number of these returnees was limited by what quarantine facilities (mostly hotels, and almost all operated by the states) could accommodate. The national border did not fully reopen until 2022. Sniping between federal and state governments, and among states, was driven by both policy differences and politics. Canberra's decision to support businessman Clive Palmer's court challenge to the Western Australian Government's closed border brought a sharp reaction in that state, and Morrison decided to pull out. His government was critical of the long Victorian lockdowns; it was also censorious of the Queensland Government's strict border policy, attacking it for denying entry to some compassionate cases. (Each of these states had a Labor government.) Australians, especially during lockdowns, became riveted to the daily news conferences given by state and territory leaders and their health officials, when case numbers and deaths were reported and restrictions and other measures were announced. These appearances elevated the profiles of both premiers and experts.

Meanwhile, the sight of long queues outside Centrelink, prompted by the lockdown, galvanised the Morrison Government to dramatically ramp up economic support. The Coalition's mantra had previously been the battle against debt and deficit. The 2019–20 budget had promised a surplus and, in anticipation, the Liberal Party had celebratory 'back in black' coffee mugs produced. The surplus would never materialise. Instead, the pandemic would put surpluses well beyond reach and send debt skyrocketing. The government was initially reluctant to embrace a wage-subsidy scheme but accepted Treasury advice to implement one – a win for experts. JobKeeper had design flaws that meant some firms that made strong profits in the pandemic received subsidies. But it was a lifeline for businesses and their workers, as was the additional financial help the government gave people on benefits and pensions. The Coalition's fiscal response was a necessary victory of pragmatism over its long-held economic ideology. The Australian economy bounced back strongly after being flattened by the pandemic. Unemployment fell to under 4 per cent in 2022.

While Australia's pandemic performance was better than that of most countries, the Morrison Government fell down on several fronts. The residential aged-care sector – a federal responsibility, although the states have a role through their public health laws – already had endemic problems and was unprepared; it saw a high proportion of the 2020 deaths. In the pandemic's second year, the vaccine rollout was initially slow. Morrison's line (adopted from a health official) that it was 'not a race' – which he later admitted had been a mistake – was frequently quoted against him. The government's initial planning relied too much on AstraZeneca, the vaccine that could be locally produced. Consequently, it had not ordered enough other vaccines. The first rollout problems arose when imported vaccines were delayed. Shortages were compounded after official health advice recommended restrictions on AstraZeneca's use. More generally, the health bureaucracy was not up to the massive rollout task; it was only after Morrison brought in a senior military officer, Lieutenant General John Frewen, to oversee the operation that it improved. But then another hitch came only months from the election: the Omicron wave hit and the government was under fire for not ordering enough rapid antigen tests.

Morrison's narrow lens on his 'woman problem'

In February 2021, a former Liberal staffer, Brittany Higgins, alleged in media interviews that before the 2019 election she had been raped by a colleague in the office of the then Minister for Defence Industry Linda Reynolds.[1] The staffers had returned to the office late at night after being out drinking. The allegation became part of a chain of events that chimed with the international #MeToo movement, and threw into relief the difficulty Morrison, with his very 'blokey' style, had in empathising with issues confronting women and in appealing to female voters.

The Higgins allegation was not the first manifestation of Parliament

House's bad culture. An affair between then Deputy Prime Minister Barnaby Joyce and one of his staffers, Vikki Campion (later his partner), led to then Prime Minister Turnbull's 2018 'bonk ban', which prohibited sex between ministers and their staff. Later that year, a Liberal MP, Julia Banks, claimed that women in the Liberal Party were routinely subjected to sexism and bullying; she defected to the crossbench.

In November 2020, an ABC *Four Corners* program exposed a 2017 affair between a minister, Alan Tudge, and his media adviser Rachelle Miller; the program also reported alleged sleazy behaviour in a bar involving another minister, Christian Porter. Morrison played down the stories about Tudge and Porter. But he could not brush off the allegation by Higgins, who claimed Reynolds had failed to properly support her and that she had been treated as a political problem. There were also questions about who knew what, and when, in the PMO. Higgins's claims came soon after Grace Tame, who as a teenager was the victim of a paedophile, had been named in January the 2021 Australian of the Year. Tame increasingly became a critic of Morrison.

Suddenly, gender issues took on a sharp political edge in federal politics.

Morrison's response was cack-handed, despite setting in train a slew of inquiries after the Higgins allegation, one of which, by Sex Discrimination Commissioner Kate Jenkins, laid bare the extent of the parliamentary workplace's toxic culture. Morrison came under fire after saying his wife, Jenny, had urged him, in relation to Higgins's allegation, to 'think about this as a father. What would you want to happen if it were our girls?'

Meanwhile, in late February 2021, the ABC reported on material sent to Morrison containing an allegation by a deceased woman that a cabinet minister had committed a historical rape. The minister was not named but Attorney-General and Industrial Relations Minister Christian Porter later identified himself publicly, totally denying the claim. The alleged incident dated back to 1988, when Porter was 17 years old and the alleged victim aged 16. The woman had committed suicide in 2020, after deciding not to proceed with a complaint to police.

In March, a large crowd of women, part of nationwide marches for justice, demonstrated outside Parliament House. In ill-chosen words

Morrison told parliament it was 'good and right' that people could gather like this, adding, 'Not far from here, such marches, even now, are being met with bullets, but not here in this country'. Aaron Patrick observed:

> In grasping and fumbling his way to recognise, accept and absorb the feminine anger directed at his government, Morrison couldn't hide his own limitations. His understanding and experience of Australian life and society made him an effective political campaigner, but also reflected the narrowness of Australian masculinity. (Patrick, 2022)

The Higgins allegation and the claim against Porter led to a ministerial reshuffle that saw Porter and Reynolds (Defence Minister) moved. Porter later went to the backbench after accepting anonymous donations for a discontinued defamation action he had brought against the ABC. He retired from parliament at the 2022 election.

Morrison would direct a series of measures to women, including arrangements to reform the Parliament House culture and initiatives to tackle domestic violence and improve women's security. He announced he and Minister for Women Marise Payne would co-chair a 'cabinet taskforce', including all the women in the ministry, to address issues of 'women's equality, women's safety, women's economic security, women's health and well-being'.

Electorally, it was all in vain. Morrison had been caught by unexpected events and his own limitations. He had failed to see issues affecting women in three-dimensional terms. He had not understood how the Higgins allegation, the claim against Porter and the exposure of the Parliament House culture would bring to the surface the much wider (and often seemingly unrelated) grievances of many Australian women. Inevitably, women became a drag on his vote.

Integrity becomes a cut-through issue

Apart from the scandals and allegations involving women, the Morrison Government was embroiled in another set of integrity issues, revolving around blatant pork-barrelling. The two examples that became notorious were the 'sports rorts' affair and the funding for car parks.

Then Sports Minister Bridget McKenzie had dispatched, before the 2019 election, $100 million in a program skewed on political grounds. The PMO had its fingers in the pie of distribution. In a January 2020 report, the Auditor-General was damning. Morrison was eventually forced to set up an inquiry by his departmental secretary, Phil Gaetjens, who did not condemn what was done as politically biased, despite noting the lack of transparency, but found McKenzie had breached the ministerial guidelines because she had not declared her membership of two relevant organisations. The $660 million national commuter car park scheme, announced in the run-up to the 2019 election, was also excoriated by the Audit Office as blatantly political.

Revelations about the misuse of both schemes intensified pressure for an integrity commission. Both sides of politics had come relatively recently to favour such a national body. In years gone by, they had argued it was not needed, because corruption was seen as more likely to be a problem at state rather than federal level. Before the 2019 election, Morrison had promised an integrity body, and during the term an exposure draft was produced. But the model, which would not allow public hearings when politicians were involved, was widely criticised. In *Keeping Them Honest*, Stephen Charles and Catherine Williams (2022) wrote scathingly, 'It would be a body with little or no ability to discover public sector corruption, and no corruption would be exposed by it'. Although consultations were held, Morrison refused to change the draft, or indeed to introduce the legislation unless Labor said it would support it. His determination that any integrity commission should be minimalist had been reinforced by the NSW Independent Commission Against Corruption's (ICAC) hearing into the relationship of that state's premier, Gladys Berejiklian with her former boyfriend, Daryl Maguire, when he was a state MP. Berejiklian later resigned, before ICAC brought down its findings. Morrison labelled ICAC a kangaroo court.

In 2021, the government was embarrassed when Liberal backbencher Bridget Archer crossed the floor to try (unsuccessfully) to get a debate on a Private Member's Bill from independent Helen Haines for an integrity commission. A commission remained an undelivered promise, which cost the Coalition votes, at a time when demand for an integrity body became a catchcry of the teal candidates. Morrison's failure had been threefold. He would not admit to inappropriate pork-barrelling; he did not carry through on his word; and he did not understand, or accept, how salient the issue had become with the Australian public.

Belated embrace of net zero by 2050

At the 2019 election, the Morrison Government had Labor on the back foot over climate policy. The opposition's policy for a 45 per cent cut in emissions by 2030 was uncosted. Labor was sending one message to electorates in the south of the country and another to coal areas in the north. But by 2021 the situation had changed dramatically. Internationally, most countries had signed up to, or were contemplating, the target of net zero by 2050. Moderate Liberals, with the climate issue biting in their electorates, told the prime minister it was politically imperative to embrace it. Morrison was also under pressure from the United States' Biden administration and the United Kingdom's Johnson Government, to whom he owed favours for the AUKUS security agreement (of which more below).

Endorsing the 2050 target required a deal with the Nationals, who had always been among the hardliners in resisting a robust climate policy. The Nationals were split. They had restored Barnaby Joyce to the leadership in June 2021, in part because they feared his predecessor, Michael McCormack, would be a 'soft touch' for Morrison on climate policy. But in the end Joyce, despite his personal opposition to the 2050 target, accepted a deal involving large dollops of promised spending for regional Australia, which was rolled out in the election campaign. Morrison took Australia's new target to the United Nations Glasgow climate conference in late 2021. But Australia did not increase its medium-term target (it gave only a projection), and was still seen as a laggard internationally. Nor were moderate Liberals helped; teal candidates used the line that whatever these Liberals thought personally on climate policy, they would vote with Joyce.

Morrison had come late to the fight to get the Coalition to endorse the 2050 target, which reinforced the impression that on policy he was often more driven by expediency than conviction. That, plus the lack of a formal enhanced medium-term commitment, left the government exposed domestically as well as internationally.

A new Anglosphere agreement for the region

Leaving aside Australia's response to the COVID-19 pandemic, when the Morrison Government's legacy is assessed, the AUKUS security agreement that the prime minister had negotiated with Joe Biden and Boris Johnson may rank as its most tangible achievement. A key aspect of the deal, unveiled by the three leaders at a virtual joint news conference in September 2021, was that Australia was promised access to the two partners' advanced technology. This included the acquisition of nuclear-powered submarines. A strong driver of the agreement was concern about China's increasing assertiveness and aggressiveness. While the agreement had clear long-term benefits for Australia, it brought a substantial short-term cost. The French were furious that their contract to supply conventional submarines to Australia had been cancelled, and French President Emmanuel Macron accused Morrison of lying to him over it. Thus, Morrison paid a significant price in personal credibility because of the secrecy surrounding the AUKUS deal; that also caused some blowback for the United States, which came under French criticism as well. The commitment to the nuclear-powered submarines left Australia with a medium-term capability gap, because of the time they would take to be delivered.

In foreign policy, the relationship with China was the most difficult challenge during the term. Relations had been deteriorating for some time. China increasingly put Australia in the 'freezer' after the Turnbull Government legislated against foreign interference and banned Huawei from participation in the 5G network. Tensions intensified substantially when in April 2020 the Morrison Government called for an independent inquiry into the origins and initial handling of the COVID-19 pandemic, which had started in Wuhan. Australia was in the vanguard of pressure for an investigation. An inquiry under the auspices of the World Health Organization took place, although it did not produce the comprehensive answers the Australian Government was seeking.

China ramped up restrictions on a range of Australian exports into the country. The Morrison Government became strident in its language about the China threat. As the election approached, its rhetoric was also driven by domestic politics, with the Coalition painting Labor as China's preferred Australian government. The Coalition's anti-China language alienated some voters of Chinese heritage in seats such as Bennelong in New South Wales, which the Liberals lost in the 2022 election.

Rising Chinese influence in the Pacific drove the Morrison Government to announce a 'new chapter in relations with our Pacific family' in late 2018. But with inadequate aid, a climate policy that alienated Pacific countries and insufficient diplomatic effort, the policy fell short. Australia was shocked when, during the run-up to the 2022 election, the Solomon Islands signed a security pact with China. Labor exploited the government's policy failure, thus effectively neutralising the Coalition's attempt to make 'national security' work to its benefit as an election issue.

After the election, the new Albanese Government launched a major effort to forge closer relations with Pacific countries, while dialogue with China resumed (partly driven by a change in China's own diplomacy).

A question of character

Not since the 2004 election, when Labor leader Mark Latham's personality came into the frame, had character been such a potent issue in a federal election as in 2022.

In March 2020, Roy Morgan conducted a survey of Australians, asking respondents to name, unprompted, politicians they trusted and distrusted. Only 8 per cent of respondents nominated Morrison as trusted, while 17 per cent distrusted him. In a repeat survey in March 2022, Morrison's trust had fallen to 6 per cent, with the distrust rising to 25 per cent. Morrison was the most distrusted politician in both surveys; the most common reasons for this distrust were telling lies and being dishonest or misleading. According to Australian National University research, in 2022 Morrison was the most unpopular Liberal leader since at least 1987, suffering a substantial fall in popularity since 2019. The Australian Election Study data 'shows that the two most important factors influencing leaders' overall popularity are honesty and trustworthiness. Perceptions that Morrison was dishonest and untrustworthy therefore disadvantaged him and the Liberals in the 2022 election' (Cameron et al, 2022).

Most damaging was that so many credible people were on the record for attacking Morrison's character. Macron's claim that the prime minister had lied to him had cut through, even though the PMO initially thought Australians would take Morrison's side. A leaked text from New South Wales Premier Berejiklian, dated from the bushfires, became public in 2022; it described Morrison as a 'horrible horrible person'. A text from Joyce, sent when he was on the backbench, condemned Morrison as 'a hypocrite and a liar'. Former prime minister Malcolm Turnbull, who became a vociferous critic of Morrison, said Morrison had a reputation for lying.

By the end, there was a widespread view that the prime minister was a man whose word could not be trusted. He also came to be seen as standing for little but survival; he was tactical rather than strategic, controlling, transactional. 'His beating heart is a focus group', was the description offered by one senior Liberal. Admitting error went against the grain but as the deteriorating electoral situation demanded it, Morrison conceded the government had not got everything right. Towards the end of the campaign, he described himself as 'a bit of a bulldozer', promising to change gears if he were re-elected. The appeal failed to resonate. It stretched believability to think he would be any different if he pulled off a second 'miracle'. More likely, it would have strengthened his deep Pentecostal conviction he was fulfilling the mission God had set for him.

After the election, startling evidence emerged of Morrison's penchant for both personal control and secrecy, and his disregard for proper process. The book *Plagued* (Benson & Chambers, 2022) and subsequent disclosures revealed that he'd had the governor-general install him into five portfolios: Health; Finance; Home Affairs; Industry, Science, Energy and Resources; and Treasury. Apart from the move into Health, the ministers concerned were unaware he was taking this bizarre course, although Resources Minister Keith Pitt subsequently discovered the PM had made himself the decision-maker in relation to a gas exploration project off the NSW coast. Vetoing a permit for that project was the only intervention Morrison made in his role as a 'co-minister' in these multiple portfolios. Morrison's unprecedented behaviour, when it belatedly came to light, shocked the public and appalled those who had been his closest colleagues in government, showing, as it did, that he had distrusted his ministers and the cabinet. The Albanese Government appointed a former High Court judge, Virginia Bell, to inquire into the extraordinary saga. In her damning report, Bell dismissed Morrison's unconvincing and contradictory explanations. She concluded 'the lack of disclosure of the appointments to the public was apt to undermine public confidence in government. Once the appointments became known, the secrecy with which they had been surrounded was corrosive of trust in government' (Bell, 2022). On 30 November 2022, Morrison became the first former prime minister in Australia's history to be censured by the House of Representatives.

Defeat on two fronts

At the election, Morrison lost support among both suburban voters and in the more urban, traditionally Liberal areas. As prime minister he had continued the realignment of the Liberal Party, begun under John Howard and continued by Tony Abbott, to concentrate its pitch on outer suburbia, the tradies, the aspirationals, the people Morrison dubbed 'the quiet Australians'. Morrison did not personally relate to many of the issues that concerned Liberal voters in the 'leafy' suburbs. These included not only climate change and integrity but also education. His government did not disguise its hostility towards universities, seeing them as harbouring and fostering left-wing views. Public universities were excluded from the JobKeeper scheme, the government arguing they had adequate resources to cope with the pandemic.

The prime minister's determination to get his own way came through in his insistence on imposing his own candidates in a number of New South Wales seats, where he ensured preselections were delayed. In Warringah, held by an independent, Zali Steggall, he had the Liberals run Katherine Deves; he thought her vociferous opposition to trans people in women's sport would resonate in Western Sydney electorates, but instead it alienated more progressive Liberal voters elsewhere.

Morrison and his ministers gambled that a combination of the government's record during the COVID-19 pandemic and the weakness of opposition leader Anthony Albanese would be enough to land a second 'miracle' result. But pandemic performance was no longer serving to Teflon-coat governments and, anyway, memories were strong about the rollout's flaws. The public marked Morrison down on crisis management. They were also looking for positive ideas about the future, and the Coalition had little to offer. Nor was its attack on Albanese as effective as the government had hoped. Albanese, learning from 2019, had made Labor a small target, both during the term and in the campaign, and he personally did not alienate voters as Shorten had done. The Liberal Party's post-election review concluded:

> Put simply, by the time of the election the Coalition had lost
> control of its brand, with the parties and their leaders being defined
> in the public's mind by our opponents. We were not in control of
> the politics, and we were unable to frame the electoral contest.
> Rather it was set by our opponents. (Loughnane and Hume, 2022)

At the election, the Morrison Government was fighting on two fronts: against both Labor and the teals. It grossly underestimated the teals, trying – insultingly – to dismiss them as 'fake' independents. It was shocked at their potency. Multiple factors contributed to the government's defeat, which cut a swathe through its moderate MPs and took out Treasurer and Liberal Party Deputy Leader Josh Frydenberg. Frydenberg had been seen as the likely new leader if the Liberals went into opposition. Up to the end, Morrison thought there was a chance of clinging to minority government. The leader who had lauded the 'quiet Australians' found it hard to believe they would come at him – a case of arrogance over evidence.

With a Coalition primary vote of 35.7 per cent, down 5.7 per cent, the Liberals lost 18 House of Representatives seats overall. On the two-party vote, Labor won 52.1 per cent to the Coalition's 47.9 per cent, which represented a swing of 3.7 per cent. In Western Australia, previously a bastion of Liberal support, the party lost five seats. In contrast to the Liberals, the Nationals retained all their House seats (and gained a senator). In the election for the Senate, the Greens expanded from nine to 12 seats. The new government would need the Greens plus one of the non-Green crossbench senators to enable it to pass legislation opposed by the Coalition. The election of progressive independent David Pocock, who took what had been a traditionally Liberal ACT Senate seat, ensured the Albanese Government of a basically friendly Senate.

Was the 2022 election primarily 'lost' by the Morrison Government or 'won' by the opposition? Of course, there was a mix of factors, including the government's longevity, which usually makes a change more appealing to voters. But the defeat appeared substantially due to many voters just wanting the government, and in particular the prime minister, to be gone, and unlike 2019, they were not put off by the opposition.

The Australian Election Study highlights longer-term shifts in voting patterns based on 'gender, generation and social class'. Women, once a mainstay for the Coalition, have moved away from it. 'Across the past three elections the gender gap in voting has been greater than in all previous elections covered by the AES [since 1987].' The generation gap saw only about one in four of the under-40s saying they had voted for the Coalition, and a record low level of support in the survey's history among this demographic for either major party. The social class breakdown showed Labor's share of the working-class vote had fallen to 38 per cent in 2022, while the Coalition had shed votes from university-educated and high-income voters. 'These shifting dynamics indicate that neither major party can rely on the support of their traditional voter base.' The election showed 'voters who are dissatisfied with the major parties are willing to support change when presented with viable alternatives' (Cameron et al, 2022).

This volume examines in detail the Morrison Government's performance between 2019 and 2022 from political, institutional and policy perspectives. Among the wide range of contributions, authors look at how the federal system and the parliament performed, the Morrison Government's management of health, aged care and economic policy during the pandemic, the bushfire disaster and climate policy, and the central question of leadership during crisis. The book is the 14th in the Australian Commonwealth Administration series sponsored by the University of Canberra on the terms of federal governments.

The overall flavour of the volume is critical of the Morrison Government. That government was faced with extraordinary circumstances: the COVID-19 pandemic created a sort of 'fog of war' for governments around the world. While the Morrison Government could claim some successes, it was ultimately felled by a combination of deficiencies, especially in the leadership of the prime minister himself.

References

Bell, Virginia. *Report of the Inquiry into the Appointment of the Former Prime Minister to Administer Multiple Departments*, Commonwealth of Australia, 2022.

Benson, Simon and Geoff Chambers. *Plagued: Australia's two years of hell – the inside story*, Pantera Press, 2022.

Boin, Arjen, Paul 't Hart, Eric Stern and Bengt Sundelius. *The Politics of Crisis Management: Public leadership under pressure*, Cambridge University Press, 2017.

Cameron, Sarah, Ian McAllister, Simon Jackman and Jill Sheppard. *The 2022 Australian Federal Election: Results from the Australian Election Study*, ANU, 2022.

Charles, Stephen and Catherine Williams. *Keeping Them Honest: The case for a genuine national integrity commission and other vital democratic reforms*, Scribe, 2022.

Loughnane, Brian and Jane Hume. *Review of the 2022 Federal Election*, Liberal Party of Australia, 2022.

Patrick, Aaron. *Ego: Malcolm Turnbull and the Liberal Party's civil war*, HarperCollins, 2022.

Savva, Niki. *Bulldozed: Scott Morrison's fall and Anthony Albanese's rise*, Scribe, 2022.

Institutions

2

DELEGATING DEMOCRACY: PARLIAMENT IN THE MORRISON ERA

Karen Middleton

O ver its term-and-a-bit in office, the Morrison Government treated federal parliament less as the centrepiece of Australian democracy and more as something between a political weapon and an inconvenience.

The pandemic's arrival in early 2020 imposed understandable restrictions on parliament's capacity to function traditionally. But the erosion of its role and of the respect within government for government's own general processes began well before that. Parliament provides the main opportunity for opposition members to challenge a government directly, to raise questions and demand answers. It is the forum in which laws are made and debated and matters of public importance raised. It also provides a particular platform for independents, minor parties and rebels in the ranks.

For Scott Morrison, with the tiniest of parliamentary majorities after 2019, parliament became a troublesome theatre. His government regularly emerged from sitting periods bruised and out-manoeuvred. From the time of his elevation to the prime ministership in August 2018, Morrison sought to change the way things were usually done, implementing measures and introducing practices that limited government transparency and accountability, both to parliament and to the Australian public.

In an early move, he made a highly unorthodox addition to the list of Cabinet committees, the 'Cabinet Office Policy Committee' – a one-person committee with Morrison its only permanent member. The updated government directory described the committee's work.

'The Committee considers major policy issues on an as needs basis, including early stage consideration of strategic issues, specialist advice on nationally significant issues and rapidly evolving situations', the directory said, explaining it conducted 'preliminary' discussions ahead of Cabinet's expenditure review committee and that Cabinet must endorse any decisions it made.

Morrison determined that meetings of the Cabinet Office Policy Committee would be covered by Cabinet confidentiality. Relying on its one-person structure, Morrison determined that virtually any meeting he attended could be declared as a Cabinet Office Policy Committee meeting, thereby protecting deliberations from external scrutiny.

Cabinet committees are established by convention, not legislation, so there was no basis for challenging this arrangement, other than through public questioning. But although questions could be asked, the secrecy cloak allowed the government to give itself permission not to answer.

The committee's existence came to light in 2019. Opposition senators grilled the government about its purpose during a Senate estimates committee hearing in early 2020. Labor's Senate leader Penny Wong questioned Finance Minister Mathias Cormann, representing the prime minister, about the committee's role and operations.

'This is an opportunity to do deep dives', Cormann explained, saying it enabled the involvement of 'a whole range of stakeholders', including backbench MPs:

Senator Wong: So it's a cabinet committee which involves people who are not in cabinet and involves, potentially, people who are not in parliament, on an ad hoc basis, as and when the Prime Minister sees fit? Is that right?

Senator Cormann: It's to ensure that the Prime Minister has the opportunity to fully inform himself and get a good appreciation of a diversity of views in an in-depth way in preparation for consideration by government in relation to these issues.

Senator Wong: But he's the only member of the cabinet policy committee?

Senator Cormann: He's the only permanent member.

Cormann went on to say the committee was 'part of good public policy development' ensuring 'the broadest possible input'.

Wong asked the deputy secretary from the Department of Prime Minister and Cabinet, Stephanie Foster, if the committee had ever made a decision.

'I don't know', Foster replied.

Wong then asked which members or senators had attended, whether any member of the Liberal Party organisation or any pollster had attended and what kinds of issues were on its agenda.

In response to the latter question, Foster used the carefully crafted form of words that had become a hallmark of public servants' responses in estimates hearings. The sentence structure left wiggle room around the facts and avoided stating whether something had *actually* occurred by stating instead what might usually be *expected* to occur: 'I would', rather than 'I did'.

'I would always have access to the agenda', Foster replied, therefore confirming neither that she had, nor that she had not, had access; only that, hypothetically, normally, she would.

Wong had also sought to clarify whether non-parliamentarians could be members of the Cabinet Office Policy Committee. Cormann confirmed that public servants were sometimes invited to meetings. Nevertheless, he took these last four questions on notice, saying he wanted to get 'technically 100 per cent accurate' and 'precise' answers and accusing Wong of 'confected outrage on things that are completely normal'.

Later that day in Question Time, Opposition Leader Anthony Albanese mocked the prime minister's special committee.

'Can the Prime Minister advise, in relation to this one-man cabinet committee, do the committee's discussions take long?' Albanese asked. 'Is there a lot of disagreement in this committee, and are the meetings of this committee held in the Prime Minister's head? Isn't this just an abuse of the cabinet designed to hide government documents?' Scott Morrison responded that the attorney-general, the deputy prime minister and the treasurer all regularly attended the committee meetings.

It took more than seven months for the Department of Prime Minister and Cabinet to formally reply to the four questions Cormann had taken on notice. When they arrived, all four written answers were identical.

'It is a longstanding practice not to disclose the operation and business of the Cabinet, including meeting attendees, as to do so could potentially reveal the deliberations of the Cabinet', the answers all said. End of interrogation.

Morrison would later use this same one-man committee as a device to cover the workings of another new construct, the 'National Cabinet'. This was a pared-down version of the old council of Australian governments, or COAG. It stripped away much of the bureaucracy surrounding the regular meetings of federal, state and territory leaders to enable more streamlined and quicker decision-making, especially through the pandemic.

The other first ministers supported the new, less cumbersome format. But the federal government's determination to maintain secrecy became its most significant feature. After persistently blocking requests made under freedom-of-information (FOI) law for documents underpinning National Cabinet decisions, Morrison's government eventually ran foul of the Administrative Appeals Tribunal on whether National Cabinet was, in fact, a 'cabinet' at all.

In a case brought by then independent senator and FOI agitator Rex Patrick in 2021, Justice Richard White ruled that it did not display the characteristics of a cabinet – being made up of members of different governments – and that Morrison's attempted administrative construct was invalid. The government then set about redrafting FOI law to entrench the secrecy provisions.

The Morrison Government downgraded the role of parliament in another, simpler way too. It just did not give it terribly much to do. Morrison went to the 2019 election promising little in the manner of legislated change and fulfilled his promise. Not a lot was legislated that moved the dial in a policy sense, with the exception of promised tax cuts and a slew of interlinked measures in national security.

The Parliamentary Joint Committee on Intelligence and Security (PJCIS), which is one of parliament's few statutorily based committees and involves only Liberal and Labor members and senators, came under huge pressure to speed up its consideration of significant and controversial legislation, particularly on access to encrypted data.

The PJCIS has a legislated responsibility to examine all national security legislation before it is passed and is often also required to conduct reviews after it becomes law. It scrutinised and reported on 23 pieces of legislation between 2019 and 2022, with two more such reviews carried over to the new parliament. It also carried out its other standing commitments and special inquiries on issues including press freedom, mandatory data retention and security risks in higher education and research.

Much of the legislation focused on increasing security agencies' reach, especially their access to private information, with the combined effect of sidestepping or overriding existing privacy protections embedded in other laws, including for journalists.

Repeatedly, two other key security watchdogs, the Inspector-General of Intelligence and Security and the Commonwealth Ombudsman, raised concerns about loose drafting and potential unacknowledged consequences – whether intended or otherwise.

On the recommendation of the PJCIS, the government made numerous amendments to address these concerns, although it took the highly unusual step of rejecting the committee's recommendations in relation to contentious changes to laws that would allow some Australians to be stripped of their citizenship. Another watchdog, the Independent National Security Legislation Monitor, conducted an inquiry into the citizenship changes, and also raised concerns.

Beyond national security, there was little in the way of significant, legislated policy change, at least not driven by the government. The loss of a vote on a migration bill in 2019 represented the first time in 90 years that a government had lost a House of Representatives vote on its own legislation. Labor and crossbenchers combined to amend a government bill and provide for the medical evacuation of refugees and asylum seekers from Papua New Guinea and Nauru to Australia, against the government's wishes.

The government had produced legal advice from the Solicitor-General that the bill was effectively a money bill and argued that the amendments made it unconstitutional. Its attempts to dissuade proponents failed and the bill passed. After it won the 2019 election, it repealed the law.

But two key promises Morrison made before the 2019 election would remain unfulfilled by the time of the next election three years later: the creation of a national integrity commission and legally protected religious freedom. Morrison had faced backbench rebellion on both.

The national integrity commission was never legislated because there was insufficient support for the restrictive version Morrison wanted to implement. The religious freedom legislation also dogged him throughout the term. The difficult politics prompted him to shelve it in the dying days of the 46th Parliament after five of his own MPs crossed the floor to back amendments protecting the rights of trans students, which conservative churches had deemed unacceptable.

Morrison had promised both the integrity commission and the religious freedom measures to address political problems but both created problems of their own, becoming twin legacies of legislative failure.

In between the two elections came the COVID-19 pandemic. This delivered logistical challenges for a parliament designed to meet in person. Government and opposition worked together to overcome legal and practical hurdles and eventually enable participation by video-link. But COVID-19 also further empowered a prime minister already inclined towards process shortcuts and a bit allergic to accountability.

The legislative basis for the most controversial decisions the government took during the pandemic, primarily the border closures, was the *Biosecurity Act*. Passed with little fanfare in 2015, this Act provided sweeping powers that overrode all other laws, state and federal.

Three months after the 2022 election, it emerged that Morrison had used the pandemic – and the extraordinary powers afforded to the health minister under the *Biosecurity Act* – to justify having himself secretly authorised by the Governor-General to administer five extra portfolios. In March of 2020, he secretly obtained administrative authority in Health, after receiving advice from then Attorney-General Christian Porter that he could do so. Soon after, he added Finance, followed a year later by the

Industry, Science, Energy and Resources portfolio and then Home Affairs and Treasury. Only some ministers knew about the first addition before it occurred and it appears none before the subsequent ones. This included Christian Porter, who by then had moved to Industry.

Only in that portfolio did Morrison appear to have used the powers to take any action, vetoing a proposed controversial gas exploration project off the New South Wales central coast. But it was the pandemic and specifically the *Biosecurity Act* that Morrison claimed as the reason for an unprecedented power grab that drew widespread condemnation, including from his own colleagues. By way of explanation once his move was revealed later, he said he believed the government had needed a back-up for Health Minister Greg Hunt – not clarifying why he thought the existing stand-in powers were not enough.

Once an emergency was declared, the *Biosecurity Act* also increased the scope for government to make laws by delegated legislation, or regulations. Many of the regulations were exempt from parliamentary disallowance, leaving parliament unable to examine, query or amend them.

Regulations are a normal part of law-making. They are adjuncts to primary laws, made effectively by government decree without a vote. The power to make regulations comes from the primary Acts to which they relate, and from the *Legislation Act* 2003. Even before the pandemic, the government had been using regulations increasingly to do things away from the public gaze, including appropriating billions of dollars for grants and making moves that might otherwise attract controversy or face parliamentary obstruction.

Three months before the 2019 election, the government made a regulation that granted certain researchers access to voters' unlisted mobile phone numbers and postcodes. Primarily explained as being for health research, it included access for registered political parties and candidates. Three years later, on election day 2022, the Liberal Party would become embroiled in controversy for sending political text messages to the mobile phones of voters in key marginal seats, alerting them to the interception of a boat carrying suspected asylum seekers – activities normally kept secret, deemed 'on-water matters' – and urging them to vote Liberal.

Once made, most regulations are subject to parliamentary scrutiny and can be disallowed through a vote in the Senate. Certain regulations are exempt, and the *Biosecurity Act* allowed the government to expand those categories and exempt a broad range of regulations from any kind of examination.

With the COVID-19 crisis as cover, the government was able to take measures under the auspices of an emergency that would have been much more difficult politically in less extraordinary times. They included, for example, relieving Australia Post of its obligation to deliver mail daily, something to which it appears unlikely to ever return.

In 2015, the then Biosecurity Bill's explanatory memorandum justified exempting regulations from disallowance by arguing it was 'more appropriate for Parliament to delegate the power to make determinations that involve technical and scientific decisions about the management of biosecurity risk to the Director of Biosecurity', who is the secretary of the Agriculture Department.

'An implication of these decisions being disallowed is that political considerations will play a role in what should be a technical and scientific decision making process', the memorandum said. 'This has the potential to frustrate the risk management processes and lead to the inadequate management of biosecurity risks.' In fact, making them non-disallowable gave political considerations a significant role. The executive government could make laws as it wished and there was very little parliament could do about it.

Among the delegated powers was the power for the finance minister to appropriate up to $5 billion in extra funds and designate how they be spent, again using regulations exempt from disallowance. Parliament had no influence.

Two Senate committees raised repeated concerns about the widening categories of activities no longer subject to examination. The Scrutiny of Delegated Legislation committee and the Scrutiny of Bills committee, both chaired by Coalition senators, challenged the governance arrangements involving both the use of non-disallowable regulations and the loose definitions that allowed certain expenditure to escape scrutiny.

These concerns pre-dated the pandemic and, in the latter case, dated back to the Labor governments of Kevin Rudd and Julia Gillard. Then, the Senate Standing Committee on Appropriations and Staffing had noted that expenditure on new programs was being incorrectly classified in appropriations bills as the 'ordinary annual services of government'. Under the constitution, the Senate cannot scrutinise or amend legislation that appropriates revenue for such 'ordinary annual services'. But new programs and projects are fair game.

The appropriations and staffing committee found in 2008 that ever since the Commonwealth had switched to accrual budgeting in 1999–2000, the division of expenditure items had been based on a wrong assumption that any spending which fell within an existing departmental outcome in the Budget should be classified as 'ordinary'.

The committee found that new programs and projects not funded in previous appropriations should be separately identified in their first year, so they could be reasonably scrutinised. It has been raising concerns ever since. In 2010, the Senate agreed the ambiguity was a problem and passed a resolution listing seven specific spending categories that should not be considered 'ordinary' and therefore should be subject to ongoing Senate scrutiny.

They were: the construction of public works and buildings; the acquisition of sites and buildings; items of plant and equipment clearly definable as capital expenditure (not including computers or building fit-outs); grants to the states; new policies not previously authorised by special legislation; items regarded as equity injections and loans; and existing asset replacement.

But in 2022, the Scrutiny of Bills committee found this was still not happening. In its Scrutiny Digest 2/22 published on 18 March 2022, the committee revealed it had written to the finance minister repeatedly since 2014, complaining that parliament was not able to properly examine government spending.

'However, the government has consistently advised that it does not intend to reconsider its approach to the classification of items that constitute the ordinary annual services of the government', the committee reported, noting this remained inconsistent with the Senate's 2010 resolution.

The committee further endorsed the work of its sibling, the Scrutiny of Delegated Legislation committee, which had been raising similar concerns about the expanded use of exempt regulations. The Delegated Legislation committee noted that the use of regulations had increased in the past several decades, finding that while during the mid-1980s, 850 disallowable regulations were made on average each year, that number was now about 1700.

But its concern was even greater in relation to how many of those regulations were being exempted from disallowance, meaning once the government had created them, parliament had no oversight role at all. The Delegated Legislation committee became so concerned about the creeping use of regulations beyond parliament's reach that it undertook two separate inquiries, in 2019 and 2021.

'As parliamentarians, we owe it to the Australian people to act independently, and to remove from the statute book delegated legislation which does not respect individual rights and liberties or the right of Parliament to control the content of the law', its 2019 report said. In both reports, it raised specific concerns about the use of what are known as 'Henry VIII clauses' – clauses embedded in regulations which actually amend the primary legislation, again without parliament casting a vote.

Among the recommendations in its report of March, 2021, the committee said that the *Legislation Act* 2003 should be amended so all exemptions from disallowance had to be contained in primary legislation, not simply added later in a daisy-chain of regulations. It found that exempt regulations should have an accompanying explanatory memorandum describing clearly how and why exceptional circumstances applied. It also recommended that all advances to the finance minister should be disallowable.

On 21 October 2021, the chair of the Scrutiny of Bills committee, Liberal senator Dean Smith, raised further concerns in parliament about new legislation that would further extend the reach of the *Biosecurity Act*. In a statement incorporated into Hansard, Smith indicated the committee was concerned that the new bill contained 'a number of coercive powers, including requiring individuals to undertake a medical examination or provide a body sample' but that it did not specify how such powers would be exercised.

Senator Smith's statement said the committee had 'heightened concerns' when instruments were exempt from disallowance, conferred broad discretion on a decision-maker, dealt with 'significant matters' or unduly impinged on personal rights and liberties. 'The committee considers that a number of provisions within the *Biosecurity Act* raise these issues, and that the COVID-19 pandemic has served to highlight the importance of parliament, and in particular the Senate, maintaining a careful and considered watch over how the legislative power that it has delegated is being utilised by the executive', Smith's statement said.

Speaking next, the chair of the Scrutiny of Delegated Legislation committee, Liberal senator Concetta Fierravanti-Wells, echoed his concerns. 'It is the committee's view that emergency delegated legislation must be subject to appropriate parliamentary oversight', Fierravanti-Wells said. 'Continuing to make instruments under the *Biosecurity Act* which are exempt from disallowance undermines parliament's constitutional role as the primary institution responsible for making law. The committee appreciates that during an emergency urgent and decisive action must be taken. However, we are now well into the second year of this pandemic, and that excuse is no longer valid. Parliament needs oversight over these critical decisions now and into the future.'

In the preceding three years, Fierravanti-Wells and her deputy, Labor senator Kim Carr, had made a crusade of pushing back against the use of legislative mechanisms that parliament could not touch, especially during the pandemic. In his own speech, Carr noted that as of mid-October 2021, the government had created 578 separate regulations linked to the pandemic. He expressed concern at the increasing incidence of lawmaking by delegated legislation – effectively by decree.

'This is not a trend we should be proud of, particularly when we consider the number of these instruments which cannot in any way be overturned through the processes of the Parliament', Carr said. 'That, to me, is a matter of deep concern. Senators, if we do not do our duty and take up our responsibilities to correct this dangerous state of affairs, we may rightly and properly be accused of negligence, and so we should be.'

Both Carr and Fierravanti-Wells expressed dismay that, 10 months after their committee had tabled its report, the government continued to ignore it. 'It is unfortunate that we are seeing a contemptuous tone grow from the executive about the concerns that this committee and its sister committee have raised', Carr lamented.

That same day, the Senate passed a motion forcing the government to respond. A week later the response was tabled. In it, the government either sidestepped or outright rejected almost all of the committee's recommendations. Simply noting many, it rejected all suggestions that pandemic-related instruments should be subject to parliamentary debate and disallowance or sunset clauses, declaring that the need for urgency and certainty made that unwise. Ahead of the 2022 election, both Senator Fierravanti-Wells and Senator Carr were dropped to unwinnable spots on their parties' respective Senate tickets and neither was returned to parliament.

Prime Minister Morrison routinely jettisoned the conventions of the Westminster system except where they allowed him to keep things secret or otherwise afforded political advantage. He brought forward the date of the Budget ahead of both elections he faced, using it as a springboard for his campaign embedded with billions of dollars in grants, particularly for Coalition target seats. The pandemic's dire economic impact helped justify abandoning the way things were usually done.

Morrison ignored protocols when they did not suit him and set the rules of the unprecedented remote parliamentary sittings to ensure they did. When Speaker Tony Smith declared there was a 'prima facie case' to refer former attorney-general Christian Porter to the privileges committee in October 2021 for potentially breaching disclosure rules by using a blind trust to fund part of his legal fees in a defamation action, the government blocked it.

It was the first time in parliament's history that the government of the day had defied a Speaker's ruling on such a referral. The issue went to a vote and the Coalition voted it down, assisted partly by the rules for remote attendance.

House of Representatives crossbenchers complained that the leader of the house, Peter Dutton, refused to count the votes of crossbenchers who were attending parliament remotely, under COVID-19 video-link arrangements.

Porter's predicament was linked to a wider issue that was to become a mark on Scott Morrison's record – his management of parliament as a workplace, especially around attitudes to women. Porter had stepped down from the ministry amid controversy around historical allegations, which preceded his time in parliament and which he denied, that he had sexually assaulted a young woman decades earlier when both were involved in university debating tournaments. After approaching police, the woman had taken her own life.

The emergence in early 2021 of separate and unrelated allegations that a Liberal staffer had been raped in a ministerial office in Parliament House in 2019 sparked a national outcry about women's safety, and demands for greater action from Morrison.

Other allegations about ministers having sexual relationships with staff contributed to a cascading political crisis, to which Morrison responded by establishing a series of inquiries. The two most significant were by Sex Discrimination Commissioner Kate Jenkins and Prime Minister's Department deputy secretary Stephanie Foster. Foster was tasked with reviewing the processes for receiving and managing complaints from people working within the parliamentary precincts.

Jenkins's more comprehensive report, *Set the Standard*, examined incidents of sexual harassment, bullying and sexual assault in Commonwealth parliamentary workplaces. As a result, the government implemented recommended changes to the employment and staff complaints processes within parliament.

Two days before he called the 2022 federal election, Morrison quietly amended his ministerial code of conduct, the statement of ministerial standards, to add six paragraphs reflecting the reviews' findings. The paragraphs codified what would constitute a sackable offence for future ministers against whom behavioural complaints were upheld. It was done without fanfare in a political environment that had become problematic around issues to do with women. After three-and-a-bit challenging years, it was a final unilateral act by a prime minister who preferred seeking forgiveness to permission but wasn't really terribly inclined towards either.

References

Albanese, Anthony. Australian Parliament. House of Representatives Hansard, 2 March 2020. Questions Without Notice, p. 2139, <parlinfo.aph.gov.au/parlInfo/download/chamber/hansardr/40515a20-4bd1-456f-a3f3-3fa9bf7ac390/toc_pdf/House%20of%20Representatives_2020_03_02_7592_Official.pdf;fileType=application%2Fpdf>.

Answers to Questions on Notice, Senate Additional Estimates 2019–20, Finance and Public Administration Legislation Committee. Questions 12–15, 24, <www.aph.gov.au/Parliamentary_Business/Senate_estimates#qon>.

Australian Government Directory 2020 (cached), <webcache.googleusercontent.com/search?q=cache:A6vvMSOmA74J:https://www.directory.gov.au/commonwealth-parliament/cabinet/cabinet-committees/cabinet-office-policy-committee+&cd=1&hl=en&ct=clnk&gl=au>.

Australian Parliament. Senate Appropriations and Staffing Committee, Ordinary Annual Services of the Government 50th report, 2010, <file:///Users/sophiemorris/Downloads/report_pdf%20(2).pdf>.

Australian Parliament. Senate Committee for the Scrutiny of Bills, Scrutiny Digest 2/22, 18 March 2022, pp. 13 and 15.

Australian Parliament. Senate Committee for the Scrutiny of Delegated Legislation, Parliamentary Scrutiny of Delegated Legislation Report 2019, Chair and Deputy Chair's Foreword, p. X.

Australian Parliament. Senate Hansard, 22 June 2010, p. 3910, <parlinfo.aph.gov.au/parlInfo/download/chamber/hansards/2010-06-22/toc_pdf/7725-7.pdf;fileType=application%2Fpdf#search=%22chamber/hansards/2010-06-22/0000%22>.

Australian Parliament. Senate Hansard, 2 March 2020, p. 76, <file:///Users/sophiemorris/Downloads/Finance%20and%20Public%20Administration%20Legislation%20Committee%20-%20Official%20-%202%20March%202020%20(1).pdf>.

Australian Parliament. Senate Hansard, Senator Dean Smith (speech presented for incorporation into Hansard by Senator James McGrath), 21 October 2021, p. 6331, <parlinfo.aph.gov.au/parlInfo/download/chamber/hansards/25181/toc_pdf/Senate_2021_10_21_Official.pdf;fileType=application%2Fpdf>.

Australian Parliament. Senate Hansard, Senator Concetta Fierravanti-Wells, 21 October 2022, p. 6332, <parlinfo.aph.gov.au/parlInfo/download/chamber/hansards/25181/toc_pdf/Senate_2021_10_21_Official.pdf;fileType=application%2Fpdf>.

Australian Parliament. Senate Hansard, Senator Kim Carr, 21 October 2022, p. 6334.

Biosecurity Act 2015. Explanatory Memorandum, <www.aph.gov.au/Parliamentary_Business/Bills_LEGislation/Bills_Search_Results/Result?bId=r5379>.

3

THE PARTIES

Chris Wallace

Turmoil on the conservative side of politics during the Morrison Government's term from 2019 to 2022, and relative stability on the progressive side, saw a change of government at its end. At the beginning of the term, the Liberal–National Coalition Government held office with 77 of 151 House of Representatives seats. At its end, the Australian Labor Party won office with 77 seats. The Coalition's net 18 seats lost and Labor's net nine seats gained, which saw power change hands, is part of a deeper shift in Australian federal party politics than is suggested by this apparently neat reversal of positions.

Labor assumed office in May 2022 with the same slim two-seat margin with which the Coalition started the previous term. This partly reflected the continuing long-run trend to declining primary (that is, first-preference vote) support for the major parties. An insurgency of well organised and funded centrist 'community candidates' in metropolitan Liberal seats saw the number of independent MPs in the House of Representatives more than treble at the 2022 election, rising from three to 10 seats, primarily at the Liberals' expense. The number of Greens MPs rose from one to four at the 2022 election, with the Greens taking seats from both major parties in metropolitan Brisbane. Geographically, a shift to Labor in Western Australia, where the party picked up four seats, and the Coalition's ability to largely hold its Queensland seats, were also notable.

The burgeoning phenomenon of centrist independents, loosely labelled the 'teals', was a striking by-product of this term of the Morrison Government. Enough metropolitan Liberal voters' frustration with, and rejection of, the party's political agenda and performance in office drove them to abandon it in favour of centrist community independent candidates who better reflected them and their values. Tactical voting by Labor supporters in historically safe metropolitan Liberal seats boosted the effect. The electoral shock was specific to the Liberals. In contrast, the Nationals held all their seats. The Coalition lost office to a steady, focused, low-key opposition led by Labor leader Anthony Albanese, who maintained party unity throughout the three-year parliamentary term.

Background

Despite parties not being mentioned in the Constitution, Australian politics has been synonymous with party politics for much of its history. The Liberal–National Party Coalition has governed for two-thirds of the post-Second World War period. The Morrison Government's surprise 2019 election win seemingly confirmed the Coalition's electoral primacy over Labor. By the 2022 election, the Coalition had governed federally for 20 of the previous 26 years. The Rudd and Gillard Governments (2007–2013) punctuated the Coalition Howard Government's reign on the one side, and the Coalition Abbott, Turnbull and Morrison governments on the other, so the scale of Labor's contemporary electoral failure federally was obscured.

The Coalition parties' surprise 2019 election win produced an air of invincibility in the political acumen of Prime Minister Scott Morrison inside the government that would prove costly. It was comparable to the hubris inside the Howard Government after its fourth consecutive win at the 2004 election, which included achievement of a Senate majority, enabling it to secure deep labour market deregulation via its WorkChoices industrial relations law. WorkChoices' extreme measures were electorally unpopular and the policy was a key element in the Howard Government's loss at the next election. The lessons of the WorkChoices overreach were forgotten, however, and Morrison governed – some elements of pandemic policy response aside – with little restraint in the pursuit of an unmitigated right-wing agenda across most portfolios. Cronyism and loose governmental standards were chronically evident.

The major parties: Labor, the Liberals and the Nationals

Labor experienced stability under Anthony Albanese, who succeeded to party and opposition leadership after the loss of the 2019 election under Bill Shorten. It was deeply demoralised after the 'certain' victory opinion polls predicted in 2019 failed to eventuate. A range of factors contributed to the shock loss, including failures of basic political strategy and craft under Shorten. Albanese was alert to the lessons of the 2019 loss and confident his strategic approach to defeating the Coalition would work. Combined with discipline in keeping the Coalition the issue rather than Labor, and a systematic improvement in his public presentation as the election drew near, Albanese's sensible political management combined with Morrison Government overreach delivered a clear if narrow victory.

Federal parliamentary Labor party unity played a role in this result, arguably for both good and ill. On the plus side, Albanese handled federal intervention in the troubled Victorian and Tasmanian state ALP branches well, and they did not create a backwash destabilising Labor in Canberra. There was also the fact that Albanese's well-fortified position in caucus deterred destabilising leadership challenges, should any rival contender emerge – something that did not happen. In this he was bolstered by the federal parliamentary Labor party rule change introduced by Kevin Rudd after his restoration as Labor leader and prime minister in 2013, discouraging leadership challenges between elections. Leadership stability helped Labor keep attention focused on the shortcomings of the Coalition parties in government. On the other hand, it kept a relatively unknown and unexciting opposition leader in place, likely contributing to Labor's low primary vote of 32.58 per cent – its lowest ever while winning a federal election – and slim two-seat majority up against what in the end was widely judged one of the worst Australian governments ever. Albanese's standing rose as the election neared and by the time the election was called he drew ahead of Morrison in net popularity terms, a factor present on the previous three times government changed hands at a federal election. After becoming prime minister, Albanese's stature and popularity rose sharply and his leadership became a strong positive for Labor. It was an example of a party choosing to elect and remain united behind a 'good enough' leader of the opposition in the interests of electoral success. But it was a close run thing.

The Coalition parties each experienced significant turbulence between victory in 2019 and defeat in 2022. The Liberals were beset by a series of scandals and criticism for, in several areas, obvious underperformance. The Nationals experienced a traumatic change of leadership which saw the controversial Barnaby Joyce restored to the position.

The Liberals' 'entryist' problem, where fundamentalist Christians joined and assumed disproportionate party influence in recent years at the expense of the party's traditional members and supporters, was thrown into high profile during this period. It revealed a historic break with the traditional nature of the Liberal Party, in which religion did not loom large other than to define 'out' groups – for example, until the late 20th century, Catholics. Morrison's ascension to the Liberal leadership, as the world's first Pentecostal prime minister, was symbolic of this. It coincided with years of steady branch stacking across Australia by and with fundamentalist Christians, with negative electoral results for the Liberals in the wider community – notably at the 2021 Western Australian state election, where the Liberals were reduced to just two seats in the lower house. This phenomenon and Morrison's relationship to it have been widely documented. Nor were the Nationals immune from the same entryist pressures. In recent decades, Catholics also reversed their previously marginal position and became increasingly influential, notably in the Liberals' NSW branch. These polarising developments changed the tone and character of the Liberal Party in a way that has made it inhospitable to many lower middle-class small business proprietors, middle-class business executives and professionals, and older Australians, who were historically its backbone. Declining support among women and millennials is also marked.

Changes in the character and personnel of the Nationals emerged fully into view during this period too. In the past, some senior Liberals were known to comment that there were too many farmers in the National Party; those same Liberals now say there are not enough, as the Nationals have come to be dominated by resource sector interests. The Nationals' climate change denialism skewed Coalition energy and environment policy in a way that contributed significantly to the loss of Liberal voters in affluent metropolitan seats, several of which were lost at the 2022 election. An internal reckoning on this is outstanding, but with the Liberal Party itself having moved decisively to the right, this may take some time to occur.

The minor parties

The Greens consolidated their presence as the principal minority party in contemporary 21st-century Australian politics during this term of the Morrison Government. The slim base of one MP, Greens leader Adam Bandt, grew into a lower house quartet at the 2022 election. This was partly due to better political presence and management under Bandt's leadership.

However, the Greens' House of Representatives expansion rested entirely on success in metropolitan Brisbane, where its party workers excelled at the same kind of community-organising approach which underwrote success in capital cities elsewhere in independent 'teal' campaigns. Teal-style community activism remained undeveloped in Brisbane compared to the southern metropolitan capitals, and the Greens offered traditional Liberal voters deserting the Morrison Government an alternative in the absence of teal-style candidates.

The Greens also benefited from the sluggish performance of Labor's underperforming Queensland state branch. Labor's already catastrophically low six-seat share of Queensland's 30 federal seats fell to five seats after losing a metropolitan seat to the Greens at the 2022 election. Labor's election review was critical of Queensland Labor's poor campaign effectiveness, which saw them outcompeted by the well-organised Greens campaign on the ground. Elsewhere, where teal-style community independents were better organised and funded, and where state Labor branches were more adept, the Greens failed to gain any seats. Caution is therefore required in seeing developments during this period as auguring a fundamental upward shift in the Greens' House of Representative presence. This does not diminish the significance of their continuing strong Senate presence, on which the Albanese Government relies, with the additional support of one other senator, to secure passage of its legislative program.

For the second consecutive election, and again despite huge campaign spending, the United Australia Party secured only one senate seat and, at least for now, appears to have expired as a significant influence on federal politics. The lone lower house MPs of the South Australian-based Centre Alliance Party and Queensland-based Katter's Australian Party were both returned at the 2022 election but showed no growth trajectory beyond maintaining their existing seats.

The independents: A quasi-party?

The rise of community independents at the expense of the Liberals was a key development during this term of the Morrison Government, which even before the 2019 election had been characterised privately by one of its own cabinet ministers as 'homophobic, anti-woman, climate-change deniers'. Disaffection among traditional Liberal voters escalated as the Morrison Government doubled down on its social conservatism and climate denialism during this term of office. There were recent examples of former actual and quasi-Liberals striking out independently. In the previous term, Liberal MP Julia Banks switched to the crossbench over bullying by Prime Minister Scott Morrison and other key Liberals. Dr Kerryn Phelps won the Sydney metropolitan seat of Wentworth vacated by vanquished Liberal prime minister Malcolm Turnbull at a by-election. Independent Zali Steggall took the traditionally Liberal seat of Warringah from former Coalition prime minister Tony Abbott at the 2019 election. An earlier demonstration still of the possibilities posed by determined centrist independents existed in the person of Cathy McGowan, who won and held the traditional rural Liberal seat of Indi as an independent in 2013, before retiring and being succeeded by fellow Indi independent activist Helen Haines in 2019.

Inspired by these examples, and increasingly outraged by the Coalition's shortcomings on climate change policy, gender equity and government integrity in particular, community independent campaigns driven by alienated Liberal voters flourished in south-eastern Australia. Contrasting with the increasingly masculinist Coalition, three-quarters of whose federal parliamentary representatives were men, the typical community independent candidate was a local woman in professional-style employment. The establishment of Climate 200, an Australian version of a US-style political action committee (PAC), was critical in the community independents' development and success, lending both funding and professional expertise to nascent campaigns judged to have sufficient prospects for success. The extra seven House of Representatives seats won by independents at the 2022 election reflected their striking success, especially set against the Greens' gain of just three seats.

Coalition critics sought to characterise the community independent campaigns as elitist, leveraging off wealthy engineer Simon Holmes à Court's founding role in Climate 200. They also sought to characterise the 'teals' as not independent at all but rather a party effectively controlled by Climate 200. This was not so. Climate 200 neither chose candidates nor itself ran campaigns. Lack of understanding of the variations within the community independent sphere nevertheless gave this line of attack some traction. The community independents are, in fact, independent, while informally sharing experiences and expertise. Labelling all as 'teals', because of the prominent use of that colour in Steggall's Warringah campaign, and later adopted in several other metropolitan independent campaigns, was misleading. The teals are those independent MPs who took metropolitan seats off the Liberals but not all of them used teal as their campaign keynote colour. The successful independent candidate for North Sydney at the 2022 election, Kylea Tink, used salmon pink. The 'Voices of' community independent groups prominent in rural and regional independent campaigns often use orange, following Cathy McGowan's example in Indi.

In 2021, with the 2022 election looming and momentum among independents and minor parties rising, the government sought to raise the hurdle for establishing new political parties. It legislated to increase the minimum membership of entities seeking party status from 500 to 1500 people. This was designed to make it harder for independent Senate candidates to achieve the party status necessary for an 'above the line' position on often voluminous Senate ballot papers. A number of independent Senate candidates nevertheless met the new requirements. One, ACT aspirant David Pocock, not only did so but displaced ACT

Liberal Senator and Morrison Government minister Zed Seselja in the second ACT senate spot at the election. Along with Dr Monique Ryan's defeat of Morrison Government Treasurer Josh Frydenberg in the hitherto safe Liberal Melbourne metropolitan seat of Kooyong, it symbolised the centrist independents' spectacular rise during this period.

What this means for the future

Consideration of 'parties as a whole' in voting decisions rose at the 2022 election, according to the latest Australian Election Study (AES) survey. While it remained only half as important a factor as 'policy issues', it was more than twice as important as 'party leaders' and 'local candidates'. The state of the Liberals during the Morrison Government's 2019–2022 term of office alienated a sufficient number of its traditional supporters in heartland seats to see it lose power.

Labor's modest two-seat majority win at the 2022 election, followed by its strong political reset in standards of policy and governance at the federal level, sets the scene for stronger party support in the future. Its low primary vote was at least partly due to tactical voting by Labor supporters in safe Liberal seats to help centrist independents defeat sitting Liberals.

The future of minor parties and independents who grew their support during this term of the Morrison Government, and consequently their parliamentary numbers at the 2022 election, is an open question. They will not have the fuel provided by a right-wing and, in the end, unpopular Morrison Government to underwrite their success. The Liberals' situation is the culmination of forces set in train in the 1980s to drive moderates from the party. This has been aided and intensified by 'entryist' behaviour by well-organised fundamentalist Christian and conservative Catholic elements who now have the dominant say in policy and in the preselection of candidates, moving it for now beyond mainstream Australia and Australians. While the Nationals did not suffer any penalty in terms of lost seats at the 2022 election, their vehement pro-fossil fuels and anti-climate change policy positions cost the Liberals support in metropolitan areas, contributing to the Coalition losing office.

Every election is there for the winning, including the next one. While the Liberal and National parties remain so far to the right of mainstream opinion, as they are now, electoral success may well elude the Coalition until it recalibrates towards the 'sensible centre', or collapses and re-emerges in some more centrist form. Labor has existed continuously as a party federally since Federation. The Liberals are the fourth iteration since then of the metropolitan wing of conservative politics in Australia. The extent of religious entryism in the Liberals may yet trigger a fifth.

References

Banks, Julia. 'Liberals pay a high price for their unholy merger with the hard right', *New Daily*, 2 December 2022, <thenewdaily.com.au/opinion/2022/12/02/julia-banks-right-wing-liberals/>.

Cameron, Sarah, Ian McAllister, Simon Jackman and Jill Shepherd. 'The 2022 Australian Federal Election: Results from the Australian Election Study', Australian National University, 9, <australianelectionstudy.org/wp-content/uploads/The-2022-Australian-Federal-Election-Results-from-the-Australian-Election-Study.pdf>.

Combet, Greg and Lenda Oshalem with Linda White and Craig Emerson. 'Election 2022: An opportunity to establish a long-term Labor government', Australian Labor Party, 5 December 2022, <apo.org.au/sites/default/files/resource-files/2022-12/apo-nid321057.pdf>.

Dyer, Jo. *Burning Down the House: Reconstructing Modern Politics*, Monash University Publishing, 2022.

Grieve, Charlotte, Nick McKenzie and Clair Weaver. 'Inside City Builders, the Pentecostal sect with lofty political goals', *The Age*, 20 November 2022, <www.theage.com.au/national/victoria/inside-city-builders-the-pentecostal-sect-with-lofty-political-goals-20221117-p5bz1x.html>.

Holmes à Court, Simon. *The Big Teal*, Monash University Publishing, 2022.

Lesley Howard and Denis Ginnivan. 'A Positive Politics: Community independents and the new wave of political engagement', *Arena* 11, September 2022, <arena.org.au/a-positive-politics-community-independents-and-the-new-wave-of-political-engagement/>.

Savva, Niki. *Plots and Prayers: Malcolm Turnbull's demise and Scott Morrison's ascension*, Scribe, 2019.

— *Bulldozed: Scott Morrison's fall and Anthony Albanese's rise*, Scribe, 2022.

Sawer, Marian and Anika Gauja. 'Party rules: Promises and pitfalls' in Anika Gauja and Marian Sawer (eds), *Party Rules? Dilemmas of political party regulation in Australia*, ANU Press, 2016.

SBS News. 'Cabinet minister Kelly O'Dwyer lashes "homophobic, anti-woman" Liberals in her party', <australianelectionstudy.org/wp-content/uploads/The-2022-Australian-Federal-Election-Results-from-the-Australian-Election-Study.pdf>.

Wallace, Chris. *How to Win an Election*, NewSouth, 2020.

4

THE AUSTRALIAN PUBLIC SERVICE UNDER MORRISON

Renée Leon

The tale of the public service under the Morrison Government is a tale of two halves: the pre-pandemic period, when the government's main focus was to control and limit the public service, and the pandemic period, when the government found it needed the public service more than it could ever have imagined.

In the beginning

It is not often that the first focus of an incoming prime minister is the public service. While there might often be administrative re-arrangements of public service departments, these are usually to allocate ministerial portfolios, or to reflect the incoming government's policy priorities. Announcements and media engagement are focused on the ministry outcomes and the policy choices, not the public service itself.

By contrast, after Scott Morrison was returned as prime minister in May 2019, even before he and his ministers had been sworn in, he called the Secretaries of the Australian Public Service (APS) together in the Cabinet room at Parliament House to set out his expectations of the public service (Whyte, 2019). It was also one of his first photo opportunities; this was not a private briefing but one to which the media were invited, to record the event and to report that the prime minister had warned the public service heads to expect performance targets, to focus on service delivery and to understand that ministers were in charge (Maiden, 2019).

These continued to be the prime minister's themes for the APS over the first year of this term – until the COVID-19 pandemic, which necessitated a greater reliance on public service advice than expected and a more nebulous view of performance targets, as vaccine rollouts and COVID-19 testing fell short of their promised targets.

But before the pandemic upended social and political expectations, Morrison was on an explicit mission to ensure the public service understood its role as he saw it. He expanded on this in a speech to the APS a few months later (Morrison, 2019), in which he set out six guideposts: listen to ordinary Australians, focus on delivering services, be accountable for performance targets, be more adaptable and innovative, display integrity and professionalism, and, above all, remember that ministers, not public servants, are to set policy – the role of the public service is to implement ministers' decisions.

Many in the public service were probably surprised that the prime minister felt he needed to emphasise that ministers decide on policy, since that was already the well-established position. Section 10 of the *Public Service Act* 1999 (APS Act) enshrines the principle of ministerial responsibility in APS values, and every public servant is drilled in the principles of accountability under the Westminster system: that the public service provides apolitical and objective advice to the government, the government decides and the public service faithfully implements the government's decisions.

Many saw the real target as being the willingness of the public service to give frank and fearless advice (Tingle, 2019). The prime minister said in his speech to the APS: 'The best teams are the ones where everyone [does] their job well rather than being in a constant running commentary about the job someone else should be doing'. While accepting that the government should receive policy advice, the prime minister cautioned that this should not involve 'providing a detached or dispassionate summary of the risks that can be logged in the "told you so" file ... The public service is meant to be an enabler of Government policy not an obstacle'.

It would be a sad day for ministerial responsibility if ministers felt that being advised of risks or problems was an obstacle to their ability to decide policy and authorise action by the public service. Having served under

17 portfolio ministers through the terms of eight prime ministers, I have seen a good deal of public service advice and ministerial decision-making, and I can attest that ministers have no difficulty contesting public service advice or ultimately making a decision contrary to that advice. Ministers, in my experience, entirely understand, as do the public servants who advise them, that decisions about policy are for ministers to make.

Morrison's speech signalled to the public service that his government did not really want to hear advice, for example, that a proposed policy had risks or that alternatives could be considered. Rather, ministers were to be the uncontradicted centre for policy ideas and generation.

Respected commentators noted that the idea that the public service was only for delivery, not advice, 'lacked subtlety':

> a government in office for any length of time needs a constantly evolving and innovative agenda, to which bureaucratic thought and expertise can contribute.

> Only an arrogant government, or one living on a temporary high after an unexpected election win, thinks it knows everything. (Grattan, 2019)

Indeed, it is a tough ask to expect a minister to know so much about their area of policy responsibility that they can generate effective policy plans without the input of experts. Of the 22-person Cabinet[1] in place before the election, for example, nine had been in their portfolio for a year or less, and a further six for less than two years – and most of the latter for only a little more than a year. Only the treasurer and the ministers for Health, Foreign Affairs and Industrial Relations had held their portfolios for more than three years.

It is therefore not a criticism of ministers to say that they cannot possibly, after a year or two of portfolio experience, know as much about the many complex areas of their portfolios as the professionals who have been collecting data and implementing policy on these matters for decades. Fortunately, they do not need to, as ministers have untrammelled access to the information and knowledge held by their departments – if only they were not being encouraged by their prime minister to consider such advice as obstacles to their control of their policy agendas.

At the time of the Morrison APS speech in August 2019, the public service was awaiting the report of an independent review into it that had been described as the most substantial root-and-branch review since the Coombs review 40 years earlier. This review was not of Prime Minister Morrison's making. It had been established by Morrison's predecessor, Malcolm Turnbull, on the advice of the then-Secretary of the Department of the Prime Minister & Cabinet (PM&C), Dr Martin Parkinson. Turnbull said at the time that the APS had a long and proud history of advising governments and serving the people well but, with global and technological developments, the time was right to review its capability, culture and operating model (Turnbull, 2018). The goal was to ensure the APS was equipped to engage with the key policy, service delivery and regulatory issues of the day.

Prominent businessman David Thodey AO, chair of the CSIRO and former CEO of Telstra, was appointed to lead the diverse public–private sector panel that would conduct the review. The review was to report in the first half of 2019, but by then Turnbull was no longer prime minister. There was speculation that Morrison was less committed to the Thodey review. He mentioned it only briefly in his speech to the APS in August, to say it had been 'a fair dinkum effort'. The review was delivered to the government in September that year but not released to the public, and there was no immediate indication as to the government's views or the likely timing of any response. In November, the public service commissioner said the recommendations of the report would be 'ambitious in nature and transformational in scope' (Easton, 2019).

Although this ambitious and transformed future had not yet been laid out, in early December 2019, the prime minister launched a substantial restructure of the public service. Eighteen public service departments were reduced to 14, with several departments abolished and several more amalgamated into 'mega-departments'. Five departmental secretaries were shown the door.[2]

The prime minister said this restructure would 'bust bureaucratic congestion and improve service delivery' (Hansard, 2019). The *Mandarin* described it as the prime minister 'showing the Secretaries Board who was boss' (Jenkins, 2019). Journalist Tom Burton, in the *Financial Review*, commented that 'Prime Ministers often adjust public service structures, but in the absence of any clear rationale or strategy other than "congestion-busting", the sudden changes sent a pall through the executive and management levels of the public service' (Burton, 2020).

Questions were asked as to what had happened to the Thodey review and why sweeping changes to the APS were being undertaken without a government response to the review. The prime minister said his restructure announcement was 'consistent entirely with the thrust of the Thodey Review' (Cheng, 2019). Yet, when the Thodey report was released, it pointed to the costs and disruption caused by such public service restructures, suggesting there were better ways to improve co-ordination and collaboration. It recommended that any such machinery-of-government changes should be principles-based, well-planned and evaluated within two years (PM&C, 2019). None of these were reflected in Morrison's December 2019 APS restructure. 'The unilateral cull was the polar opposite of what Thodey had proposed when his panel recommended a more professional regime for managing the performance of secretaries and agency CEOs', observed Tom Burton (2020).

A week later, the prime minister released the Thodey review, which was a thorough and thoughtful analysis of the challenges and opportunities for the APS. It concluded that the APS was not broken but needed significant transformation to be ready for the changes and challenges in the decade ahead. It found that the APS needed clear, unified purpose and priorities, investment in capability and enabling systems, and greater capacity for rapid change (PM&C, 2019a).

The report's 40 recommendations laid out a plan for a more united and outward-facing public service; better digital and data capability to provide outstanding services and advice; strong investment in people and systems to underpin the required transformation; and a determined focus on implementing the recommendations. These recommendations built on a substantial body of reform work that had already been underway within the APS over the preceding two years, led by the Secretaries Reform Committee under Finance Secretary Rosemary Huxtable.

The government also announced its plan for APS reform, titled 'Delivering for Australians', at the same time as it released the Thodey review. The plan was not framed around the recommendations of the Thodey review, but based on the six guideposts the prime minister had outlined in his August speech to the APS. The formal response to the Thodey review was attached as a somewhat unrelated appendix.

The government's response to the Thodey report's recommendations is illuminating on several fronts. While the government mostly agreed to implement the recommendations on the APS improving its own arrangements and performance, it firmly rejected recommendations that would affect the prime minister and the government's executive powers, such as a legislated code of conduct for ministerial advisers, a proposal to include experienced public servants in ministerial offices, rules for Cabinet to ensure programs and policies were evaluated and the evaluations published, a more robust evidence base for government spending decisions, and limits on the prime minister's ability to terminate departmental secretary appointments without cause. The recommendation that machinery-of-government changes be well-planned and evaluated was merely 'Noted', with the somewhat cool explanation that 'decisions on machinery of government changes are a matter for the Prime Minister' (PM&C, 2019b, p. 22).

While most APS-focused recommendations were agreed or part agreed, those that were rejected sought to strengthen the arm of the public service, such as legislating for the management roles of the Secretaries Board, the head of PM&C and the APS Commissioner; amending the APS Act to embed the Westminster principles and strengthen action on integrity; and lifting the arbitrary limit the government had placed on public service numbers (the 'ASL cap').

In most cases, where a recommendation was rejected or partly rejected, the government's response was said to be on the advice of the Secretaries Board itself. As it happens, by this time, there had been a changing of the guard at the top of the public service. The government had installed Phil Gaetjens as head of PM&C and chair of the Secretaries Board, in place of distinguished economist and career public servant Dr Martin Parkinson. Gaetjens was a long-time Liberal Party political adviser, including as chief of staff to Morrison during his time as minister from 2015 to 2018. With Gaetjens at the helm once the Thodey review landed, perhaps it was not surprising that the advice of the Secretaries Board came to align so smoothly with the government's preferences.

PM&C announced that it was getting on with implementing the government's APS reform agenda, with a 'sprint' to be conducted in early 2020 to plan the sequencing of reforms (PM&C, 2019c). But crises greater than the government's tussle with the public service soon assumed much greater prominence.

And then the problems began.

From December 2019, raging bushfires devastated Australia's east coast. Some 30 million hectares burned, thousands of properties were destroyed, and more than 30 people were killed. For weeks, communities across eastern Australia suffered hazardous air quality due to the extent of the smoke blanketing the country. Tourism operators lost their peak summer season revenue as holiday visitors fled from orange skies and burning bush.

Before the nation had finished fighting the fires, the COVID-19 virus began to circulate. The first cases were detected in Australia in February 2020. In March, the World Health Organization declared the onset of a pandemic. Australia's international borders were closed to most arrivals on 20 March, and those who were permitted to enter were required to undergo quarantine, first at home and later in designated hotels. State governments declared public health emergencies and ordered non-essential businesses to close. Schools transitioned to online learning. Much of the economy entered the quietude of lockdowns, while the health system prepared to deal with a spreading infection for which there was as yet no vaccine and no cure.

In April 2020, the Secretary of PM&C announced that work on implementing the government's APS reform agenda was suspended indefinitely as it needed to focus on the response to the COVID-19 pandemic.

The pandemic response required much from the public service. From the early days, the public service was advising on health measures and border protection. Australians in Wuhan, China, the centre of the outbreak, were evacuated to Christmas Island. Pandemic plans were activated. Personal protective equipment (PPE) was released from the national stockpile, and infection-control training amplified across the health workforce. New arrangements were invented to ensure international arrivals were quarantined. With the pandemic declaration and imposition of extensive lockdowns, the economy faced cataclysmic contraction.

Suddenly, a government that was keen on individual choice and market forces had to reach for all the levers of government intervention, and needed advice from its public service as to how to deploy them. Other chapters in this volume detail the effects of COVID-19 on the economy and on the health and aged-care sectors. But across every area of community life, public service advice and action were needed. International border closures necessitated detailed work on repatriating Australians stranded overseas, developing humanitarian and skills exemptions, and supporting international students. Changes in health advice meant regular adjustments to rules about social distancing and the wearing of masks, and the development and broadcasting of consistent public information. The effects of business closures on wages and business revenue required generous and wide-ranging economic support from the government. New policies and practices were needed almost daily, on everything from visiting rules in aged care, to infection-testing arrangements, childcare attendance, Medicare rebates for telehealth, mental health services, university funding, domestic violence responses, protection of remote Indigenous communities, unemployment benefits, cybersecurity for working and studying from home, corporations rules to enable online shareholder meetings, support for Australia's Pacific Island neighbours, and so much more.

Commentators noted that, despite its 2019 statements, the government was now relying more than ever on the public service, and the public service was rising to the challenge (Dingwall & Rollins, 2020). An academic analysis of the importance of 'agency' in supporting innovation in the public service noted that 'the often novel responses to the global pandemic show just how resilient "agency" is in the public sector, and how important it is to our collective safety and welfare' (Ayres et al, 2021). By the end of 2020, Canberra-watchers noted that 'the Coalition government [had] appeared to learn that its bureaucracy was suited to something other than following orders. Public appetite for good government boomed in the pandemic. Meeting that demand involved listening to a well-trained, expert bureaucracy. The Prime Minister's patronising message in August 2019 that public servants should implement rather than advise on policy seemed from another era' (Dingwall, 2020).

In his 2020 end-of-year speech to the top levels of the APS, Morrison praised the public service for rising to the pandemic challenge. However, he characterised that successful response as vindication for his advice that the APS should focus on implementation, as though the public service had not also had to rapidly develop the new systems and policies that it had implemented. There was a single reference to the involvement of 'Treasury officials' in the development of the substantial economic support package, a package which the prime minister said was 'the product of Ministers' (Morrison, 2020).

The minister for the public service, Ben Morton, managed to find some further recognition for the public service, including for its policy role. Reflecting on the COVID-19 response in early 2021, Minister Morton said that 'in 2020, we witnessed our Australian Public Service at its best ... brokering sound policy, finding practical solutions, working across silos, removing barriers to get the job done' (Morton, 2021). And Minister Morton introduced his own gloss to Morrison's portrayal of ministers as the policy brains and public servants as the implementers: 'It is this that 18 months ago the Prime Minister talked of when he laid out his expectations of his Ministers and of the APS, that ... we act as a team. *Ministers leverage the experience, professionalism and capability that you bring*, and the APS delivers Government decisions' (Morton, 2021, italics added). Perhaps it was some small acknowledgment that ministers actually did have to rely on the public service's experience and professional skills to develop the government's policy response to the crises Australia was facing.

Despite the scale of the APS effort in responding to the pandemic, the public service did soon resume work on implementing the Thodey review recommendations to which the government had agreed. Former Secretary Stephen Sedgwick was engaged to undertake work on the Thodey review integrity recommendations. PM&C announced (PM&C, 2020) that Secretaries had agreed to support a number of Thodey-inspired capability-building initiatives, based on approaches already being developed to respond to COVID-19. These included:

- greater interdepartmental cooperation, resource sharing and staff mobilisation
- accelerated digital transformation
- an APS 'surge reserve', and
- investment in skills needed for the future.

Over 2020–21, the APS Commission launched a review of classifications to address the Thodey recommendation to streamline management and reduce hierarchy; an APS Workforce Strategy, said to be the first whole-of-enterprise approach to strategic workforce management across the public service (APS Commission, 2021a); the APS Mobility Framework (APS Commission, 2021b); the APS Surge Reserve (APS Commission, 2021c), designed to facilitate rapid transfers of staff to meet changing demand; and the APS Academy, implementing the Thodey recommendations for capability development in the APS.

Although summarised only briefly here, this has been an extensive body of work. Yet the Morrison Government made almost no mention of APS reform achievements, nor the extent to which the Thodey review was, or was being, implemented. The PM&C 2021 Annual Report stated in low-key terms that 44 of 50 initiatives contained in the government's APS reform agenda had been achieved or were on track (PM&C, 2020–21, p. 119), but the Morrison Government seemed to show no interest in this achievement.

The public service did a great deal of good work that enabled the government to respond effectively to the pandemic. But it was not aided by the systematic degrading of capability and capacity that had occurred over the preceding years. Well before Morrison set out his APS expectations, successive Coalition governments had committed to the goal of reducing the size of the public service as part of its smaller government agenda (Cormann, 2015; Cormann, 2016; Cormann, 2017.)

After slashing the public service by 11 000 jobs in 2013–14, the Abbott Government had committed to keeping the number of public service positions at the level of 2006–07, the last year of the Howard Government, by imposing a staffing cap. In the 2015–16 Budget, the number of APS positions budgeted for each agency became its upper limit of public service staff for the agency: the average staffing level (ASL) cap,[3] a figure that was set to be reduced each year. Although the ASL cap was touted as a means to achieve 'budget repair', it did not in fact bear any relationship to budgetary reductions. Agencies that were tasked to deliver new or renewing government programs continued to receive the necessary budgetary allocations to do so, but were prohibited from engaging public servants to do the work. Instead, the APS had to outsource the work or engage contracted staff from labour-hire companies who were not counted in the ASL cap.

It was a strange, twilight version of 'smaller government'. The scale of government spending, and hence government's role and outputs, increased rather than decreased during the Coalition's most recent three terms in office.[4] The Abbott, Turnbull and Morrison governments had spent as much, or more, on programs and activities, but increasingly administered their outputs via private-sector means rather than the APS. While this shift commenced under the Abbott and Turnbull governments, the effects of the ASL cap became cumulatively more pressing over time and resulted in significant use of alternative forms of labour under Morrison.

A 2018 Senate Committee report received evidence that government spending on labour contractors had more than doubled across a sample of 24 agencies between 2012–13 and 2016–17 (JCPAA, 2019, referenced in Senate, 2021). A further Senate Committee inquiry in 2021 reported that spending on contractors increased from about $289 million in 2013 to $2.1 billion in the 2020 calendar year (Senate, 2021). The 2021 report found, for example, that over 40 per cent of the workforce of the Department of Veterans' Affairs comprised labour-hire staff. The National Disability Insurance Agency (NDIA), operating with about half the number of public servants intended in its original design, had spent $190 million on labour hire in 2020–21, a further $97 million outsourced to 'delivery partners' and $30 million on a privatised call centre run by Serco (Morton, 2021).

While labour hire became the go-to method for maintaining necessary levels of service delivery staff, the ASL cap also drove reductions in policy staff, resulting in the 'hollowing out of strategic policy skills' identified in the Thodey review. As policy and management capability was degraded, work on policy and strategy increasingly went to consulting firms. In 2012–13, the federal government spend on the largest seven consulting firms came in at just under $400 million; by 2020 the amount had trebled to $1.2 billion (<consultancy.com.au>, 2021a). Ironically, even the design of the APS Academy, intended to cultivate core capabilities in the public service, was contracted out to the private sector (Canales, 2021).

The Australia Institute calculated that the amount spent on consultants in 2020 could hire 12000 public servants – about the same number as Coalition governments had cut from the public service since 2013 – and would also have the benefit of keeping their knowledge and capability within the departments that serve the government (Browne, 2021).

Consultants were prominent in the government's efforts to respond to the pandemic crisis. External consultants, principally Boston Consulting Group, were paid nearly $3 million for the COVID-Safe App, for example (<consultancy.com.au>, 2021b). McKinsey was paid $660000 in relation to Australia's vaccine strategy for four weeks of 'collaboration and participation' in a range of activities, though not any actual advice (Farrell & McDonald, 2021). McKinsey was later paid $3 million to advise the Department of PM&C about 'maximising economic and social opportunities as the COVID-19 vaccine progresses', and $2.4 million to advise the Health Department on IT services to support the vaccine rollout. Consultancy PWC was paid $11.4 million to be the Health Department's primary partner in managing the vaccine rollout program. McKinsey was paid $1.4 million by the Department of Employment to examine post-COVID labour force gaps in the Australian economy. Labour market analysis was a core Department of Employment capability until not so long ago.

Was the expenditure on consultants money well spent? The COVID-Safe App developed with the aid of Boston Consulting Group was widely pilloried. It detected only a handful of cases not traced by existing capability and was found to have increased workload for state contact tracers (Vogt et al, 2022). Despite the significant spend on consultants to plan and prepare the vaccine strategy, the rollout was beset by delays, leading to Australia's population being left mostly unvaccinated as fresh waves of COVID-19 infection swept through during winter 2021. Not surprisingly, many have observed that a properly resourced APS could have been far more effective (Duckett & Stobart, 2022).

As the Morrison Government's term approached its end, the APS had every reason to be proud of its efforts and achievements in the face of both disdain from its ministers and the extraordinary demands of a pandemic. But public servants are weary, and the APS has struggled to maintain essential skills in the face of deep cuts and political inroads. In the very last days of the 2022 election campaign, Morrison announced that the entire cost of the Coalition parties' campaign promises would be met by public-service cuts, a further blow to APS hopes that its pandemic performance would be the basis for some reinvestment.

The war on the public service, waged over nearly a decade of Coalition government, is not unique to Australia. In the United Kingdom, the home of the Westminster tradition, Boris Johnson's government saw off numerous senior civil servants who resigned in protest at maladministration (Payne, 2020) or under pressure of ministerial hostility (Syal, 2020). Lord Kerslake, head of the civil service from 2011–14, spoke of 'a diminishing trust between the civil service and ministers ... and an unwillingness to give the honest advice that's needed' (Syal, 2020), and a senior civil servant, writing under protection of anonymity, described the government's 'relentless, remorseless and world-beating destruction of [civil service goodwill]' (*Guardian*, 2020). The origins of the deteriorating relationship between ministers and civil servants have been traced back to former prime minister Margaret Thatcher, who sought to recast the role of civil servants from providers of impartial advice, to 'enthusiastic deliverers of [ministerial] policy ideas or ideology' (King & Crew, cited in Murphy, 2020) – a playbook that now sounds rather familiar.

The United States, already more accepting of political appointees than Westminster governments, saw full-blown attacks on public service advice and reputation under former president Donald Trump (Rhode, 2019), who both publicly, and through intermediaries, attacked public servants who provided advice or evidence that conflicted with the president's views or political expectations. The attacks were so extreme that *Time* magazine recognised as the 2019 'Guardians of the Year' the public servants who, despite the risk of loss of career and public attacks, showed courage and integrity as whistleblowers or in giving evidence to public inquiries (Calabresi et al, 2019). Academics described Trump's approach to the public service as part of a deliberate undermining of public institutions 'accompanied by a rhetoric of delegitimization', and described the sidelining of experts through the appointment of unqualified public service chiefs who actively undermined the mission of the organisations they were appointed to lead (Moynihan, 2021). The false characterisation of public servants as part of a 'deep state' that is acting improperly to undermine the government culminated in an order signed by Trump shortly before his loss of office in the 2020 election, to allow the sacking of public servants considered to be disloyal to the government (Rein et al, 2020).

The increasingly overt agenda of recent conservative governments to reduce the role and undermine the capacity of the public service has morphed from a preference for small government and light regulation to a concerted effort to limit evidence and expertise as the basis for government action, with significant implications for effective governance and public trust. It is an agenda that was not supported by the alternative government, which generally expressed greater respect for the traditions of public service.

In Opposition, Labor vowed to restore public service capability if elected, promising to end the ASL cap and slash the by-now annual $3 billion Coalition government spend on contractors and consultants. The election of the Albanese Government in May 2022, and its appointment of Thodey review member Dr Glyn Davis AO as head of PM&C, was a hopeful portent that those promises would be fulfilled. It will be a long road to recovery.

Note: This chapter was written with invaluable research assistance from Mr Liam Lander.

References

APS (Australian Public Service) Commission. 'APS Workforce Strategy 2025', 18 March 2021a, <www.apsc.gov.au/initiatives-and-programs/aps-workforce-strategy-2025>.

APS Commission. 'The APS Mobility Framework', 29 April 2021b, <www.apsc.gov.au/initiatives-and-programs/aps-mobility-framework>.

APS Commission. 'APS Surge Reserve', 15 March 2021c, <www.apsc.gov.au/initiatives-and-programs/aps-mobility-framework/aps-surge-reserve>.

Ayres, Russell, Wendy Jarvie and Trish Mercer. 'Public Sector Informant: The public service can innovate, when we let it', *Canberra Times*, 2 November 2021, <www.canberratimes.com.au/story/7487124/the-public-service-can-innovate-when-we-let-it/>.

Browne, Bill. 'Talk isn't Cheap: Making consultants reports publicly available via Senate order'. *The Australia Institute*, September 2021, <https://australiainstitute.org.au/wp-content/uploads/2021/10/P1079-Talk-isnt-cheap-Order-for-the-production-of-consultants-reports-Web.pdf>

Burton, Tom. 'Can the Australian public service reform itself?', *Financial Review*, 4 March 2020, <www.afr.com/politics/federal/can-the-australian-public-service-reform-itself-20200224-p543oj>.

Calabresi, Massimo, Vera Bergengruen and Simon Shuster. 'Guardians of the Year – Public Servants', *Guardian*, 2019, <time.com/guardians-of-the-year-2019-public-servants/>.

Canales, Sarah Basford. '"Embarrassing": Government racks up $500k contractor bill in two months to build its new APS Academy', *Canberra Times*, 3 May 2021, <www.canberratimes.com.au/story/7226440/embarrassing-new-public-service-academy-racks-up-500k-contractor-bill-in-two-months/>.

Cheng, Amy. 'Overhaul of APS sees cuts to govt depts', *Government News*, 5 December 2019, <www.governmentnews.com.au/overhaul-of-aps-sees-cuts-to-govt-depts/>.

Consultancy.com.au. 'Federal government spend on big 7 consulting firms tops $1 billion', 30 March 2021a, <www.consultancy.com.au/news/3213/federal-government-spend-on-big7-consulting-firms-tops-1-billion>.

Consultancy.com.au. 'BCG's fees for COVIDSafe app surpass $1 million mark', 21 July 2021b, <www.consultancy.com.au/news/2341/bcgs-fees-for-covidsafe-app-surpass-1-million-mark>.

Cormann, Mathias. 'Preface, Agency Resourcing Budget Paper No. 4 2015–16', Commonwealth of Australia, 2015, <archive.budget.gov.au/2015-16/bp4/00_BP4_consolidated.pdf>.

Cormann, Mathias. 'Preface, Agency Resourcing Budget Paper No. 4 2016–17', Commonwealth of Australia, 2016, <archive.budget.gov.au/2016-17/bp4/Budget2016-17_BP4.pdf>.

Cormann, Mathias. 'Preface, Agency Resourcing Budget Paper No. 4 2017–18', Commonwealth of Australia, 2017, <archive.budget.gov.au/2017-18/bp4/Budget2017-18_BP4.pdf>.

Dingwall, Doug and Adrian Rollins. 'COVID-19 forces us to re-learn the importance of good government', *Canberra Times*, 1 April 2020, <www.canberratimes.com.au/story/6706810/covid-19-forces-us-to-re-learn-importance-of-good-government/>.

Dingwall, Doug. 'Demand for good government boomed in 2020', *Canberra Times*, 26 December 2020, <www.canberratimes.com.au/story/7046486/demand-for-good-government-boomed-in-2020-will-the-coalition-deliver/>.

Duckett, Stephen and Anika Stobart. 'What do we get for the millions spent on COVID consultancies?' Grattan Institute, 10 May 2022, <grattan.edu.au/news/what-do-we-get-for-the-millions-spend-on-covid-consultancies/>.

Easton, Stephen. 'Are the planets aligned for APS reform, or is it more like a perfect storm?', the *Mandarin*, 27 November 2019, <www.themandarin.com.au/121421-are-the-planets-aligned-for-aps-reform-or-is-it-more-like-a-perfect-storm/>.

Farrell, Paul and Alex McDonald. 'A consultancy firm was paid $660,000 to advise on Australia's COVID-19 vaccine strategy. But a government official said they provided no "specific advice"', *ABC News*, 3 June 2021, <www.abc.net.au/news/2021-06-03/federal-government-mckinsey-covid-vaccine-strategy-advice/100185786>.

Grattan, Michelle. 'Scott Morrison can learn a lot from public servants, but will he listen?' *ABC News*, 19 August 2019, <www.abc.net.au/news/2019-08-09/scott-morrison-can-learn-a-lot-from-public-servants/11398456?utm_campaign=abc_news_web&utm_content=link&utm_medium=content_shared&utm_source=abc_news_web>.

Guardian. 'Editorial: Goodwill is the civil service's lifeblood – this bullying government is using it up fast', 16 December 2020, <www.theguardian.com/commentisfree/2020/dec/16/goodwill-lifeblood-civil-service-bullying-public-servants-europe>.

Hansard. 'New structure of government departments', 5 December 2019, <parlinfo.aph.gov.au/parlInfo/search/display/display.w3p;query=Id%3A%22media%2Fpressrel%2F7064930%22>.

Jenkins, Sharon. 'Out of the blue: PM shows the Secretaries Board who's boss', *The Mandarin*, 6 December 2019, <www.themandarin.com.au/122204-out-of-the-blue-pm-shows-the-secretaries-board-whos-boss/>.

Maiden, Samantha. 'PM warns public service of "congestion busting" ahead', the *New Daily*, 23 May 2019, <thenewdaily.com.au/news/election-2019/2019/05/23/scott-morrison-public-service/>.

Morrison, Scott. 'Speech, Institute of Public Administration', 19 August 2019, <pmtranscripts.pmc.gov.au/release/transcript-42366>.

Morrison, Scott. 'Speech to APS Virtual Forum', 25 November 2020, <pmtranscripts.pmc.gov.au/release/transcript-43149>.

Morton, Ben. 'Speech to the APS, State of the Service Roadshow', 19 February 2021, <webarchive.nla.gov.au/awa/20220427042811/https://ministers.pmc.gov.au/morton/2021/speech-aps-state-service-roadshow>.

Morton, Rick. 'How private management consultants took over the public service', the *Saturday Paper*, 9–15 October 2021, <www.thesaturdaypaper.com.au/news/politics/2021/10/09/how-private-management-consultants-took-over-the-public-service#hrd>.

Moynihan, David. 'Populism and the deep state: The attack on public service under Trump', in Michael W Bauer, B Guy Peters, Jon Pierre, Kutsal Yesilkagit and Stefan Becker (eds), *Democratic Backsliding and Public Administration: How Populists in Government Transform State Bureaucracies*. Cambridge University Press, 2021.

Murphy, Peter. 'Why it matters that so many senior civil servants are quitting under Boris Johnson', *The Conversation*, 2 September 2020, <theconversation.com/why-it-matters-that-so-many-senior-civil-servants-are-quitting-under-boris-johnson-145257>.

Payne, Sebastian, George Parker, Peter Foster and Jim Pickard, 'Top UK government lawyer quits over Brexit withdrawal agreement changes, *Financial Times*, 8 September 2020.

PM&C, Department of. *Our Public Service, Our Future. Independent Review of the Australian Public Service*, Commonwealth of Australia, 2019a.

PM&C, Department of. 'Delivering for Australians. A world-class Australian Public Service: The Government's APS reform agenda', Commonwealth of Australia, 2019b.

PM&C, Department of. 'Open letter to the Australian Public Service – December 2019', 13 December 2019c, <www.pmc.gov.au/resource-centre/government/open-letter-australian-public-service-december-2019>.

PM&C, Department of. 'Open letter to the Australian Public Service – September 2020', 4 September 2020, <www.pmc.gov.au/resource-centre/government/open-letter-australian-public-service-040920>.

PM&C, Department of. *Annual Report 2020–21*.

Rein, Lisa, Josh Dawsey and Toluse Olorunnipa. 'Trump's historic assault on the civil service was four years in the making', *Washington Post*, 23 October 2020, <www.washingtonpost.com/politics/trump-federal-civil-service/2020/10/23/02fbf05c-1549-11eb-ba42-ec6a580836ed_story.html>.

Rhode, David. 'Public servants are starting to respond to Donald Trump's false attacks', the *New Yorker*, 14 October 2019, <www.newyorker.com/news/daily-comment/public-servants-versus-donald-trump>.

Senate, Finance & Public Administration References Committee, 'APS Inc: undermining public sector capability and performance', November 2021.

Syal, Rajeev. 'Number of UK civil servants leaving Whitehall rises by 9% in a year', *Guardian*, 28 August 2020, <www.theguardian.com/politics/2020/aug/28/number-of-uk-civil-servants-leaving-whitehall-rises-by-9-in-a-year>.

Tingle, Laura. 'Scott Morrison has the public service and accountability in his sights, but what's behind the rhetoric?', *ABC News*, 27 July 2019, <www.abc.net.au/news/2019-07-27/scott-morrison-accountability-public-service/11351262>.

Turnbull, Malcolm. 'Media release, Prime Minister Malcolm Turnbull, and Minister for the Public Service Kelly O'Dwyer', 4 May 2018, <parlinfo.aph.gov.au/parlInfo/search/display/display.w3p;query=Id:%22media/pressrel/5943423%22;src1=sm1>.

Vogt, Florian, Bridget Haire, John Kaldor and Linda Selvey. 'The COVIDSafe app was designed to help contact tracers. We crunched the numbers to see what really happened', *The Conversation*, 5 February 2022, <theconversation.com/the-covidsafe-app-was-designed-to-help-contact-tracers-we-crunched-the-numbers-to-see-what-really-happened-172242>.

Whyte, Sally. 'Scott Morrison to public service bosses: Expect performance targets', *Canberra Times*, 23 May 2019, <www.canberratimes.com.au/story/6178463/morrison-sends-a-pointed-message-to-public-service-bosses/>.

5

THE MORRISON GOVERNMENT AND AUSTRALIAN FEDERALISM

Alan Fenna

The period from May 2019, when the 46th Parliament was elected, to April 2022, when it was dissolved, was a particularly dynamic one for Australian federalism. The COVID-19 pandemic, together with continuing partisan differences over climate-change policy, brought the states to the fore and injected a fresh vitality into the federal system and intergovernmental relations. For the first time, the pandemic even led to the state premiers being rated ahead of the prime minister as the country's most powerful figures by the *Australian Financial Review Magazine*'s 'power issue' (Coorey, 2021). At various points, the Morrison Government was clearly on the back foot in its dealing with the states. These events are unlikely to alter the long-term process of centralisation, but they did run counter to the trend and provided a reminder that the states continue to be important in the federal system.

As active as this period was in Australian federalism, the Morrison Government was not, though, itself particularly active in federal matters. Only three initiatives stand out, and one of those occurred during the previous parliament: modifications to water down Australia's system of horizontal fiscal equalisation; proposals for a greater Commonwealth role in disaster management; and a shift from the Council of Australian Governments (COAG) to 'National Cabinet'.

Fiscal federalism: Fair shares?

The defining characteristics of Australian federalism's fiscal arrangements are a high degree of vertical fiscal imbalance, whereby the Commonwealth enjoys exclusive access to the main tax bases; extensive use of the 'spending power' to influence policy in areas of state jurisdiction through conditional or 'tied' grants; and a thorough-going system of horizontal fiscal equalisation, whereby the GST revenues are distributed to the states so as to ensure a common fiscal capacity. By contrast with some preceding governments, there was little action in respect to the first two of these under Scott Morrison's leadership but a significant change to the third.[1]

Since the Commonwealth introduced the Goods and Services Tax (GST) in 2000, Australia has practised a form of 'direct' equalisation, in which a given pool of state and territory funds is divided up according to an equalising formula, as determined by the Commonwealth Grants Commission.[2] The Commonwealth made no contribution from its own budget and thus any gain for one jurisdiction was a loss to another. The net contributors had always been New South Wales and Victoria until the resources boom transformed Western Australia into a substantial contributor jurisdiction as well. Massive windfall revenues from minerals exports were driving down its share of the GST revenue dramatically, and pressure soon mounted from Western Australia for the Commonwealth to relax the strict principles of equalisation in that state's favour (eg Porter, 2011).[3]

The Commonwealth's earlier response to such demands had been the tried-and-true one of commissioning an inquiry, one that ended up endorsing the status quo (GSTDR, 2012). This time it assigned the task to the Productivity Commission, an institution whose firm intellectual basis in economics meant it was bound to be more ambivalent about wealth sharing (Fenna, 2011). And so it was, recommending that the system be diluted to bring about 'reasonable' rather than full equalisation (PC, 2018, p. 39).

As treasurer in the Turnbull Government, Morrison (2018) enthusiastically embraced the Productivity Commission's recommendations, a commitment reaffirmed once he became prime minister himself (Morrison & Frydenberg, 2018). By the middle of November 2018, the government had passed legislation enshrining the rule that no state would receive less than

70 per cent of its per capita share – regardless of how disproportionately that might reward them.[4] This broke with the longstanding principle of Australia's equalisation system that it should equalise fully – bringing advantaged jurisdictions down and disadvantaged ones up to a common level. It also required the Commonwealth to start dipping into its own pockets to make up some of the difference for recipient jurisdictions, though the commitment to ensuring there would be no losers was extended only to 2027.

Quite how extreme might be the consequences of such a move became glaringly evident in 2020–21 when, as other states were battling with the severe budgetary effects of the pandemic, Western Australia recorded the largest budget surplus in its history and the second largest in the history of any state, and then repeated this in 2021–22. A substantial part of those surpluses was due to the 70 per cent floor on GST share.[5]

Real reform to federal financial relations – such as an increase in the rate and base of the GST or, more ambitiously, income-tax sharing, as mooted by New South Wales (NSW Treasury, 2020) – got no more traction than had a number of ideas that had bubbled up in the past (Fenna, 2017).

Climate change: The states step up

As treasurer in the Turnbull Government, Morrison (2017) had also appeared in parliament, proudly displaying a lump of Australia's dirtiest energy source, declaring: 'This is coal. Do not be afraid. Do not be scared. It will not hurt you'. It was a stunt that encapsulated the Coalition's stand on climate change since Tony Abbott had won the 2013 election vociferous in his determination to 'axe the tax' on carbon emissions the Gillard Labor Government introduced in 2012.[6] While as prime minister Morrison dialled down the celebration of all things coal, that nonetheless set the tone for the government's approach to climate change and, in particular, its refusal to introduce any measures that might penalise Australia's existing comparative advantage in the exploitation of hydrocarbons. Natural gas was instead touted as the saviour transition fuel, but its merits were widely contested (eg Wood & Dundas, 2020). Reinforcing this was the adamant position of the National Party.[7]

While all this might have been bad for the climate, it was good for federalism – opening the way for the states and territories to fill the policy void (Fenna, 2023). Notwithstanding the long-run drift of power to the Commonwealth (Fenna, 2019), the states retain abundant capacity to introduce mitigation policies of their own. This is particularly the case since electricity generation is the leading source of greenhouse-gas emissions in Australia and remains in state hands. The states are very much at the coal face. Moving in to compensate for Commonwealth government inaction, they all adopted emissions-reduction targets matching or exceeding net zero by 2050 and set in place a range of programs expediting the shift to renewable energy.

Typically, this compensatory action reflected the partisan divide, with Labor states leading the way. However, it also reflected differing circumstances, with South Australia being best positioned and taking the most ambitious steps (McGreevy et al, 2021). More awkward for the Morrison Government was when the Coalition Government in New South Wales converted to climate action, prompting another round of verbal sparring. The Commonwealth eventually came on board, committing to net zero by 2050 at the 26th United Nations Climate Change Conference, held in Glasgow. This was to be achieved, though, 'the Australian way' – that is, without punitive measures such as a carbon tax (Australian Government, 2021). Even then, National Party members made it clear that the commitment was weak.

Bushfires: More centralisation?

The severe bushfire season of 2019–20 tested Australia's arrangements and division of roles and responsibilities concerning natural disasters. While management of such events is an established responsibility of the states, and each has its own police, ambulance, emergency services and fire brigade organisations, disasters may be of a breadth, severity or duration such as to exceed state capacity or readiness. In that event, it has long been accepted that the Commonwealth will supply assistance.

The extent and severity of the fires was such as to require substantial assistance from the main emergency management service the

Commonwealth has at its disposal, the Australian Defence Force (ADF). Such assistance included navy vessels rescuing beleaguered residents in fire-stricken coastal zones, and was 'one of the largest domestic ADF operations in our history', according to the prime minister (Morrison, 2020a). The cross-border extent of the fires also presented challenges for the states.

Having been burnt by public opinion for taking a back seat as the fires raged out of control over the Christmas period, Morrison was asserting the view by the end of January 2020 that the Commonwealth should be granted a more prominent role in disaster management. Having protested that 'I don't hold a hose, mate' in response to complaints about his being away vacationing, Morrison argued a month later that it was time there was a 'legal framework that would allow the Commonwealth to declare a national state of emergency' (Morrison, 2019, 2020a). A Royal Commission inquiry was soon launched to flesh out this proposition, delivering its report only eight months later (RCNNDA, 2020). A National Emergency Declaration Bill was introduced into parliament on 3 December 2020, enacted within a week and assented to on 15 December. Its implications for Commonwealth–state relations were minimal and it did nothing to address state concerns about such practical matters as the intergovernmental Disaster Recovery Funding Arrangements, as raised for instance by the New South Wales premier (Perrottet, 2022).

The pandemic: Federalism redux

The bushfires were not over before it became apparent that Australia was facing a potentially even greater emergency: the new coronavirus from China that was threatening the world (Fenna, 2021). By contrast with the bushfires, this was a threat for which the Commonwealth had sweeping national emergency powers – or, at least, claims for itself such powers. The Commonwealth's *Biosecurity Act* 2015 provides statutory authority to 'give any direction, to any person ... to prevent or control' the entry or spread of disease (s. 478(1); see also Lee et al, 2018). However, as with the bushfires, it is the states who own, control or regulate almost everything of relevance to managing a pandemic, and each has its own Public Health Act with provisions for such an event. As with the bushfires, too, the natural and agreed-upon role of the Commonwealth is to provide co-ordination and support. The main difference lies in the importance of the external border, which is regulated and controlled by the Commonwealth.

The states responded with alacrity and it became apparent almost immediately that as far as internal management was concerned, the *Biosecurity Act* was redundant. For instance, on 16 March Victoria declared a 'state of emergency' under its *Public Health and Wellbeing Act* 2008 while the Commonwealth declared a 'human biosecurity emergency' on 18 March (McLean & Huf, 2020). This set the tone for the ensuing two years of battling the pandemic, with the states out in front and the Commonwealth resisting or trailing. It also set the scene for a new phase in peak-level intergovernmental relations. The pandemic's reinvigoration of Australian federalism was evident in several ways. First of all, it was the states that imposed lockdowns and other controls to limit the spread of the virus. Second, the states were able to defy the Commonwealth in the stringency of their measures. Third, the switch to frequent and far more consensual first ministers' meetings indicated that the two levels of government were on a much more equal footing than was usual.

States *versus* Commonwealth

In taking charge to such an extent, the states were regularly at odds with the Commonwealth, particularly about the appropriate severity of control measures, and that tension persisted well into 2021 as new outbreaks continued. Whether it was lockdowns, school closures or border closures, the Commonwealth frequently expressed its frustration and its desire to see the economy – for which it bears primary responsibility – re-opened. Its draconian powers in the *Biosecurity Act* were of little assistance in that regard. Resolute action by state governments was strongly supported by public opinion, and they prevailed throughout.

There was no action more expressive of Australian federalism's revival than state border closures. On the face of it, these were flagrantly at odds with the unambiguous language of section 92 of the Constitution and were deplored by the Commonwealth. On 15 March 2020, the

Western Australian Government declared a state of emergency, closing the border three weeks later. Following rejection of his request for a travel exemption, Clive Palmer – who had significant mining interests in the state but was based in Queensland – brought a case to the High Court. The Commonwealth joined the challenge, antagonising Western Australia and other states, only to withdraw when the savageness of the second wave hitting Victoria became apparent.[8] The High Court upheld the closures as a legitimate exception to the requirements of section 92 three months later.[9]

States *or* Commonwealth?

There were also challenges at the operational boundary between the Commonwealth and the states. The most significant concerned quarantine, a major component of the control strategy through into early 2022. Quarantine is an enumerated Commonwealth power under section 51; however, it is a concurrent power, and its implementation involves access to and administration of significant accommodation resources, and this put it into state hands. Mismanagement of quarantine gave rise to the deadly second wave in Victoria in 2020, and questions continued to arise about its handling (CHQI, 2020). There were other areas where one level of government or the other erred, most notoriously when a somewhat halting start to the Commonwealth's vaccine rollout in early 2021 led to the prime minister protesting to widespread incredulity that 'It's not a race'. However, these were not issues of federalism per se.

States *and* Commonwealth

The first case of COVID-19 in Australia, a passenger arriving in Melbourne from China, was confirmed on 25 January 2020. COAG (2020) met on 13 March, agreeing to various co-operative measures and reaffirming the division of responsibilities laid down in a series of agreements and protocols going back more than a decade. This was the 48th meeting of COAG, but only the second of the Morrison Government.[10] Immediately afterwards, the prime minister announced that COAG would be suspended in favour of a weekly first ministers' meeting, to be called 'National Cabinet'. This was much more collegial in character than COAG's summit-style events, and provided an important consistency of messaging as well as overarching policy coherence. The states, and several commentators, welcomed this development, praising National Cabinet's consensus-based decision-making and the way it 'established national principles that recognise the sovereignty of states and territories to implement policies according to local circumstances' (Victoria, 2020).

At the same time, other commentators, particularly those on the right, and some experts, expressed impatience with the fact that National Cabinet decisions were not binding and that the states followed the 'roadmap' at their own speed. National Cabinet outcomes were accused of being 'a "decision" in name only', presenting a mere 'fig-leaf of unity' (Duckett et al, 2020; see also SCC19, 2022). This deviation from the practice of rule by Commonwealth diktat might seem, however, quite consistent with norms of federalism.

What's in a name? National Cabinet was more a case of operational change and re-branding than of institutional change. A cabinet is only such by virtue of the combination of party discipline and collective ministerial responsibility to parliament, neither of which pertains in this case. This reality was confirmed by the Administrative Appeals Tribunal when an unsuccessful attempt was made to shelter National Cabinet records from freedom of information requests.[11] The government's response was to make an attempt at endowing National Cabinet with privileged status via legislation, but the Bill did not proceed beyond second reading before parliament was dissolved in 2022.[12]

National Cabinet had not been operating long before the prime minister announced with great fanfare that it would supersede COAG permanently, promising that the new arrangement 'will change the way the Commonwealth and states and territories effectively and productively work together' (Morrison, 2020b).[13] For the prime minister, it was to be a 'congestion busting process', putting a stop to 'endless meetings that do not result in action'. National Cabinet continued through the rest of the Morrison Government's term, though meeting less frequently. No post-congestion achievements were registered, but it did outlast the government. The incoming Labor Government held a National Cabinet meeting soon after taking office and expressed a newfound conviction that the meeting should be shrouded in Cabinet-like confidentiality.

In Sum

The three most salient developments in Australian federalism under the Morrison Government were the implementation of a compromise system of fiscal equalisation, together with a stark demonstration of what consequences might follow; a more active role for the states as a consequence of the Morrison Government's stand on climate change combined with the impact of the pandemic; and the replacement of COAG with a more informal and frequent heads-of-government meeting, National Cabinet. It was a significant period for Australian federalism, with the system's federal nature being given a major boost, but the Morrison Government's initiatives with regard to the system were limited.

National Cabinet was a notable new variation in Australia's practices of executive federalism, one that corresponded to the extraordinary circumstances of the time. There were several reasons it worked so well: the states so heavily occupied the emergency management and health fields and were thus equal partners; having a federal as distinct from a unitary approach was effective and was recognised as such by public opinion; the pandemic eclipsed all other issues; and the pandemic was much less a zone of ideological conflict than most public policy questions. Once the conflict, messiness, complexity and difficulty of Australia's shared governance issues return, so, one must assume, will the normal difficulties and procedures of intergovernmental relations.

References

Australian Government. *The Plan to Deliver Net Zero: The Australian way*. Commonwealth of Australia, 2021, <www.industry.gov.au/sites/default/files/October%202021/document/the-plan-to-deliver-net-zero-the-australian-way.pdf>.
CHQI, COVID-19 Hotel Quarantine Inquiry. *Final Report and Recommendations*, Government of Victoria, 2020.

COAG, Council of Australian Governments. *Communiqué*. Commonwealth of Australia, 2020.

Conran, Peter. *Review of COAG Councils and Ministerial Forums: Report to National Cabinet*, Commonwealth of Australia, 2020.

Coorey, Phillip. 'Morrison has been unseated by the premiers', *Australian Financial Review Magazine*, 1 October 2021.

Duckett, Stephen, Hal Swerissen, Will Mackey, Anika Stobart and Hugh Parsonage. *The Course of COVID-19 in Australia: Submission to the Senate Inquiry into the Australian Government's response to the COVID-19 pandemic*, Grattan Institute, 2020.

Fenna, Alan. 'Fiscal equalisation and natural resources in federal systems', *Public Policy*, 6 (1/2), 2011, pp. 71–80.

— 'The fiscal predicament of Australian federalism', in Mark Bruerton, Tracey Arklay, Robyn Hollander & Ron Levy (eds), *A People's Federation*, pp. 134–46, Federation Press, 2017.

— 'The centralization of Australian federalism 1901–2010: Measurement and interpretation, *Publius* 49(1), 2019, 30–56, <doi.org/10.1093/publius/pjy042>.

— 'Australian federalism and the COVID-19 crisis', in Rupak Chattopadhyay, Felix Knüpling, Diana Chebenova, Liam Whittington and Phillip Gonzalez (eds), *Federalism and the Response to COVID-19: a comparative analysis*, pp. 17–29, Routledge, 2021.

— 'Federalism and climate governance in Australia', in Alan Fenna, Sébastien Jodoin and Joana Setzer (eds), *Climate Governance and Federalism: A Forum of Federations comparative policy analysis*, Cambridge University Press, 2023.

Fenna, Alan and Geoff Anderson. 'The Rudd reforms and the future of Australian federalism', in Gabrielle Appleby, Nicholas Aroney and Thomas John (eds), *The Future of Australian Federalism: Comparative and interdisciplinary perspectives*, pp. 393–413, Cambridge University Press, 2012.

GSTDR, GST Distribution Review. *Final Report*, Department of the Treasury, 2012.

Lee, HP, Michael WR Adams, Colin Campbell and Patrick Emerton. *Emergency Powers in Australia*, 2nd edn, Cambridge University Press, 2018.

McGreevy, Michael, Colin MacDougall, Matt Fisher, Mark Henley and Fran Baum. 'Expediting a renewable energy transition in a privatized market via public policy: The case of South Australia 2004–18', *Energy Policy*, 148 (A), 2021, pp. 1–14.

McLean, Holly and Ben Huf. *Emergency Powers, Public Health and COVID-19*. Parliament of Victoria, 2020, <www.parliament.vic.gov.au/publications/research-papers/send/36-research-papers/13962-emergency-powers-public-health-and-covid-19>.

Morrison, Scott. *The Alan Jones Breakfast Show*, John Stanley, 2GB Radio, 2019.

— 'All better off from fairer way to share the GST' (Media Release, 5 July), 2018 <sjm.ministers.treasury.gov.au/media-release/069-2018/>.

— 'Address, National Press Club', 29 January 2020a, <www.pm.gov.au/media/address-national-press-club>.

— Canberra: House of Representatives Hansard, 2017.

— Media Release, 29 May 2020b, <www.pm.gov.au/media/update-following-national-cabinet-meeting>.

— and Josh Frydenberg. 'Legislating a fairer way to distribute the GST (Media Release, October 1), 2018.

NSW Treasury. *NSW Review of Federal Financial Relations: Final report*, State of New South Wales, 2020.

PC. *Horizontal Fiscal Equalisation*, Productivity Commission, 15 May 2018.

Perrottet, Dominic. 'Federal–state haggling over disasters must stop', *The Australian*, 29 April 2022, p. 1.

Porter, Christian. 'The Grants Commission and the future of the federation', *Public Policy*, 6(1/2), 2011, pp. 45–70.

RCNNDA, Royal Commission into National Natural Disaster Arrangements, Commonwealth of Australia, 2020, <naturaldisaster.royalcommission.gov.au/publications/royal-commission-national-natural-disaster-arrangements-report>.

SCC19, Select Committee on COVID-19. *Final Report*, Senate, 2022.

Treasury, Department of. 'Budget Paper No. 3: Economic and fiscal outlook,' in *Western Australia State Budget 2022–23*, Government of Western Australia, 2022.

Victoria, Government of. Victorian Government Submission to the Senate Select Committee on COVID-19, Government of Victoria, 2020.

Wood, Tony and Guy Dundas. 2020. *Flame Out: The future of natural gas*. Grattan Institute, 2020.

6

THE MORRISON GOVERNMENT AND THE MEDIA

Katharine Murphy and Matthew Ricketson

The 2019–2022 Morrison Government, which ended in emphatic rejection by the electorate on 21 May 2022, marked a turning point in relations between government and the media in Canberra. The public has also rejected the crocodile deathroll politicians and journalists have been engaged in for at least a decade, whereby political spin and journalistic 'gotcha' moments mutually reinforce each other in a dispiritingly downward spiral. There is a hunger for a public discourse that is not driven by 'winning the day' as media advisors claim, or by journalists pointing to every policy's problems while rarely offering solutions. Whether government–media relations will change substantively under the Albanese Government is yet to be seen, but the Morrison Government's term of office saw the exhaustion of the business-as-usual approach to political communication. Events that occurred during the Morrison term played a role in shaping government–media relations, of course; so too did memories of how inadequately the press gallery had reported the misogyny towards the nation's first female prime minister, Julia Gillard, a decade earlier.

In early 2021, *Australian Financial Review* (AFR) journalist Aaron Patrick evidently felt a disturbance in the force. Patrick had worked for his masthead in Canberra's parliamentary press gallery earlier in his career. Based in Sydney, Patrick looked back on his old stomping ground with a certain amount of confusion. A report by Samantha Maiden, political editor of News.com.au, of a serious allegation by former Liberal Party staffer Brittany Higgins against a work colleague – an allegation that later became the subject of criminal proceedings – resulted in Scott Morrison enduring the most difficult period of his prime ministership since his ill-judged, ill-concealed family holiday to Hawai'i during the catastrophic summer bushfires of 2019–20. The federal parliament was experiencing a #MeToo moment, and women around Australia, sensing a significant cultural reckoning, were gathering at protest rallies, in greatest number in Canberra. For his part, the prime minister was engaged in political damage control rather than in listening and learning. Several political commentators in Canberra called out this failure. From Sydney, though, Patrick was witnessing what he characterised in his 31 March article as a 'schism through political journalism' and 'a shift in the centre of gravity from the male perspective to the female' (Patrick, 2021). In his eyes, the coverage by 'a new female leadership' was 'angry' and 'often strayed into unapologetic activism' (Patrick, 2021).

This observation was confusing at several levels, given that at least three of the women Patrick named – Laura Tingle, Karen Middleton and Katharine Murphy (co-author of this chapter) – had worked alongside him in the Canberra press gallery and, in fact, before he had arrived there. All three had served as bureau chiefs and political editors. Thus, the question was not so much where these women with their 'new', 'female' perspective or 'leadership' had suddenly emerged from, but why Patrick had apparently failed to notice them and their contributions when working alongside them. As might have been predicted, Patrick's apparent confusion and discomfort caused a minor ruckus among AFR readers – an enlightened bunch – and among engaged followers of politics more broadly. But his news feature – ostensibly about Samantha Maiden – contained a useful new fact. Patrick reported that Morrison, during a press conference in which the prime minister's aim had been to offer a mea culpa about failing to grasp the enormity of the times, in a terse exchange with a journalist, had levelled a veiled and, as it turned out, false allegation against Maiden. Maiden had been the first to report an alleged sexual assault in Parliament House, on 15 February.

The tone-deaf reaction to Maiden's story by some of Australia's most powerful men had riled many Australian women. It is highly unusual for a prime minister to behave in the way Morrison had behaved on that day, so perhaps unwittingly, Patrick was chronicling two interesting developments: a more combative reporting environment between a prime minister and Canberra-based political reporters, and a related shift in tone. For Patrick, the political reporting he was consuming out of Canberra evidently felt different. This insight sat at the root of his clumsy reportage. Something was different – the dynamic was more adversarial, less 'clubbish', less access-driven, less characterised by the run-of-the-mill 'he said, she said' reportage of journalism's so-called 'golden age', at least among the female correspondents. Hence the charge of 'activism'. Important as it is to disclose that one of this chapter's authors became, in Patrick's eyes, an angry activist, it is more important to note that the issue of how women responded to a government – and a news media – that wanted them to remain invisible and quietly accepting of the status quo became a defining issue of both the Morrison Government of 2019–2022 and its relationship with the media.

Gender equality was one of the issues that the female candidates, dubbed the 'teal independents' – Kate Chaney in the electorate of Curtin, Zoe Daniel in Goldstein, Monique Ryan in Kooyong, Sophie Scamps in Mackellar, Allegra Spender in Wentworth and Kylea Tink in North Sydney – campaigned on strongly, and successfully, in the lead-up to the 2022 election. The other two issues they had in common were the need for urgent action on climate change and integrity in government. These issues had differing origins and trajectories. Gender inequality has been a longstanding concern but was catapulted on to the national political stage, first by the revelations of sexual assault mentioned, then by allegations in February 2021 that a cabinet minister had raped a young woman many years before entering parliament. Where these events marked, even scarred, the Morrison Government's term of office, the major political parties had been locked in a rancorous 'forever war' over action on climate change for more than a decade. Integrity in government did not need to become a defining issue but it did, because before the 2019 election the Morrison Government had promised to create an independent national integrity commission, then took most of the term to develop a Bill for it that was roundly criticised by integrity experts. Morrison squibbed the test of having the Bill debated in parliament, then used the election campaign to tell the public he had not broken an election promise but that in any case integrity commissions end up being kangaroo courts.

If the three issues had different origins, what united them was that the Morrison Government and the mainstream media ignored (gender equality) or downplayed (climate change) or distorted (the demonising of the teal independents) them during the election campaign. And yet, as the stunning electoral success of the teal independents showed, they were issues that voters in these seats, and many others for that matter, cared about and in which they found the government wanting. These gaps, omissions and failures on the part of the government and the news media reveal something important about both. In the chapters about the media in the past two volumes of this series, which aims to chronicle Commonwealth administrations, we have discussed the questions: how do you govern in a seemingly ungovernable environment, and how do you get your message out when the noise constantly drowns the signal? Here, we examine how the Morrison government interacted with the news media and, in doing this, we ask another question that seems pertinent since the electorate spoke on 21 May 2022: where were people getting their news and information from that would prompt such a forceful repudiation of the government's communication strategy?

It is useful to begin by charting Morrison and his government through the prism of media management. Did this prime minister operate using different methods, and were these methods provocative enough to trigger a minor insurrection from press gallery journalists?

Morrison came to power by orienteering along a thin track. Malcolm Turnbull, his predecessor, had split the Liberal Party. When the right faction moved against Turnbull in 2018, Morrison scrambled up a path through the middle. He became leader and held a ragtag government together, assembling an election pitch that cast himself as an opposition leader on a quest to defeat the Labor leader Bill Shorten, as the 'Bill Australia can't afford'. Morrison had managed to hold power and to lead the Coalition into his second term as prime minister. Morrison's ascension extinguished the after-dark passions of Sky News. Sky's evening stable of conservative blowhards had roiled through much of Turnbull's leadership. To them, Morrison appeared a more acceptable figure – not a beloved one, but certainly more acceptable than Turnbull. National affairs became less noisy, even on Ray Hadley's famously shouty 2GB radio program in Sydney. An unspoken media rule for Australian prime ministers is to keep the News Corporation Australia (News Corp) tabloids and Rupert Murdoch's national broadsheet, *The Australian*, well watered with tips, leaks, drops and mid-deliberation kite flying. Morrison was so cemented in this practice that by the end of the government's term it was commonplace among commentators to regard News Corp as virtually an arm of the Coalition Government and, during the election campaign, to argue that the company's outlets had been engaged not in news reporting and analysis but propaganda (Muller, 2022a; Muller 2022b; *Media Watch*, 2022a; *Media Watch*, 2022b). The election result crystallised two important points: first, that News Corp's publications have substantially less influence than they – and others – have long assumed (Simons, 2022) and, second, perhaps related, that the Murdochs, whether on the basis of ideology or commercial self-interest, or both, have built a business model not on news but on 'delivering a predictable product to its niche audience of alienated, older whites, mobilising their resentments over status anxiety, and cutting through the complexities of the modern world with simple affirmations of their prejudices' (Tiffen, 2022).

By the standards of his predecessors, Morrison gave few long-form interviews to newspaper journalists, though these have become essentially a relic of a bygone age. More pertinently, Morrison did so few interviews with the Australian Broadcasting Corporation's (ABC) flagship current affairs programs on radio or television between 2019 and 2022 that it became a talking point, especially when he eventually consented, in the last week of the election campaign, to an interview with Leigh Sales on *7.30*. What Morrison may have gained by avoiding tough questions he lost by inadvertently drawing attention to his unwillingness to be subjected to them, thereby feeding the perception he was allergic to taking responsibility for his government's actions. He made himself available to radio stations frequently, and his press office – which possessed the art of curating the sort of imagery that would present Morrison as an avuncular and non-threatening leader in the good times, and buttoned-down and sober in the bad times – was highly attentive to the needs of nightly television news.

Morrison also forged a return to Sky News by avoiding the ideologues and fronting up to speak to Paul Murray every now and then in the evenings. Murray has strong ideological beliefs but presents to his audience as a plain-speaking populist – a neat fit with the Morrison brand.

Morrison's press office during the 46th Parliament was an active shop, mainly professional, mostly courteous, sometimes helpful. During the first wave of the COVID-19 pandemic in 2020, Morrison moved beyond his regular media habits and held a series of background briefings for bureau chiefs in Canberra's parliamentary press gallery, in an attempt to shape the coverage of the fast-moving public health crisis. These briefings, witnessed by a handful of Morrison's policy and press staff, taking notes, were held in the cabinet room. Morrison clearly found these briefings useful, as did journalists trying to cover the crisis in real time and on multiple platforms. If this was a high point of the government's relations with the media, it did not last. The press office, run by a former senior journalist with the *Daily Telegraph*, Andrew Carswell, ran into turbulence that became a turning point when federal parliament experienced its #MeToo moment in 2021. In February that year, the Ten Network journalist Peter Van Onselen told the ABC that the prime minister's office was 'backgrounding against' the partner of the Liberal staffer who had raised an allegation of sexual assault in a ministerial office in Parliament House. 'The internals are just shocking … I can let your listeners know that the Prime Minister's office has been backgrounding that her partner, her now partner, has a vendetta, or a gripe might be the better way to put it, against the government because of him being a former public servant', Van Onselen told ABC Radio National's *Breakfast* program. 'That might not technically be victim blaming, but I tell you what, it is grubby.' The former government staffer at the centre of the storm made a formal complaint to Morrison's chief of staff, John Kunkel, which triggered an investigation into the behaviour of staff in the press office. Katharine Murphy was one of three journalists Kunkel interviewed for that inquiry; other journalists did not respond or refused the invitation. In a four-page letter to the prime minister, released publicly in May 2021, Kunkel declined to make a finding that the prime minister's office had briefed against the former government staffer's partner, citing a lack of firsthand evidence and the seriousness of the allegation. Kunkel concluded that he was 'not in a position to make a finding that the alleged activity took place' (Kunkel, 2021, p. 4). But he also warned the allegations served as 'an important reminder of the need for [the prime minister's] staff to hold themselves to the highest standards' (Kunkel, 2021). His was one of several reports and inquiries that together gave a sheen of accountability but masked an absence of substantive change.

On media policy, as in many other policy areas, the Morrison Coalition Government was characterised by inactivity and a preference for announcements over delivery. Apart from a minor, partly successful foray into assisting financially struggling regional and rural media outlets, the government's energy was devoted, first, to responding to intense lobbying by commercial media companies and, second, to antagonising the ABC. Taking the second issue first, Patrick Mullins and Matthew Ricketson (co-author of this chapter) argued in their book, *Who Needs the ABC?* (2022), that relations between the Morrison Government and the ABC were at least as bad as they had been under the two previous Liberal prime ministers, Malcolm Turnbull (2015–18) and Tony Abbott (2013–15). The ABC's funding had continued to be cut, its arms'-length governance process for appointing board members was trashed and government MPs routinely called the publicly funded national broadcaster 'the enemy' (Ricketson & Mullins, 2022). The government did not act on the motion to privatise the ABC, passed at the Liberal Party's federal council by a two-thirds majority in 2018, but then Communications Minister Mitch Fifield's response that this was not government policy was hardly a ringing endorsement of the ABC as a valued national cultural institution. Morrison, at that time treasurer in the Turnbull Government, reiterated Fifield's point but could not resist a cheap quip, that some Australians 'may think the Labor Party already owns it'.

During the 2022 election campaign, the ABC, far from being an entrenched locus of anti-Coalition bias, as the government and its supporters in the Institute of Public Affairs (IPA) and News Corp outlets repeatedly claimed, was criticised by those on the progressive side of politics for relying on Coalition talking points in framing news stories and being unduly harsh on Labor and the Greens (Quinn, 2022). The criticism, from an apparently unlikely source, pointed to the potentially corrosive internal effects on the ABC's editorial culture of nearly a decade of hostility from successive Coalition governments. Research conducted for *Who Needs the ABC?* (2022) by former ABC executive and current PhD candidate, Michael Ward, provided a factual basis for what many had intuited: since the ABC's change from being a commission to a corporation in 1983, Liberal–National Party Coalition governments have consistently cut its funding overall, while Labor governments have increased it (Ricketson & Mullins, 2022).

The Morrison Government's major media policy initiative was to take seriously the calls by commercial media companies, led by News Corp, to do something about how their advertising revenue had been siphoned off by online companies, most notably Google and Meta, which owns Facebook and Instagram (Grueskin, 2022). The issue of the commercial media's crumbling business model, especially print media, had been around for at least a decade and had been the subject of government and parliamentary inquiries – to little effect. This time, though, the government asked the Australian Competition and Consumer Commission (ACCC), a well-resourced agency that reports to Treasury, to investigate. ACCC's comprehensive, 617-page report, released in July 2019, showed that online advertising had grown as a share of all advertising, from 25 per cent to 53 per cent between 2012 and 2018. As of 2019, Google and Meta were receiving two-thirds of all online advertising revenues in Australia, and the proportion was rising (ACCC, 2019). The transfer of wealth from one commercial company to another would not normally worry the ACCC, but in this instance it did, because the shrinking revenue was affecting the media companies' ability to produce journalism, especially public-interest journalism, whether that was covering news from courts and local councils or funding expensive investigative projects. Such journalism is a public good, the report stated, and not just for its direct audience or readership. 'Journalism provides broader benefits to society, including to individuals who do not consume it' (ACCC, 2019). Public-interest journalism holds the powerful to account, campaigns for social goals, keeps a record for society and provides a forum for discussing ideas.

The ability of the major media companies – News Corp, Fairfax Media (which merged with the Nine Entertainment Company in late

2018) and Seven West Media – to invest in public-interest journalism had been compromised, the ACCC found. It studied the 12 national and metropolitan daily newspapers published in Australia, and found that between 2001 and 2018 the total number of articles published had declined by 11 per cent, and that the decline in the number of articles on topics associated with public-interest journalism had been steeper (ACCC, 2019).

The ACCC was not the first to notice that Google and Meta had built a 'phenomenally better mousetrap' than the legacy media companies in capturing the public's attention and selling that leverage to advertisers, but their success led to them becoming global technological behemoths: among the 10 biggest companies in the world, with market capitalisation many times that even of Rupert Murdoch's global media empire (Ricketson & Mullins, 2022). The ACCC did, however, come up with a smart strategy to do what regulators in other countries had been largely unsuccessful in doing – forcing Google and Meta to compensate media companies for use of their content. The News Media and Digital Platforms Mandatory Bargaining Code was an arbitration process, underpinned by legislation, that would force Google and Meta to the negotiating table. More to the point, it was a final offer, or 'baseball', arbitration process. Under this process, the negotiating companies can make a final offer, one of which the arbitrator chooses before making its decision, which is binding and thereby reduces the likelihood of ambit claims. The Morrison Government passed the necessary legislation in early 2021, prompting a sharp response from Google and Meta, in particular, which briefly stripped news stories from people's Facebook feeds. The cack-handed move backfired, drawing widespread public condemnation, and rendering its founder, Mark Zuckerberg, as a comic Dr Evil-like figure. Gradually, the two companies began to negotiate with media companies, especially large ones like News Corp and Nine, but also with smaller companies such as Schwartz Media, publisher of the *Monthly* and the *Saturday Paper*, and Private Media, publisher of the online news website Crikey.com.au. By late 2021, Google and Meta had agreed to pay an estimated $200 million annually to media companies over the following three years.

The architect of the News Media and Digital Platforms Mandatory

Bargaining Code, Rod Sims, stepped down from his role at the ACCC in early 2022, becoming a public policy professor at the Australian National University. Sims wasted no time in publishing a paper outlining why the code was an important reform (Sims, 2022). He acknowledged that the code had been criticised on numerous grounds, listing 14, including that the enabling legislation had not actually been applied to Google and Meta, but acted as a lever to ensure they would negotiate with media companies; that most of the deals were negotiated in secret, with little public transparency; and that smaller media outlets such as *The Conversation* had little success persuading Meta even to return their calls. Sims rebutted the arguments, primarily on the grounds that the code was never intended to solve all the problems facing public-interest journalism and that the final-offer arbitration process was necessary to overcome the significant power imbalance between Google and Meta, and the media companies, and to force them to the negotiating table. Further, he said, the code had enabled the employment of more journalists (Sims, 2022).

Sims' paper also drew attention to an important piece of information that partially answered the question we posed earlier in this chapter: where were people getting their news and information from that would have prompted such a forceful repudiation of the government's communication strategy? Much has been written about the potentially damaging effects of misuse of social media to spread misinformation and disinformation, and there is little doubt at least some damage has been done. That social media occupies at least as much space in the overall news and information ecology as the mainstream media has become a clear trend. The 2021 Digital News Report, released by the University of Canberra's News and Media Research Centre, shows the proportion of people who consume news and information through their social media feeds has risen by five percentage points, to 23 per cent (Park et al, 2021). Among Gen Z respondents, this figure is more than half – 54 per cent (Park et al, 2021). What is less clear is the extent to which people are reading or watching news and information shared by friends or other sources but originating in the news media. Sales of daily print newspapers have been declining for years, but the number of people accessing newspapers' online websites has grown rapidly over the same period. Sims (2022) points to Nielson's online news rankings, which show the top 10 sites are all mainstream news media outlets, headed by ABC Online with more than 11 million unique users each month, followed by Nine.com.au and News.com.au.

The ABC's 2021 annual report outlines the extent to which the national broadcaster has moved well beyond radio and television. ABC Online has been the country's most popular news website since the beginning of 2020. The ABC delivers content on YouTube that reaches 22.6 million monthly unique viewers. On Facebook, its content reaches 6.1 million monthly unique users, and on Instagram it reaches 3.5 million users, mostly Australians aged under 45 years, with a skew toward women. Podcasts produced from local ABC Radio content, Triple J and Radio National, are downloaded millions of times each month, with Radio National, the pioneer of the popular new form in Australia, seeing 7.8 million monthly unique downloads (ABC, 2021). Some of this content is re-purposed short-form radio and television material but a sizeable amount of what is published on ABC Online is created specifically for it. An increasing amount of that is long-form feature material that used to be the sole province of newspapers and magazines.

Many consumers also access short, smartly produced TikTok videos, such as those created by Matilda Boseley for *Guardian Australia*, which regularly attract hundreds of thousands of viewers, her sharp insights founded in solid reporting and fact-checking. The easy availability online of the sources of news, such as reports by parliamentary committees and non-government agencies, enables anyone to follow up the details behind the headlines. How people voted at the 2022 federal election at least suggests that a hefty proportion of the population was preoccupied with the issues of gender equality, action on climate change and integrity in government, and went looking for news, views and information about them. Encouragingly for the media, and those who study it, good journalism brought to the public revelations about gender inequality. Without Samantha Maiden's work, we would not know about an alleged sexual assault in a federal minister's office; without Louise Milligan, we would not know about an allegation of a historical rape by a cabinet minister.

The discouraging news is that much of the news media industry is unwilling or unable to reflect on its work, to learn from the past and improve coverage. For instance, horse-race journalism, a form of reporting in which politics is presented as resembling a sporting event, has been decried for more than four decades but there is still an awful lot of it around (Broh, 1980). In response to the two major political parties' strategies of avoiding campaigning on their record (the Coalition) or curling into a small ball to avoid being wedged (Labor), much media coverage, as Judith Brett (2022) writes, obsessed over 'Who won the day on the campaign trail? Who forgot a crucial number? Who looked more convincing cosplaying a tradie?'. Just as the electorate seemed to send the two major political parties a loud message in May 2022, about the need to do politics better, they seemed to be sending the mainstream media, with its overreliance on high-vis televisual dumbshows and underplaying of urgent policy issues, a similar message. Do better; we need you.

References

ABC. *Annual Report 2020–2021*, 21 October 2021, <about.abc.net.au/wp-content/uploads/2021/10/ABC10150_00_v14_FILM_WEB-a11y_FINAL2-1.pdf>.

Australian Competition and Consumer Commission (ACCC). (2019). *Digital Platforms Inquiry – Final Report*, <www.accc.gov.au/publications/digital-platforms-inquiry-final-report>.

Brett, Judith. 'Spoiling for victory', the *Monthly*, May 2022, pp. 10–11.

Broh, C Anthony. 'Horse-race journalism: Reporting the polls in the 1976 presidential election', *Public Opinion Quarterly*, 44 (4), 1980, pp. 514–29, <doi.org/10.1086/268620>.

Grueskin, Bill (2022). 'Millions of dollars for news, shrouded in mysterious deals', Judith Neilson Institute for Journalism and Ideas, 10 March 2022, <jninstitute.org/news/millions-of-dollars-for-news-shrouded-in-mysterious-deals/>.

Kunkel, John. Letter to the Prime Minister, 25 May 2021, <cdn.theconversation.com/static_files/files/1591/Kunkel_Report.pdf?1621992704>.

Media Watch. ABC TV 'Teal threat', Episode 14, 16 May 2022a, </www.abc.net.au/mediawatch/episodes/teal/13884036>.

— ABC TV. 'Election '22', Episode 15, 23 May 2022b, <www.abc.net.au/mediawatch/episodes/election/13895010>.

Muller, Denis. 'As News Corp goes "rogue" on election coverage, what price will Australian democracy pay?', *The Conversation*, 9 May 2022a, <theconversation.com/as-news-corp-goes-rogue-on-election-coverage-what-price-will-australian-democracy-pay-181599>.

— (2022). 'How the "reality distorting machinery" of the federal election campaign delivered sub-par journalism', *The Conversation*, 25 May 2022b, <theconversation.com/how-the-reality-distorting-machinery-of-the-federal-election-campaign-delivered-sub-par-journalism-183629>.

Park, Sora, Caroline Fisher, Kieran McGuinness, Jee Young Lee and Kerry McCallum. *Digital News Report: Australia 2021*. News & Media Research Centre, University of Canberra, <apo.org.au/node/312650>.

Patrick, Aaron. 'PM caught in crusade of women journos', *Australian Financial Review*, 31 March 2021, <www.afr.com/companies/media-and-marketing/pm-caught-in-crusade-of-women-journos-20210326-p57eee>.

Quinn, Karl (2022). 'Biased against the left or right? The social media onslaught targeting the ABC', *Sydney Morning Herald*, 1 May 2022, <www.smh.com.au/culture/tv-and-radio/biased-against-the-left-or-right-the-social-media-onslaught-targeting-the-abc-20220429-p5ah5k.html>.

Ricketson, Matthew and Patrick Mullins. *Who Needs the ABC? Why taking it for granted is no longer an option*, Scribe, 2022.

Simons, Margaret. 'News Corp's biased reporting ultimately backfires', the *Age*, 16 May 2022, p. 30.

Sims, Rod (2022). 'Instruments and objectives; Explaining the News Media Bargaining Code', 23 May 2022, Judith Neilson Institute for Journalism and Ideas, <jninstitute.org/wp-content/uploads/2022/05/Rod-Sims_News-Bargaining-Code_2022.pdf>.

Tiffen, Rodney. 'Will News Corp change its approach after Labor's election win? Not if the US example is anything to go by', *The Conversation*, 30 May 2022, <theconversation.com/will-news-corp-change-its-approach-after-labors-election-win-not-if-the-us-example-is-anything-to-go-by-183650>.

Policy

7

THE (MIS)MANAGEMENT OF
THE COVID-19 PANDEMIC

Stephen Duckett

The Morrison Government was re-elected on 18 May 2019, and for most of its term Australian politics was dominated by the response to the SARS-CoV-2 virus, which causes COVID-19. This chapter discusses how the Morrison Government managed its health sector-related COVID responsibilities. In brief, the answer is, poorly.

Overall, COVID-19 outcomes in Australia have been good, with over 7 million cases and more than 8000 deaths by the end of the term (May 2022). Most deaths occurred in 2022 following the progressive lifting of restrictions after the release of the National Plan.

Australia had a comparatively low number of pandemic deaths in 2020 and 2021, estimated by Prime Minister Morrison as 40 000 deaths averted (Morrison, 2022) although independent estimates were less than half that (COVID-19 Excess Mortality Collaborators 2022). This success was a result of public health measures that suppressed infection rates in the first two years of the pandemic, when the COVID-19 strains were more virulent. Importantly, the effects of the pandemic were experienced unevenly, both economically and in terms of health effects, with people in low socioeconomic groups, particularly women, faring worse.

However, the states did not always manage their responsibilities well. There were quarantine breaches, most notably in Victoria, failures in managing cruise ship arrivals and in testing and tracing. Despite this, for most of 2020 and 2021, it was state implementation of public health measures – supported by the Australian public, which endured lockdowns and border controls – that led to Australia's good overall outcomes in the pandemic, not federal government actions. The Morrison Government can claim little credit for Australia's success. In fact, it mostly hindered the states' successful responses to the pandemic or bungled its own. The Morrison Government's response to the pandemic has been discussed in more detail elsewhere (Duckett, 2022).

A new virus – four roles for the national government

The national government had four health-related responsibilities during the COVID-19 pandemic: to steer the response through effective national political leadership; to manage external borders; to protect residents of residential aged-care facilities; and to approve, procure and distribute personal protective equipment (PPE), tests and vaccines. State governments are responsible for determining the appropriate public health measures and implementing them – including managing the border quarantine arrangements and the testing, tracing and isolation regimen – and managing the hospital response. States are also responsible for developing strategies to mitigate mental health and other effects of restrictions.

Effective national leadership

The SARS-CoV-2 virus ('coronavirus') was first identified in Wuhan, China, in December 2019; Australia had its first case in January 2020. An effective response to the COVID-19 pandemic required a range of strategies and skills. Sagan et al (2021) identified 'steering the response through effective political leadership' as the first of a list of 20 strategies. Sriharan et al (2022) identified three 'crisis leadership' competencies required for effective leadership during pandemics: task competencies (eg communication and collaboration); adaptive competencies (eg decision-making); and people competencies (eg empathy and awareness). Unfortunately, all three were weak or missing at the national level, which resulted in ineffective decision-making (a failed National Cabinet), the undermining of state strategies, and a political – rather than evidence-based – National Plan, which the government was unwilling to review as circumstances changed.

Given that pandemics do not respect borders, a key competency in a pandemic response is collaboration (Sriharan et al, 2022). This is especially true in the Australian federation, where power is shared.

Early March 2020 saw increasing cancellations of events, and states beginning to make unilateral calls about the pandemic response. Media attention focused on state premiers and chief health officers as the key decision makers and sources of information about the pandemic response, with the prime minister and health minister Greg Hunt relegated to catch-up roles.

The National Cabinet, created on 13 March 2020, dealt the prime minister in to discussion of state decisions, and gave the states political cover for difficult choices in the early stages of the pandemic. But because the National Cabinet was set up in haste, there were no real rules for its operation. Any outcome of a National Cabinet meeting was a 'decision' in name only: behind the fig leaf of unity, each state and territory went its own way, while the Commonwealth ran a critique from the sidelines. Federal ministers actively undermined decisions taken by the prime minister's National Cabinet colleagues. This 'white-anting', which started almost immediately and continued throughout the pandemic, delegitimised public health measures, especially movement retrictions such as lockdowns and state border closures.

For example, in 2020 then-Education Minister Dan Tehan attempted to induce private schools to open, despite state closure orders; the prime minister placed overt pressure on states to end lockdowns early; and the government intervened to support mining oligarch Clive Palmer's bid to overturn Western Australia's border closures. This action featured prominently in Western Australia during the federal election and undoubtedly contributed to Labor's success in that state.

The following year, the prime minister continued his jawboning to argue that states should open up quickly after the release of the 2021 National Plan. The prime minister also undermined the social licence for a strong state public health response by 'dog-whistling' support for anti-vaccination demonstrators.

The National Cabinet could have been a forum for an effective dialogue between leaders; perhaps it could have functioned to promote an effective dialogue with the public about the nature of the risks of COVID-19. But although the meetings did take place, there was no consensus-building dialogue and no comprehensive or coherent national response to the crisis. Instead, the Commonwealth and the states pursued inconsistent policies that hindered management of the pandemic.

The prime minister obtained National Cabinet endorsement for the 'National Plan to transition Australia's National COVID-19 Response' on 6 August 2021. The plan was obscured by a 'veil of vagueness' (Gibson and Goodin, 1999), and was hedged in qualifiers. It only applied in a given state when Australia as a whole – and that state – met specific targets, a constraint that was subsequently ignored in the Morrison Government's rhetoric. There was an approximation tilde in front of the first vaccination target, the list of measures for each phase was preceded by the uncertain verb 'may', and the measures themselves were expressed in vague terms. The plan did not address key bones of contention, such as state border closures.

The plan foreshadowed a progressive relaxation of restrictions once two vaccination thresholds for the population aged 16 years and older were attained: approximately 70 per cent and 80 per cent, representing about 56 per cent and 64 per cent of the total population, respectively. These population thresholds were well below those thought to be required to achieve 'herd immunity', and were presumably politically determined, with the aim of bringing an end to state public health measures as soon as possible.

The government's rhetoric then weaponised the low thresholds. State governments and public health experts sceptical of the plan's effectiveness were challenged with: 'If not 70, then when?' The government slowly framed the policy choice as a crude dichotomy: either follow the plan and 'live with COVID', or face continuing lockdowns. A more nuanced public health strategy, including the use of masks, density limits and ventilation requirements, was erased from the agenda.

The policy rhetoric shifted after the plan's release, especially from the Commonwealth and the Coalition New South Wales governments: the message was that, with vaccination, all other restrictions could be removed. In retrospect, the release of the National Plan marked an important transition: public health measures began to be relaxed regardless of infection prevalence. It marked the end of the 'control', or 'elimination', era, and a shift to the 'live with COVID' era, and the political acceptance of the death rate that entails.

Although the published plan included the caveat that 'The Plan is based on the current situation and is subject to change if required', it did not change as circumstances did. This was apparent even at the most trivial level – for example, the 16+ age denominator for opening was not adjusted when children aged 12–15 years became eligible for vaccination. There were also no changes when Omicron, a significantly more transmissible variant than Delta, became dominant. The lack of adaptive competency was demonstrated in this failure to adapt the plan to a changing environment. A key narrative during the pandemic – especially among those advocating for a 'live with COVID' approach – was that COVID-19 was no worse than a bad influenza season.

On the worst case scenario, in the Doherty Institute modelling the government used in support of the 70 and 80 per cent coverage targets in the population aged 16+ years, relaxing certain restrictions at the 70 per cent (16+ years) threshold would be expected to lead to fewer than 20 deaths on any day in the three months after opening up, with an estimated 2710 deaths after six months. These daily and total worst-case estimates were quickly exceeded in 2021, but the plan was not revised. In the first four months of 2022, there were only 25 days when the death toll was under 20. The effect of waning vaccine efficacy was even more significant, but again the government did not adjust the plan.

The Morrison Government failed to provide effective national leadership during the pandemic. The failure to adapt the National Plan in the light of changing circumstances was driven by ideology and politics. The government consistently attacked and undermined state public health measures, and could not pivot from that stance in response to changes in the environment and the reduction in effective vaccination protection.

Managing external borders

Then Commonwealth Chief Medical Officer Dr Brendan Murphy recommended a border closure to China a few weeks after the virus was identified, which the government announced on 31 January 2020. This reduced the number of infected people arriving in Australia, and is estimated to have delayed widespread transmission of the virus by about four to six weeks.

From mid-March 2020, the government also required all arrivals – including returning Australians – to self-isolate and then, later, to be quarantined for a two-week period. Caps on international arrivals – matched to quarantine availability – forced airlines to cancel flights and limit passengers on flights that did arrive. Despite the obvious advantages of using purpose-built quarantine facilities, the Commonwealth was slow to support states to build them.

Overall, the Morrison Government made the right call on the initial border closure, but its subsequent leadership was weak, particularly in terms of supporting quarantine and managing the return of Australians stranded overseas.

Protecting residents of residential aged-care facilities

Since 2011, the Commonwealth has had sole funding and regulatory responsibility for aged care, and could therefore be expected to have been proactive in managing providers' preparation for, and response to, the pandemic. It was not.

Residential aged-care outcomes were tragic: 7 per cent of all COVID-19 cases and 75 per cent of all deaths in the first year of the pandemic were of people living in residential aged-care facilities (Australian Institute of Health and Welfare, 2021). The Morrison Government attempted to play down the significance of the death toll in aged care (and the death toll of older Australians in the community), qualifying announcements of deaths by referring to the approximately 40 per cent of the population who 'had underlying conditions', or claiming that many of those who had died in residential care had been 'palliative'. This approach represents an ageist failure to demonstrate empathy; a critical 'people competency' required in a pandemic (Sriharan et al, 2022).

The Morrison Government's response was subject to excoriating criticism in a special report from the Royal Commission into Aged Care Quality and Safety (Royal Commission into Aged Care Quality and Safety, 2020), discussed in more detail in chapter 9.

Personal protective equipment, tests and vaccines

The Commonwealth Government was responsible for approving, procuring and distributing personal protective equipment (PPE), tests and vaccines. Again, this was an area where the Morrison Government fell short, particularly in the case of vaccine rollouts.

The pandemic quickly disrupted every element of global supply chains for PPE. All countries scrambled simultaneously to source supplies, or belatedly to develop manufacturing capacity, and shortages of PPE were common across the world in the early stages of the pandemic.

One area of failure was in managing the national medical stockpile, the source for the initial urgent supply of PPE. The national stockpile had been allowed to run down immediately preceding the pandemic. The Department of Health did not have good systems in place for emergency procurement and, possibly as a result, inconsistent due-diligence checks of suppliers impeded its ability to procure equipment effectively. Many providers in both primary care and hospitals felt exposed because of the lack of PPE. Even in mid-2020, PPE was in short supply in Australia, and less than half of requests for supply from the national stockpile were being met.

The first stage of pandemic control is testing to identify who is infected, so they can isolate or be quarantined to prevent further infections, and to enable tracing of their contacts. 'TTIQ' – for Testing, Tracing, Isolation and Quarantine – became a ubiquitous acronym. Tracing, isolation and quarantine became state responsibilities, carried out with varying effectiveness, with the Commonwealth's role in this area limited to its COVID-Safe mobile app. The app was much hyped but proved to be useless.

Tests for infection with SARS-CoV-2 were developed quickly, but testing kits were initially in short supply globally. Overall, Australia had a good testing rate throughout the pandemic.

The Morrison Government negotiated a generous payment with private diagnostic providers for the standard polymerase chain reaction (PCR) test, which included supervised collection of the sample. The alternative method, self-collection, was used in the United Kingdom for symptomatic people and approved by the United States Food and Drug Administration but was not introduced in Australia. The negotiated payment to private pathology providers was about double what was paid to state-owned public providers and led to soaring profits for the private companies.

A new generation of testing, rapid antigen tests (RATs), became available in mid-2020. Unlike PCR tests, RATs provided results within minutes, and were rolled out internationally in mid-late 2020. A perfect storm emerged in late 2021, when the more transmissible Omicron variant took hold. Public health protections were being wound back, and more people began to travel and gather over the Christmas break. Infections skyrocketed, and so did demand for tests. COVID-19 testing became the 2021 Christmas barbecue stopper. Inordinate delays occurred as people waited hours for PCR tests and days for results. Laboratories were overwhelmed, and some tests were not reported on at all. Governments responded by relaxing testing rules and promoting the use of RATs. In the absence of a nationally managed supply arrangement, unscrupulous providers rationed RATs with price gouging.

The testing debacle of the summer of 2021–22 was the result of the previous 18 months' failure of strategy. Although RATs are not perfect, their use in population screening and asymptomatic testing had become widespread internationally by late 2020. The Therapeutic Goods Administration (TGA), the independent regulator that is a unit of the Commonwealth Department of Health, was slow to approve any change in a testing regimen that had proved so lucrative for private pathology companies. Representatives of pathology providers had consistently argued against testing strategies, such as self-PCR testing and the use of RATs, which would cut into their revenue streams.

The head of the TGA sheeted home the failure of the testing strategy to the government in September 2021, before the full scale of the problem was publicly apparent: '... we can't formally make an approval decision until we get a signal from the government', Professor Skerritt said. 'It's a decision for the government' (Gould, 2021).

The vaccine rollout was unambiguously a Commonwealth Government responsibility. It was described as a 'phenomenal failure in public administration' (Macmillan, 2021) and 'the worst national public policy failure in modern Australian history' (Bongiorno, 2021). Widely publicised delays in the rollout produced the 2021 word of the year: 'strollout'.

Everything that could go wrong with Australia's vaccination program did go wrong. The highly politicised procurement strategy put Australia at risk in the event that vaccines fell over, which they did; the vaccination rollout began months after rollouts in the United Kingdom and the United States, so by mid-2021 Australia was among the worst performers internationally in terms of proportion of the population vaccinated. Initial vaccination targets were not met; the choice of vaccination channels was driven by politics; logistics and vaccination prioritisation failed; the rollout of vaccinations to residential aged care and disability facilities was a slow-moving tragedy; and communications about approvals and changes in approvals created uncertainty and fuelled vaccine hesitancy in the population.

However, this litany of failure did not stop Health Minister Hunt, who had determined the procurement strategy, from describing the vaccination outcomes in early October 2021 as having 'exceeded our expectations' and 'a huge national achievement' (Hunt, 2021a). The public's assessment was not so positive. The percentage of the population rating the 'federal government's response to the Covid-19 outbreak' as quite good or very good dropped shortly after the vaccine rollout began falling from the high 60 or low 70 per cent approval range to the high 30 or low 40 per cent range in August 2021.

Vaccine procurement was, at least initially, a media bonanza for the Morrison Government. Media releases flowed regularly, and politicisation of the vaccine rollout went as far as having the Liberal Party logo included on vaccine announcements. But positive stories disappeared in 2021 when the public wanted vaccines in their arms, not more announcements.

During much of 2020, vaccines remained a promise. It was not clear whether a vaccine against SARS-CoV-2 would be developed, and if so, when. In an environment of uncertainty, the optimal strategy is to 'hedge one's bets', and that is what most countries did, spreading their investments and plans over multiple technologies, from multiple countries. A presentation to the Morrison Government by consultancy group McKinsey in August 2020 confirmed this as the international standard for procurement strategy. The government ignored this evidence, instead primarily investing in a two-vaccine strategy. Both its preferred vaccines (AstraZeneca and a University of Queensland potential vaccine) had strong Australian links. The 'buy Australian' strategy may have been developed because of fear of breakdowns in supply chains if all vaccines had to be procured internationally. But it quickly unravelled.

Because of the initial narrow procurement strategy, no vaccine alternative was immediately available in sufficient quantities when things went awry. The government eventually seized on the Pfizer vaccine as a solution to supply and hesitancy problems, which led to a mad scramble to purchase supplies from Pfizer directly, and from other countries that had near-expiry Pfizer supplies.

The result of the government's poor procurement decision-making was that, in contrast to other countries that had started their vaccination programs in late 2020, the Australian vaccination program started late, was implemented slowly and ultimately faltered. The experience in most countries was that the rate-limiting factor for vaccine coverage was demand – the result of vaccine hesitancy. In contrast, in Australia the rate-limiting factor was supply: there was not enough vaccine supply to meet demand until September 2021. Australia ranked last in the OECD in terms of proportion of the population vaccinated in the middle of 2021, and its ranking did not improve significantly until the supply problems were overcome later that year.

The vaccine rollout strategy was influenced by the political and epidemiological environments of late 2020 and early 2021. The government's view at the time was that the virus was essentially under control, which created an air of complacency about how quickly the vaccination program should proceed once vaccines became available. In March, the prime minister famously excused the slow start and early missed targets by describing the vaccination rollout as 'not a race'. Health Minister Hunt accepted that it was a race, but 'a marathon, not a sprint' (Hunt, 2021b).

Any perceived threat of outbreaks was de-emphasised in planning. The political assumption at the time was that even with a February start to the vaccine rollout, most Australians would be vaccinated by late 2021. The government could then call an early election for November or December 2021, at which it would coast to victory, basking in the electorate's gratitude for a successful vaccination program and a return to a life close to the pre-pandemic normal.

However, despite adopting a slow rollout strategy, the federal government continued to set ambitious goals, but only achieved 15 per cent of the initial end-March vaccination target. Midway through the vaccination program, blame was shifted onto the Commonwealth Department of Health for the failures of the rollout. Administration of the program was militarised as part of an attempt to deflect political attention. Nevertheless, the public still held the government accountable. Not for nothing did 'strollout', a typically Australian and laconic critique of the government's performance, became the 2021 word of the year.

The communications about vaccine-supply arrangements, and whether the public would have a free choice of vaccines, was poor from the start. Reports of complications and deaths following use of the AstraZeneca vaccine began to emerge in Europe in early 2021. Deaths associated with AstraZeneca were rare but nevertheless widely reported, contributing to vaccine hesitancy.

In response to the accumulating evidence about adverse events, the relevant government advisory group, Australian Technical Advisory Group on Immunisation (ATAGI), initially issued reassuring statements, but shifted its position to a recommendation that Pfizer was 'preferred' for people aged under 50 years. ATAGI's cautious approach was informed both by the immediate risk–benefit ratio (including low contemporary prevalence of SARS-CoV-2) and the fact that the recommended alternative vaccine, Pfizer, was in short supply because of the procurement strategy failures.

As reports of adverse events accumulated, ATAGI revised its advice to preference Pfizer for people under 60 years. Within 30 minutes of ATAGI's statement, Health Minister Hunt publicly announced it – but without any additional communications plan, and in apparent disregard of the fact that Pfizer remained in short supply. Not surprisingly, public acceptance of AstraZeneca tanked, exacerbating supply constraints and fuelling vaccine hesitancy.

Changing advice as additional information becomes available is the right call for any government. But the overall messaging in the first six months of the vaccination program was uncoordinated, sometimes confusing, and poorly designed. The reasons for changed advice were poorly explained, with the result that trust in AstraZeneca plummeted, even among those aged 60 years and older, just as infections were beginning to increase again with the Delta variant.

The slow start and slow rollout of the vaccination program were costly. A better program could have saved lives, reduced the burden on health systems and staff, and averted an estimated $31 billion in damage to the economy (Holden & Leigh, 2022). The human costs of the bungled procurement and rollout were significant. With an alternative procurement strategy, the mid-2021 lockdowns could perhaps have been avoided, with weeks and perhaps months of fewer restrictions, fewer effects on children and fewer mental health issues.

Australia's vaccination program has attracted a thesaurus of negative adjectives. The key issue now is understanding what caused these failures.

The government obviously wanted to be a 'cleanskin': not to have to bear any of the responsibility. The creeping militarisation in administering the vaccine rollout in mid-2020 sent the signal that the public service was to blame, and could not manage the implementation.

The attribution of responsibility for the failure of the rollout to the Department of Health has also been advanced by independent commentators (Maskell-Knight, 2022; Podger, 2022), who highlight that successive governments, following the neoliberal playbook, had stripped out the policy and administrative capacities of the public service. Others have suggested the failures were a consequence of the clientism approach favoured by the Morrison Government across a range of portfolios, including Health. However, there is a chicken-and-egg problem to disentangle here: certainly, the government was quick to hire consultants;

however, it is unclear whether they were hired because the government preferred to heed their advice (Minister Hunt had previously worked for McKinsey), or because the department was incapable of providing timely advice. But it is clear that the cascade of failure started with the policy design. Advised by an expensive kleptocracy of consultants, the vaccine-procurement strategy was clearly a political one. Poor decision-making in procurement was a critical distal cause. It led to the slow rollout because of the failure to procure sufficient vaccines.

Another strategic mistake was to emphasise a privatised Commonwealth distribution strategy through general practitioners (GPs) and pharmacists rather than to embrace state distribution through mass vaccination hubs. Again, this appears to have been a politically driven, credit-claiming choice that created logistical challenges.

The testing debacle was clearly one driven by political decisions, potentially the result of lobbying by pathology company rent-seekers. The head of the TGA called out the political nature of the process when he admitted that having to wait for government signals was the reason for slow decision-making.

The public health policies the Morrison Government pursued were often in competition with those pursued by the states, and state public health measures were undermined as a result. The different federal strategy was, again, politically and ideologically driven, reflecting different priorities about the importance of business and economic interests when compared to public health concerns.

Finally, the communication failures were mainly of politicians' making. It is too easy to see problems on the ground and assume that the failures are all administrative. It is important to consider the strategic choices that increased the likelihood of implementation failure.

Nonetheless, there were obvious bureaucratic failures. The Aged Care Royal Commission trenchantly criticised the aged-care regulator for failing to take sufficient action when outbreaks occurred; a continuing failure that is still in evidence at the time of writing (mid-2022).

Overpromising and Underdelivering

Many countries found it difficult to adapt and respond to the COVID-19 pandemic, and all countries are looking to learn how to handle shocks in the future.

Australia, led by the state premiers, got a lot right, and this led to significant numbers of deaths averted in 2019 and 2020. But the Morrison Government's performance was not so good. It failed in three of its four key pandemic responsibilities: national leadership was poor, impeding and undermining the public health response; the aged-care response was a tragedy; and the government failed to ensure adequate supply and distribution of PPE, tests and vaccines. The only bright spot was border control, and even here the plight of stranded Australians was not handled well.

The key problems underlying this sorry saga are politicisation and politically driven decision-making – with the consequential failures in implementation – and issues related to federal–state coordination.

The failures of implementation may not have been inevitable or as egregious if the initial strategic choices had not been so political. The politicisation of the federal response affected every element of the Morrison Government's approach. The government pledged to underpromise and overdeliver, but did the opposite. Its relentlessly optimistic political messaging made it harder for the government to admit its mistakes, to learn from them and reset its agenda.

Australia's decentralised public health system served the country well. That Australia performed so well, at least up to the release of the National Plan, is a tribute to the strengths of the states. The states provided leadership and made the tough decisions that controlled the virus and delivered the outcomes that led to international praise. But the Morrison Government's record in management of the pandemic was very poor indeed. Lessons must be learnt and new systems developed to ensure that the weaknesses exposed during the pandemic provide a basis for better planning and better pandemic responses in the future.

References

Australian Institute of Health and Welfare. *The first year of COVID-19 in Australia: direct and indirect health effects*. AIHW (Canberra), 2021, <www.aihw.gov.au/reports/burden-of-disease/the-first-year-of-covid-19-in-australia/summary>.

Bongiorno, Frank. 'A little jab, now and then: The federal government's handling of vaccinations shows how much damage has been done to the public sector', *Inside story*, 2021, <insidestory.org.au/a-little-jab-now-and-then/>.

COVID-19 Excess Mortality Collaborators. 'Estimating excess mortality due to the COVID-19 pandemic: a systematic analysis of COVID-19-related mortality, 2020–21', the *Lancet* 399 (10334): 1513–1536, 2022. <doi.org/https://doi.org/10.1016/S0140-6736(21)02796-3>.

Duckett, Stephen. 'Public Health Management of the COVID-19 Pandemic in Australia: The Role of the Morrison Government', *International Journal of Environmental Research and Public Health* 19 (16): 10400, 2022.

Gibson, Diane, and RE Goodin. 'The veil of vagueness: a model of institutional design', in *Organizational and institutional factors in political life: Essays in honour of Yohan P Olsen*, edited by Morton Egeberg and Per Laegreid, Oslo: Scandinavian University Press, 1999.

Gould, Courtney. 'TGA admits delay in at-home testing until vax rates higher was deliberate.' *NCA Newswire*, 27 September 2021, <www.news.com.au/world/coronavirus/australia/tga-admits-delay-in-athome-testing-until-vax-rates-higher-was-deliberate/news-story/43626bc665945d721d532a9f62713a6c>.

Holden, Richard, and Andrew Leigh. 'The race that stopped a nation: Lessons from Australia's COVID vaccine failures', *Oxford Review of Economic Policy*, 2022.

Hunt, Greg, 'Minister Hunt's Press Conference in Canberra on 5 October 2021 with an update on COVID-19 and net-zero emissions targets', 5 October 2021, 2021a, <www.health.gov.au/ministers/the-hon-greg-hunt-mp/media/minister-hunts-press-conference-in-canberra-on-5-october-2021-with-an-update-on-covid-19-and-net-zero-emissions-targets>.

— 'Press Conference in Canberra about COVID-19 cases and vaccination rollout in Australia', 18 March 2021, 2021b, <www.health.gov.au/ministers/the-hon-greg-hunt-mp/media/press-conference-in-canberra-about-covid-19-cases-and-vaccination-rollout-in-australia>.

Macmillan, Jade, 'Malcolm Turnbull criticises Australian COVID-19 vaccine rollout, particularly mixed messaging on AstraZeneca', *ABC News*, 1 July 2021, <www.abc.net.au/news/2021-07-01/malcolm-turnbull-criticises-australian-covid-19-vaccine-rollout/100260940>.

Maskell-Knight, Charles, 'Why the Department of Health has proven tragically inept', *Pearls and irritations* (blog), 2022, <johnmenadue.com/why-the-department-of-health-has-proven-tragically-inept/>.

Morrison, Scott, 'Why I love Australia', Liberal Party of Australia on YouTube, 2022.

Podger, Andrew, 'Rebuilding Australian Public Service capability – Part 2', *Pearls & Irritations*, 23 February 2022.

Royal Commission into Aged Care Quality and Safety, *Aged care and COVID-19: A special report*, Royal Commission (Canberra), 2020.

Sagan, Anna, Erin Webb, Martin McKee, Scott L Greer, Marina Karanikolos, Gemma A Williams, Jonathan Cylus, Erica Richardson, Ruth Waltzberg, Suszy Lessof and Josep Figueras, *Health systems resilience during COVID-19: Lessons for building back better*, Copenhagen: European Observatory on Health Systems and Policies, 2021.

Sriharan, Abi, Attila J Hertelendy, Jane Banaszak-Holl, Michelle M Fleig-Palmer, Cheryl Mitchell, Amit Nigam, Jennifer Gutberg, Devin J Rapp and Sara J Singer, 'Public Health and Health Sector Crisis Leadership During Pandemics: A Review of the Medical and Business Literature', *Medical Care Research and Review* 79 (4): pp. 475–486, 2022, <doi.org/10.1177/10775587211039201>.

8

ECONOMIC POLICY IN THE 46TH PARLIAMENT

Richard Holden

What odds might have been obtained for the following bet, if placed in 2019? 'The incoming Liberal Government's Treasurer will deliver a balanced budget, appear in public with merchandise and a music video promoting the slogan "Back in the black", then ditch his party's "Debt and deficits" mantra to spend more than $300 billion over two years to save Australia from the worst economic crisis in a century, and will eventually be bundled out of office as well his own electoral seat.'

Fairly long odds, one might suggest. Yet that is the central narrative in the economic policy story of Australia's 46th Parliament. It is an act in two parts: first, the brief moment when it achieved budget balance, due to significant 'bracket creep' and moderate fiscal restraint, and second, the overwhelming fiscal force that saved the Australian economy during the pandemic but jettisoned any notion of budgetary balance.

Both acts speak to the challenges facing the current and future parliaments. For all the Morrison Government's discussion of fiscal restraint in the pre-pandemic period, its success in achieving a balanced budget was achieved through increases in income tax, in the form of bracket creep. This is most starkly evident in the total revenue raised as a proportion of gross domestic product (GDP), climbing from 23.4 per cent in 2012–13 to 25.3 per cent in 2018–19. Spending restraint was modest, at best, with expenditure rising from 25 per cent of GDP to 26 per cent, and then clawed back to 25 per cent over the same period.

This does not bode well for future governments. Income tax – already high and one of the least efficient forms of taxation – has been the only real driver toward budget balance. And since the briefest of returns to a predicted budget surplus, the embedded spending commitment in our three largest entitlement programs has become clear: spending on the National Disability Insurance Scheme (NDIS) is (based on the October 2022 budget) forecast to grow at more than 12 per cent per annum and already it costs more than Medicare. After 30 years of compulsory superannuation – which, regardless of the original intention, ought to be largely a replacement for rather than a supplement to the age pension – 80 per cent of retirees now receive the pension or part-pension. This will cost $62 billion by 2025–26, or roughly 10 per cent of budgetary spending.

If there is any good news in the aggregate economic statistics, it is that the government's additional spending during the COVID-19 pandemic, on top of the 2008 stimulus, still leaves its balance sheet in good shape. Australia's net debt is low, relative to almost all other advanced economies, with our debt estimated at half that of the famously thrifty German government, one-third of the United Kingdom's and less than one-third of that of the United States (Trading Economics, 2021; Holden and Dixon, 2022).

The Morrison Government's fiscal position evolved during the 46th Parliament, ultimately shaped by the most important economic event of the term: the COVID-19 pandemic and the government's fiscal response. In addition, one of the more important issues prior to the pandemic was infrastructure spending; the current state and future viability of our three largest entitlement programs – the age pension, Medicare and the NDIS.

Fiscal position: Net debt

The fiscal history of Australia since the mid-1990s goes roughly like this. The fruits of Hawke–Keating economic reforms combined with the revolution in information and communications technologies to reduce Australia's already modest net debt to GDP, from 18.1 per cent to –3.4 per cent in 2008. The financial crisis of 2008, and the Rudd–Henry (then Treasury Secretary) stimulus package in response, drove net debt up to 10 per cent of GDP. Following this, a period of drift set in with increased spending by the Gillard Government and a lack of significant financial reform by the Abbott Government saw debt rise to 18 per cent of GDP. As shown in Figure 8.1, under the leadership of Finance Minister Cormann and a series of Coalition treasurers from 2015–2020, net debt stabilised until the onset of the COVID-19 pandemic. The Morrison Government's policy response to the second great crisis of the 21st century added a further 15 per cent debt to GDP, leaving the country at 33 per cent net debt to GDP.

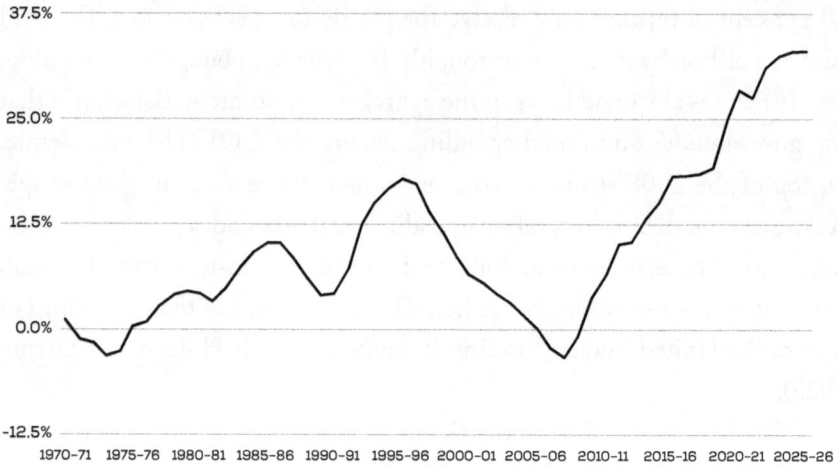

Figure 8.1
Australia's net debt to GDP, 1970–2025

NOTE Percentages for 2022–23 and 2024–25 are estimates.

Although the rise in net debt since the Global Financial Crisis has been rapid, Australia's overall fiscal position is very strong, with net debt low relative to almost all other advanced economies. Australia is peculiar among advanced economies in that the public narrative is that all government debt is bad, and that any debt accrued to weather a crisis needs to be 'paid back'. This sensibility, which has no basis in economic theory, was neatly captured in an interview by former National Party leader John Anderson with former treasurer Peter Costello, which included statements such as 'Debt eventually needs to be paid back' and 'Growing debt is a tax on our youth' (Anderson in Costello, 2021).

Perhaps this narrative comes from the highly unusual confluence of circumstances in 2006, in which Australia did wipe out government debt. As economics teaches, the benefit of spending today must be balanced against the cost of servicing that spending tomorrow. In other words, Mr Anderson's aforementioned phrase, 'Growing debt is a tax on our youth' is not wrong, but it is incomplete. Yes, debt is a tax on younger generations, but it is also a dividend to them through the provision of social and physical infrastructure, an advanced education and training system, and strong employment opportunities. It is also worth remembering that not all debt is created equal and, in particular, debt accumulated to avoid the worst ravages of global economic crises is particularly desirable. This point was made at length by Edmond, Holden and Preston (2021, p. 558), who observe:

> At times of full employment, additional government spending tends to crowd out private-sector spending, driving up interest rates, which in turn undermines the effectiveness of the stimulus. But in current conditions with the economy far from full employment and interest rates low, crowding-out effects are likely to be small.

Indeed, this view is supported by the best empirical evidence, including by Auerbach and Gorodnichenko (2012) and Caggiano and co-authors (2015).

In light of this – the correct standard of evidence – government spending during the pandemic was entirely appropriate. Such spending could have been more effective in its targeting, and the debt issuance from this increased spending could have been better managed. But these are areas for improvement rather than criticisms of the fiscal response.

Yet emergency spending – which has an especially high marginal benefit – is different from continuous spending in the 'ordinary course of business'. To that end, while the large increases in debt during the pandemic were justifiable, this certainly does not mean that debt levels do not matter. Indeed, one of the great challenges facing the 47th and future parliaments is how to get the approximately $40 billion a year 'structural' budget deficit under control.

Australia's fiscal response to the COVID-19 pandemic

The defining feature of economic policy in the 46th Parliament was the massive fiscal response to the COVID-19 pandemic. The 2021–22 budget revealed that the total government spending during the pandemic was $311 billion. This represents approximately 15.6 per cent of annual GDP, or nearly 8 per cent per annum for two years.

The major components of the spending are well known. The roughly $90 billion JobKeeper wage-subsidy program helped maintain the connection between workers and employers while cushioning the blow of government-mandated and self-imposed lockdowns. The JobSeeker program provided expanded unemployment benefits. There was an early program to boost business cashflows, which supported 800 000 businesses and not-for-profit organisations with payments of as much as $100 000 each, costing around $35 billion. Businesses were also allowed to fully expense rather than depreciate capital items, and were permitted to 'carryback' losses against past profits – measures that cost around $50 billion. Health spending naturally increased dramatically, to fund everything from expanded capacity in intensive care units to vaccine purchases.

While the total dollar figures are important, understanding the underlying philosophy of this fiscal support is equally important. Very early on in the pandemic, Treasury and the treasurer made clear that they understood the enormity of the challenge the nation faced. Spending was large, it was immediate and it was delivered extremely effectively (in the case of JobKeeper) through the single-touch payroll system. It was a tour de force in administrative efficiency.

Certain industries were excluded from the JobKeeper program, which was highly unfortunate and, in some instances, appeared to be vindictive. The arts industries suffered mightily and, although they comprise a disparate sector with business models that do not fit easily into government funding categories, should and could have been treated vastly better. The university sector was essentially excluded from JobKeeper, leading to large layoffs and further cutbacks in the quality of education offerings.

Perhaps the most contentious of all during the pandemic was the absence of a 'clawback' mechanism on JobKeeper, so that businesses supported in anticipation of hard times might have had to repay funds received if it turned out, after the fact, that they did not need those funds. This was viewed as a design flaw in some quarters, and the Labor Opposition prosecuted the case very effectively. By some estimates, as much as $20 billion went to businesses that, ex post, fared well enough that they did not need assistance. Indeed, the politics of the matter 'devolved into a populist riot desperate to expose which recipient experienced rising revenue after the fact, which paid executive bonuses, which paid foreign dividends, and so on' (Hamilton & Holden, 2021).

A different perspective on Labor's approach to this issue is that the animating principle of fiscal support measures such as JobKeeper was to ensure that unemployment did not rise too high and that businesses were not forced to the wall. The very success of such an approach is ensured by people's belief in its effectiveness, such that the economy will be 'okay', which justifies that belief and drives a self-fulfilling prophecy. Or, in the language of game theory, it leads society to coordinate on the 'high output' equilibrium rather than the 'low output' equilibrium (Akerlof & Holden, 2019).

The most extraordinary aspect of the Morrison Government's fiscal response was that it involved a volte-face on decades of political branding, which had lauded balanced budgets, irrespective of circumstances, as virtuous and saw debt and deficits as not just evidence of poor economic management but also as morally wrong.

In fact, this was a moment that could have changed Australian politics in the economic realm. But two things happened to prevent that. First, the Labor Party could not restrain itself from pointing out the Coalition's hypocrisy and repeatedly highlighted the 'trillion dollars of debt' it had incurred. Second, the key architect of the economic plan during the pandemic, Treasurer Josh Frydenberg, lost his seat of Kooyong at the 2022 election – and many of his moderate colleagues suffered the same fate. There is the real prospect of the entire episode being written off as sui generis.

Infrastructure and other spending

In 2019, Josh Frydenberg's first budget as treasurer committed $100 billion to infrastructure spending, including $42 billion over the forward estimates. In his budget speech, the treasurer underscored this with the statement that 'Cranes, hard hats and heavy machinery will be seen across the country'. For a time this was true, but then the pandemic hit, and with it came some obvious slowdowns in major projects due to public health measures. Yet Treasurer Frydenberg also knew the government had to pump money into an economy staring at the possibility of 15 per cent unemployment. Thus, subsequent budgets sought to increase spending on infrastructure.

It quickly became clear, however, that there were supply limitations on how much physical infrastructure spending could be implemented quickly. Some major projects require working closely with, or are largely determined by, the states and territories. Large projects take years of planning, consultation, land acquisition and the like. There is a relatively fixed supply – at least in the short term – of qualified workers for construction projects. And Australian construction costs are high by international standards, making cost–benefit analyses harder to satisfy than in many other jurisdictions (see Cella, 2017).

The 46th Parliament did not make sufficient progress on consideration of infrastructure more broadly as physical and social infrastructure. Education spending at all levels came under continued pressure; the manifest failings of the aged-care system were grimly exposed (see Royal Commission into Aged Care Quality & Safety, 2021); and the National Broadband Network continued to be slower yet more expensive than analogous infrastructure in most advanced (and many not-so-advanced) economies. Indeed, Australia ranks 57th in the world in this critical piece of 21st-century infrastructure (World Population Review, 2022).

The future of entitlement programs: Age pension, NDIS and Medicare

The 46th Parliament highlights the nation's major entitlement programs. Not only did the pandemic emphasise the crucial role of these programs but it also exposed many of the gaps in their long-term growth rates (Holden & Dixon, 2022).

The three largest entitlement programs in Australia (other than assistance to the states, which is essentially an accounting line item) are the age pension, Medicare and the NDIS.

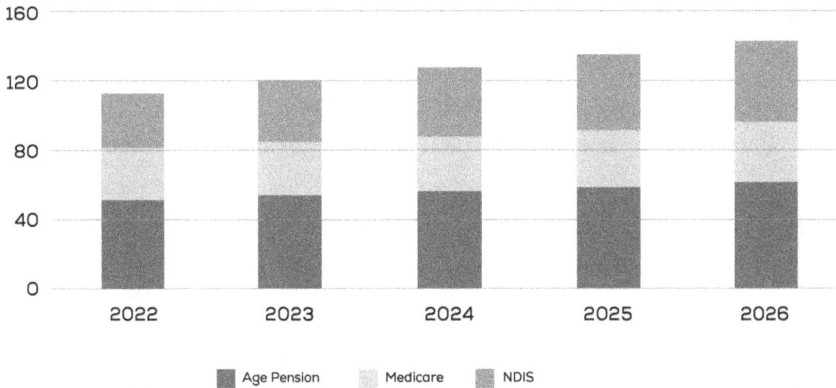

Figure 8.2
Estimated spending on major entitlement programs ($billion).

Medicare and the age pension have long been part of the fabric of the Australian social welfare state. They are central pillars in providing a 'dignified social minimum' to all Australians (Holden & Dixon, 2022). That said, as Figure 8.2 shows, based on figures from the May 2022 Budget, these programs are growing at 3.6 and 4.6 per cent a year, respectively. Medicare is sustainable. However, the age pension, which is growing at 4.6 per cent per annum, is exceeding a reasonable, long-term estimate of government revenue growth. It will thus increasingly consume a larger share of the federal Budget.

The NDIS is a relatively new program, having been introduced during the Gillard Government. It is a vital means of providing dignity to a large number of Australians. It is also an important social insurance program. Yet the May 2022 Budget forecast it to grow at 10.6 per cent per annum, and it already costs more than Medicare. The October 2022 Budget updated this growth rate to more than 12 per cent per annum. It is expected that expenditure on the NDIS will be double that of Medicare relatively soon. This is patently not sustainable, but raises difficult, perhaps wrenching, questions about eligibility, the benefits provided and the efficiency with which they are provided.

Of course, these arguments about sustainability presume that government cannot just 'print money' without consequence to pay for such programs. Proponents of a radical, informal theory known as Modern Monetary Theory (MMT) suggest that there are no effective limits on the sustainability of government spending programs.

Modern Monetary Theory starts with an obvious point that is neither new nor controversial: that a government that can issue debt denominated in its own currency (such as Australia) will always be able to finance a budget deficit by simply creating whatever number of new Australian dollars is required. In this way, the government can never fail to make payment on AUD-denominated liabilities. Since any deficit – however large – can always be financed through the printing of money, the idea of a budget deficit is, to use US economic commentator and proponent of MMT Stephanie Kelton's term, a 'myth'. This is all well known.

The key question this raises is, when and under what circumstances a government is likely to run into an inflationary spiral because it has ignored deficits budgets. Supporters of MMT deny that inflation can spiral out of control, even when an economy is below full capacity. Yet history shows that runaway inflation is not just a phenomenon of dysfunction or external shocks; even well-functioning economies can experience large increases in inflation when there is a structural deterioration in underlying fiscal capacity (eg in its capacity to raise taxes or to cut spending). This happened in France in the early 1980s, Aotearoa New Zealand in the mid-1980s, and both Germany and South Korea in the early 1990s.

The fundamental problem with MMT is that there is only a finite number of real economic resources that can be extracted through seigniorage, which is the difference between the face value of physical money and the cost to produce it. Or, to put it another way 'one can only get so much juice out of a lemon'.

All of this goes to highlight what mainstream economists have long known: that the total amount of net government debt *does* matter and that deficits are not a myth but an important constraint on what governments can prudently do. This is why it is crucial to focus on the government's 'structural' deficit. Financing government spending for ongoing programs like Medicare and the NDIS from newly issued debt is doing nothing more than putting off the inevitable: either a cut in spending or an increase in taxes.

Tax increases can occur through inflation or conventional taxation measures. The 'fiscal theory of the price level' (see, for instance, Cochrane, 2023) teaches that newly issued debt – however it is financed – leads to an increase in the overall size of the government's consolidated balance sheet (effectively Treasury plus the Reserve Bank). Whether this new spending and debt are inflationary ultimately depends on fiscal backing. If the new debt is matched with future increases in taxes, then it will not be inflationary; if it is not matched with increases in taxes, then it will be inflationary.

Is 35 per cent net debt to GDP too high? This is a more difficult question to answer. But Australia's fiscal history since the 1990s has demonstrated that debt is very hard to 'pay down' and increasingly difficult to 'shrink away' as a share of GDP through robust economic growth, but it is easy and necessary to increase debt in times of crisis such as was the case in 2008–09 and 2020–21. At a minimum, we should not let lazy politics and fear of reform let debt continue to drift upward outside of a genuine macro-economic crisis.

What that leaves is a $40 billion structural budget deficit. As pointed out elsewhere (Holden, 2022) the scale of this problem means that only large reforms to expenditures or taxes can bridge the gap. Australia already has high rates of personal income tax and, since those are a disincentive for people to work, are not a good place to look for extra revenues. Three possibilities beckon. One is enacting a 'progressive GST' as previously advocated (Holden & Dixon, 2022). This involves increasing the rate and broadening the base of the GST, but with a $7500 to $10000 GST-free threshold for each adult Australian. This would be progressive – it would help lower income-earners the most – but would also deliver a net $40 billion that could be spent on personal income tax cuts and reduction of the deficit. A second possibility is cutting back on superannuation tax breaks. Australia spends around $25 billion a year on these, yet 80 per cent of people still retire on to the pension, or part pension. This double-dipping, whereby people take the superannuation tax break *and* the age pension, should be removed. Finally, as previously stated (Holden, 2022):

> … we provide more than $13 billion per year in tax breaks for negative gearing. That drives household debt up and housing affordability down. It reduces the financial stability, but increases intergenerational inequities. Negative gearing is a bad idea. Which is why we are the only country that has such a perverse system.

The 46th Parliament sat during an extraordinary period in Australian economic, social and political history. Overall, the fiscal response to the pandemic was exemplary. This chapter has outlined some minor quibbles to that general assessment. The first is that the term-structure of government debt issuance could have been better. In particular, Australia should have issued more long-term government bonds – of at least 30-year duration – to lock in the benefits of low interest rates during the pandemic. Second, the country was not sufficiently prepared to roll out the JobKeeper program and, understandably given the urgency of enacting the program, it erred on the side of inclusion in parts of the population, and significantly against inclusion in others. Both lessons can and should be learnt in advance of the next major fiscal crisis Australia is likely to face.

But there is a broader set of lessons that many hope that Australia can learn from the 46th Parliament. The extraordinary challenges faced highlight the importance of fiscal policy in general, and how it should be rebooted to better serve the nation. Australia is a nation that tends to fetishise headline budget deficit (or surplus) numbers rather than to focus on how government spending – or lack thereof – serves the Australian people in the long term. Fiscal policy should be judged by the outcomes they are expected to deliver, rather than by a set of accounting numbers.

Edmond, Preston and Holden (2022) argue that there are four elements to a new fiscal approach that Australia should embrace:

1. Acknowledge that fiscal policy is a useful, rather than merely necessary, tool and that it plays an important role in stabilising the economy. As they argue: 'In the short run we need aggressive fiscal stimulus to get us out of recession. In the medium run, fiscal policy should be deployed (with monetary policy; more on this below) to achieve price stability and full employment.'
2. The budget should separate 'emergency' and 'ordinary' expenditures: 'The government should continue to use the emergency budget as needed to ensure a recovery is achieved. Any need to demonstrate fiscal prudence should be confined to the province of the ordinary budget.'
3. Even with ordinary expenditures, there needs to be a distinction between the 'cyclical' component of the budget bottom line and the 'structural' budget balance. The cyclical component 'is necessarily affected by automatic stabilisers and ordinary amounts of discretionary spending', whereas 'the underlying "structural" budget balance ... reflects the [Commonwealth's] long-term fiscal position'.
4. There should be a commitment not to raise taxes against debt issued for emergency expenditures for at least 30 years if such expenditures are financed by 30-year bonds.

It is not advisable to look for silver linings in a global pandemic that has wrought such devastation, even in Australia, where good public health and economic policy muted the worst ravages of the COVID-19 pandemic. But if there is one benefit for economic policy from this period, it is that the positions of the left and right of the economic debate in Australia have been clarified, while the centrist position that underpinned the country's fiscal strategy was shown to be highly successful.

The deficit-hawk position that the optimal level of government debt is zero and always needs to be 'paid back' has not only been shown to be frivolous: it has been explicitly jettisoned by the Liberal Party. Reinstating its 'Debt and deficits' mantra should not and will not be easy. The left's view that all spending is good spending, and that debt does not matter at all has also been shown to be an intellectually bankrupt notion.

Going forward, Australia must focus on what spending can be used to enhance the lives of current and future generations – a collective obligation – and how we might enact sensible policies to keep debt at a level at which overwhelming fiscal force can be used should the country face another crisis like the COVID-19 pandemic.

References

Akerlof, Robert and Richard Holden. 'Capital Assembly', *Journal of Law, Economics and Organization*, 35(3), 2019, pp. 489–512.

Auerbach, Alan J and Gorodnichenko, Yuriy. 'Fiscal multipliers in recession and expansion', *Fiscal Policy After the Financial Crisis*, NBER, 2012, pp. 63–98.

Caggiano, Giovanni, Efrem Castelnuovo, Valentina Colombo and Gabriela Nodari, 'Estimating fiscal multipliers: News from a non-linear world', *The Economic Journal*, 125(584), 2015, pp. 746–76.

Cella, Lauren. 'How does Australia compare globally in costs for construction?', *Infrastructure*, 20 March 2017, <infrastructuremagazine.com.au/2017/03/20/how-does-australia-compare-globally-in-costs-for-construction/>.

Cochrane, John H. *The Fiscal Theory of the Price Level*, Princeton University Press, 2023.

Costello, Peter. 'Growing debt is a tax on our youth', 2021, <www.youtube.com/watch?v=EfNLpGCG8q4>.

Edmond, Chris, Richard Holden and Bruce Preston. 'Should we worry about government debt? Thoughts on Australia's COVID-19 response', *Australian Economic Review*, 53(4), 2020, pp. 557–65.

Hamilton, Steven and Richard Holden. 'ALP takes the low road on JobKeeper', *The Australian*, 23 September 2021.

Holden, Richard. 'We'll have to think bigger on budget repair', *Australian Financial Review*, 24 March 2022.

Holden, Richard and Rosalind Dixon. *From Free to Fair Markets: Liberalism after COVID-19*, Oxford University Press, 2022.

Royal Commission into Aged Care Quality and Safety. *Final Report: Care, dignity and respect*, Commonwealth of Australia, 2021, <agedcare.royalcommission.gov.au/publications/final-report>.

Trading Economics, 'Public sector net debt to GDP', 2021, <tradingeconomics.com/country-list/government-debt-to-gdp>.

World Population Review, 'Internet speeds by country 2022', 2022, <worldpopulationreview.com/country-rankings/internet-speeds-by-country>.

9

AGED CARE UNDER THE MORRISON GOVERNMENT

Brenton Prosser

Public crises can be a crucible that burns away all but the core structural, economic and social dilemmas political leaders face. They can also foreground the strategies of political leaders in accepting, deflecting, rejecting or denying political blame. The crisis of COVID-19 and aged care is an apt example of Scott Morrison's political trial by fire.

That said, aged care did not become a national issue overnight. Concerns reach back to 1975, when a report by the Social Welfare Commission stressed the importance of the autonomy, dignity and human rights of older Australians. These concerns were echoed ten years later in the McLeay Report. Now, reviewing the findings of the 2021 Royal Commission into Aged Care Quality and Safety, the commissioners could well have written every word of these earlier reports.

Prime Minister Morrison cannot be held solely to blame for the current aged-care dilemma. However, the scope of this collection sees us look at the strategies and policies Morrison and his ministers employed, consider the outcomes of the Royal Commission he established, and explore how he responded as blame grew at the federal level.

The origins of the Royal Commission

Within weeks of becoming prime minister in 2018, Morrison announced a Royal Commission into Aged Care Quality and Safety (Hutchens, 2018). The mistreatment, abuse and neglect of Australians living in aged-care facilities had been in the public consciousness for some time. The use of kerosene baths – an archaic treatment for scabies – on residents at Riverside Nursing Home had been a major issue for the Howard Government and remains a symbol of elder abuse and the challenges of aged care in Australia.

Following decades of scandals and subsequent inquiries into aged care, the Royal Commission was a significant development that could have framed Morrison's leadership. A positive frame depended, of course, on how the government would respond to the commission's findings. It provided a profound opportunity for reform to aged care in Australia; a reform that could have built a better system to protect, care for and support some of the most vulnerable members of our society.

The Royal Commission's findings and the government's response

After more than 10 500 submissions, 6800 calls and submissions from 641 witnesses, the Royal Commission made 148 recommendations in its final report. Ultimately, those recommendations called for fundamental reform to the provision and regulation of aged-care services in Australia. At the heart of the calls for change lay the need to replace the existing *Aged Care Act* 1997 (Cth) with one that was human-rights based. This would enshrine the rights of older Australians to self-determination, respect and receipt of quality care.

The Morrison Government's response to the Royal Commission's report was released in May 2021, but it did commit to new legislation based on the commission's first three recommendations. By this time, however, the government was beleaguered by issues surrounding its response to the COVID-19 pandemic. Aged-care residents had suffered enormously from prevarication, delays in procuring vaccines and the government's failure to prioritise their health and safety. By the time the government responded formally, almost 700 aged-care residents had died from COVID-19.

The commissioners did not agree on the best governance structure for a renewed approach to aged care. Commissioner Pagone favoured a regulatory framework that would be independent of ministerial and departmental oversight, while Commissioner Lynelle Briggs AO recommended (and the Morrison Government preferred) a regulatory framework based within the broader governmental structure. However, both commissioners were united in their assessment of the way successive governments had prioritised minimising costs over providing quality care for vulnerable older Australians. As Commissioner Briggs stated:

> [a]fter years of critical reviews, it took the Oakden catastrophe in South Australia to expose again the cracks in the aged care system. Over the 2 years of our inquiry, we have catalogued the failures of the system, shining a light on the egregious abuse, mistreatment and neglect that we discovered. The COVID-19 pandemic reminded us all again of the crisis in aged care in this country and of the failure of our leaders to take responsibility for what happens in this system. (Volume 1, 2021)

Such insights highlight the deep and abiding crisis in aged care. The commission's findings represent a story of the policy and regulation failures of consecutive governments. Both major political parties must share the blame. It is ironic that when the Howard Government introduced the current aged-care legislation in 1997, its intention was to tighten care standards, but instead it privatised and commercialised much of the aged-care sector, which would later contribute to the contemporary crisis.

Leap forward 25 years, and community outrage forced the Morrison Government to call a Royal Commission to consider the apparent failures of Howard's legislation. It found that while the profits for some had soared, care had plummeted for many. That the Morrison Government had failed to respond to the Royal Commission's findings in either a timely or proactive way (both before and during the global pandemic) allowed this situation to continue.

The Morrison Government's policy response

Since Federation, the Commonwealth has become increasingly involved in aged care, with postwar pensions, direct funding to providers from the 1960s, and the expansion of home and community care from the 1980s. This was followed by the centralisation, privatisation and marketisation of aged care in 1997. The Australian Government then took over responsibility for setting and evaluating standards of (non-government) residential aged care services, and for funding, although with some financial contribution from residents. Most aged care service provision is outsourced to private or not-for-profit providers, while states and territories are responsible for associated health and hospital services, particularly at times of health crisis.

Since 1997, the focus of policy has been on improving efficiency and quality through competition, as well as on expanding consumer-directed care. Largely, this has been pursued following the argument that older Australians want independence and to remain in their homes. In recent years, government has expressed concerns that some providers have used control of funding and services to 'game' the system, which further justified the shift towards market models, client independence and 'choice'. However, this has not been without challenge. Royal Commissioner Pagone reported concerns that Howard's changes, inherited by Morrison, were primarily to reduce Commonwealth expenditure by shifting costs, rather than improving care or independence:

> ... there has never been an assessment of how much money is required
> to deliver high quality care. Moreover ... the indexation arrangements
> applied to aged care payments over the last twenty years have
> systematically reduced the real value of the funding ... quality care
> has decreased, at least in part, because we ... have decreased funding
> levels in real terms over the last twenty years. (Volume 1, 2021)

Meanwhile, Commissioner Briggs offered a more contemporary assessment – shared by many in the sector – that the current market model is ill-suited to quality in aged care:

> The aged care system has suffered from sequential attempts by
> governments to define it as a market in its own right ... these
> market-based reforms that redefine the people who use aged care as
> 'consumers' who 'direct' their own care by purchasing services from
> businesses in a 'competitive market' have resulted in more confusion
> than before. (Volume 1, 2021)

As is often the case with complex public policy, it is likely that both approaches could be plausibly and legitimately argued. More importantly, this highlights an ongoing tension where focusing on the individual potentially obscures deep structural issues and the implications of policy decisions of political leaders.

There have been more than 20 inquiries into aged care over the past 25 years. The findings have largely been the same. The supply of care is struggling to keep up with growing demand and consumer expectations. An ageing population that is living longer is presenting with increasingly complex, chronic and costly medical conditions. The aged-care workforce is low paid, low skilled and hard to attract in regional areas. While many providers supply quality care, examples of unacceptable care practices persist. Aged-care recipients continually face unwieldy and difficult-to-navigate systems, as well as difficulty in securing the services they require.

The response from governments over the past 25 years has been to focus attention on the failures of providers. The 'go to' response of federal governments when things go wrong has been to single out individuals or private providers for public criticism, then regulate new quality standards. Such accountability is not without merit, but what has resulted is a highly regulated sector in which abundant regulations do little to quell deeply persistent problems. As Karen Hitchcock (2015) highlighted in her compelling *Quarterly Essay*, this is one of the most highly regulated sectors and yet that has little effect on the deeply persistent problems in Australia. This assessment has been reiterated by numerous inquiries and reports in the years that followed. Many have said it, but Commissioner Briggs said it well:

> Perhaps the most shocking part of this is that the problems in our aged care system are not new. There have been more than twenty substantial official inquiries into aspects of the aged care system over the past twenty years. Many of these inquiries have made similar findings and offered similar recommendations for improvement. The responses by successive governments have failed to tackle the underlying problems. (Volume 1, 2021)

The Morrison Government both inherited and continued this convention of blaming the providers during the early months of its second term. However, this approach became less and less tenable in the face of a Royal Commission and a pandemic.

COVID-19 and the Royal Commission

It is quite possible that the Morrison Government, after instigating the Royal Commission in 2018, did not expect to still be in power when its findings were released. Even if this was not the case, it could not have anticipated the effects of the COVID-19 pandemic on the nation and, particularly, on the aged-care sector.

The first week of March 2020 saw the announcement of the first death in a NSW aged-care facility. By 18 March, both New South Wales and Victoria had announced restrictions on aged-care facilities. Days later, the newly formed National Cabinet announced $444.6 million in temporary funding to support aged-care providers and strengthen the industry, including specific mechanisms to reinforce the workforce.

Hindsight reveals that governments were unprepared and early measures were inadequate. By May 2020, there had been outbreaks in three aged-care homes, while cases in Victorian residential facilities skyrocketed from mid-July. By August, 12 Victorian facilities were in lockdown, and accusations of 'hubris' and 'inaction' were made between federal and state ministers and health officials. It was in this context that the Royal Commission expanded its investigation to include COVID-19 from September 2020.

Several submissions to the Royal Commission presented the COVID-19 pandemic as exacerbating structural and funding concerns, and these caught media attention. One concern was the lack of funding to allow the federal regulator to exercise its powers, an issue further high-lighted by the impact of COVID-19 on the sector. Another prominent concern was the federal decision to relax a provision that prevented aged-care workers from working across multiple sites. Motivated by staff shortages, it saw casual and part-time staff spread the virus through multiple facilities. This restriction was reintroduced in aged-care hot spots in May 2021.

Another example was early federal government reticence about introducing mandatory vaccination for aged-care workers. Personal resistance to vaccination among the sector's lower-skilled, largely migrant workforce resulted in low vaccination rates. Adding to this was the Morrison Government's inefficient supply of vaccines. This contributed to higher infection rates in staff and transmission rates to residents. The situation was addressed with mandatory vaccination requirements from November 2021.

Both examples highlight how COVID-19 illuminated deeper structural issues for the sector, for which no single provider could be held responsible. They were further highlighted by the Royal Commission recommendations. The message was clear – the aged-care system needed to be rebuilt, not tweaked, with workforce pay, conditions, skills, effective regulation, training and registration at the core. All of these are federal responsibilities.

Perhaps most awkward for the Morrison Government were recommendations for better pay for aged-care workers and the introduction of a levy through the taxation system to support required aged-care reforms. The government rejected the Royal Commission's options for achieving this, but they became part of public debate, including a Health Services Union submission to the Fair Work Commission for a permanent 25 per cent pay rise. Hence, the outcomes of the Royal Commission presented the government with a difficult political and policy challenge.

Responses to blunders, budgets and blame

The Morrison Government's responses to national attention on its handling of aged-care policy during this term marked a necessary shift from previous government approaches. The previous approach of blaming providers was hard to sustain, given ministerial blunders, minimalist budget responses and rising levels of blame on the Commonwealth.

Minister for Aged Care and Senior Australians Richard Colbeck had a memorable second term, one his government likely preferred to forget. On three different occasions he attracted national attention for what many described as major blunders. He was forced to apologise at a Senate hearing in August 2020 after being unable to provide the number of people who had died in residential aged-care facilities. In June 2021, Colbeck was unable to inform Senate Estimates how many aged-care workers had been vaccinated, but reassured them he was comfortable with worker vaccination rates as part of the Morrison Government's priority push. Later, in January 2022, Colbeck was found to have attended three days of an Ashes Test after declining to appear in front of the Senate's COVID-19 committee. None of these events played well publicly for the Morrison Government. Interestingly, this did not result in a strong response from Morrison. Instead, the prime minister told the media that he understood the public criticism of Minister Colbeck's actions, but he still had 'confidence' in him; effectively, leaving the minister to ride out his blunders.

More substantially, the Morrison Government was conservative in its Budget responses to the findings of the Aged Care Royal Commission and the impact of COVID-19. The 2020 and 2021 Budgets focused on expanding the minimum numbers of funded homecare packages by over 100 000, while experts explained it was not a matter of numbers but effectiveness (Duckett, 2020). Such a response also failed to address the pairing of low-care packages for people with high care needs. The 2022 Budget came with a commitment to continue the measures promised in 2021 (additional access to healthy food and professional time etc), along with better access to pharmacists in residential facilities, vocational training for workers in the sector and a once-off $800 wage payment to workers. Again, in practical terms, this fell well short of the Royal Commission's recommendations.

In light of these responses, the long-term challenges and the Royal Commission using terms such as 'crisis' and 'neglect', it is hard to depict the Morrison Government's response as a policy success. A long-held convention within the political studies literature is that due to the relative cost versus benefit, political leaders tend to seek to avoid blame, above seeking to take credit. The strategies they employ to achieve this are made all the more complex in multi-level (for example, federal) systems.

In response, I explore the blame avoidance strategies that Morrison mobilised, to see whether they changed anything. My analysis is, in fact, that they did. Blame was shifted up the political hierarchy, from a focus on singular 'bad' providers to actors within state and federal governments. This aligns with scholarly arguments that times of crisis are more likely to broaden perspectives that 'point back in time' or 'up the (political) hierarchy' (Brändström & Kuipers, 2003). Attention shifted away from blaming providers and on to state and federal leaders. The question, then, is 'How did the Morrison Government respond?' The answer is that it employed three different strategies.

The first strategy was denial. From the earlier stages, the government did not accept that there was a crisis (Speers, 2020). Early in the pandemic, Senator Colbeck rejected claims from aged-care providers of personal protective equipment (PPE) shortages, 'dismiss[ing] concerns that ill-equipped and undertrained staff had contributed to the spread of COVID-19 in aged care homes' (Visontay, 2020). In April 2020, before the huge outbreaks, Prime Minister Morrison highlighted the low number of coronavirus infections in aged care, to claim there was not a crisis and also to put pressure on facilities to let family members visit their residents (McCauley, 2020). Health Minister Greg Hunt expressed similar sentiments, saying that Australia's 'two significant outbreaks' in residential aged care were 'so far below our best-case expectation that I say a prayer of thanks virtually every day' (McCauley, 2020). However, as the crisis deepened this form of denial became less tenable. Ultimately, this led to Morrison's admission of crisis in the sector in early 2022, while responding to calls to bring in Defence personnel support (as had been the case with other recent disasters).

A second strategy was what Hood (2011) calls 'lightning rods' – public experts to whom authority is given to add legitimacy to a topic. We have seen this at work on multiple levels during the COVID-19 pandemic, as chief health officers were rolled out to give authority, and at times credibility, in disputes between ministers. Ostensibly, the Morrison and other governments shifted themselves out of the spotlight by saying that they were only doing what the experts were telling them. At key points during the crisis, this depoliticisation strategy was revealed. It was most evident in clashes between chief health officers over students returning to school, but also evident in disagreements regarding mandatory vaccination of visitors to aged-care homes. These clashes challenged the 'we are just following the science' approach. Rather, the independence of these lighting rods was dampened by political influence. As policy shifted from 'keeping COVID out' to 'living with the disease', the prominence of these lightning rods faded, just as their daily televised briefings ceased in late 2021.

A third strategy might be called 'scapegoating'. This was seen on more than one occasion, but most notably when the prime minister labelled the second wave of outbreaks as 'the Victorian wave' (Davey, 2020). This was continued in June 2021, when federal ministers suggested that the pandemic in Victorian aged-care facilities was due to a percentage of elderly people not getting their jabs (Connolly, 2021). Another version of this was when Morrison sought to present the outbreak in aged care as a state public health issue rather than a federal responsibility (Murphy, 2020). Similarly, when asked whether he felt personally responsible for deaths in aged care, Senator Colbeck avoided blame, saying deaths were 'ultimately caused by COVID-19' (Hurst, 2020). This approach of seeking to shift blame between levels of government in a federal system became the most persistent throughout the pandemic. The Morrison Government had some success in shifting blame to the states, particularly Victoria. Further, as legal proceedings against providers began to emerge in 2022, public attention looked less to Morrison's government and more towards the status quo of governments devolving responsibility to non-government scapegoats.

It was clear that perhaps a range of blame strategies was being employed. These examples included blaming:

- the Victorian community (Murphy, 2020; Visontay & Boseley, 2020; Deery & Rose, 2020);
- the aged care sector (White, 2020; Lunn, Baxendale & Caisley, 2020);
- an unsuitable workforce (Rose & Minear, 2020).

This speaks to a deeper trend in Australian aged care. Looking to the history of aged care in Australia, it is an issue that has been identified as in crisis for over thirty years (Royal Commission, 2020). And yet, a historical review conducted by the author has found no example of a minister (federal, state or territory) taking responsibility or losing their role. Even the aforementioned use of kerosene baths, which is infamous in Australia, and the scandal around the response of the Commonwealth Department did not result in the direct sacking of the responsible minister. Hence, it can be posited that the key feature of the long-term Australian aged-care crisis is a churn of blame generation without acceptance of responsibility by any public individual. It is this convention to which Morrison appealed.

Yet, the COVID crisis introduced a new dynamic. Repeated public outcry, growing media attention and Royal Commission recommendations focused attention on structural and policy factors, as well as the Australian government, for a time, but this attention soon ebbed away. One reading of this is that the resilience of long-term blame conventions will trump the impact of short-term blame attribution practices and presentation strategies.

A missed opportunity

A fascinating insight from the Morrison Government's response to emerging aged-care policy challenges during its second period in office was that when the convention of blaming providers lost currency, it employed a range of other blame-shifting strategies. These strategies seemed effective in the short term. However, the federal election results in 2022 may see historians class the Morrison Government's carriage of aged-care policy as a negative. It is true to say that the Morrison Government inherited much of the volatile aged-care dilemma, and it would also be overstating things to say the Labor Party's more expansive policy won it the election. However, it is also fair to say that the Morrison Government missed the opportunity to make aged care a positive of its term.

Note: I wish to acknowledge the important contributions of Amanda Smullen, Gabriel Helleren–Simpson and Phillipa Brennan in the conceptualisation of this chapter.

References

Australian Law Reform Commission. *Report 131: Elder Abuse – A National Legal Response*, 2017, <www.alrc.gov.au/publication/elder-abuse-a-national-legal-response-alrc-report-131/>.

Braithwaite, John, Toni Makkai and Valerie Braithwaite. 'Regulating aged care: Ritualism and the new pyramid', *Leadership in Health Services*, 22(4), 2009, pp. 340–54.

Brändström, Annika and Sanneke Kuipers. 'From "normal incidents" to political crises: Understanding the selective politicization of policy failures', *Government and Opposition*, 38(3), 2003, pp. 279–305.

Connolly, Anne. 'Aged care, COVID vaccination blame game hits a new low – and residents are collateral damage' *ABC News*, 2 June 2021, <www.abc.net.au/news/2021-06-02/covid-19-aged-care-vaccination-roll-out-blame-game/100181486>.

Cowie, Tom. 'Hidden camera captures attack on elderly man by carer at Adelaide nursing home', *Sydney Morning Herald*, 26 July 2016, <www.smh.com.au/national/hidden-camera-captures-attack-on-elderly-man-by-carer-at-adelaide-nursing-home-20160726-gqdnh5.html>.

Davey, Melissa. 'Daniel Andrews brushes off PM's "Victoria wave" claim after 297 new Covid cases and nine deaths', the *Guardian*, 29 July 2020, <www.theguardian.com/australia-news/2020/jul/29/daniel-andrews-brushes-off-pms-victorian-wave-claim-as-state-records-nine-more-deaths>.

Deery, Shannon and Tamsin Rose. 'Andrews blames spike on mass failure to isolate', *Herald Sun*, 23 July 2020, p. 8.

Duckett, Stephen. 'The budget must address aged care – here are 3 key priorities', *The Conversation*, 30 September 2020, </theconversation.com/the-budget-must-address-aged-care-here-are-3-key-priorities-146678>.

Hitchcock, Karen. 'Dear Life: On caring for the elderly', *Quarterly Essay 57*, 2015, <www.quarterlyessay.com.au/essay/2015/03/dear-life/extract?msclkid=71cae692b49111ecb5a450301e8ceeeb>.

Hood, Christopher. *The Blame Game: Spin, Bureaucracy, and Self-Preservation in Government*. Princeton University Press, 2011.

Hurst, Daniel. 'Aged care minister Richard Colbeck says he's not personally responsible for 700 Covid deaths', *Guardian*, 27 October 2020, <www.theguardian.com/australia-news/2020/oct/27/aged-care-minister-richard-colbeck-says-hes-not-personally-responsible-for-700-covid-deaths>.

Hutchens, Gareth. 'Scott Morrison announces royal commission into aged care after string of scandals', *Guardian*, 16 September 2018, <www.theguardian.com/australia-news/2018/sep/16/morrison-to-announce-royal-commission-into-aged-care-after-string-of-scandals>.

Lunn, Stephen, Rachel Baxendale, and Olivia Caisley. 'Aged and confused in care', *The Australian*, 28 July 2020, p. 5.

McCauley, Donna. 'Don't lock aged care residents away from their families, PM says', *Sydney Morning Herald*, 21 April 2020.

Murphy, Katharine. 'Scott Morrison's persistent effort to sidestep accountability for aged care is utterly transparent', *Guardian*, 19 August 2020, <www.theguardian.com/australia-news/2020/aug/19/scott-morrisons-persistent-effort-to-sidestep-accountability-for-aged-care-is-utterly-transparent>.

Rose, Tamsin and Tom Minear. 'Deaths were avoidable', *Herald Sun*, 31 July 2020, p. 10.

Royal Commission into Aged Care Quality and Safety. *Final Report: Care, Dignity and Respect: Volume 1 Summary and recommendations*, Commonwealth of Australia, 2021, </agedcare.royalcommission.gov.au/publications/final-report>.

Senate Standing Committee on Community Affairs. *Effectiveness of the Aged Care Quality Assessment and Accreditation Framework for Protecting Residents from Abuse and Poor Practices, and Ensuring Proper Clinical and Medical Care Standards are Maintained and Practiced*, Commonwealth of Australia, 2019, <www.aph.gov.au/Parliamentary_Business/Committees/Senate/Community_Affairs/AgedCareQuality/Interim_report>.

South Australian Independent Commissioner Against Corruption. *Oakden: A Shameful Chapter in South Australia's History*, 2018, <www.icac.sa.gov.au/publications/published-reports/oakden>.

Speers, David. 'Aged Care Royal Commission's findings have been batted away. But huge problems remain for Morrison', *ABC News*, 4 October 2020, <www.abc.net.au/news/2020-10-04/aged-care-royal-commission-covid-government-cop-blame/12725246>.

Visontay, Elias. '"Significant risk of dying": Australian aged care workers accuse minister of playing down safety concerns', *Guardian*, 27 July 2020.

Visontay, Elias and Matilda Boseley. 'Victoria records 484 new coronavirus cases on worst day of outbreak', *Guardian*, 22 July 2020, <https://www.theguardian.com/australia-news/2020/jul/22/victoria-records-484-new-coronavirus-cases-and-two-deaths-in-australias-worst-day-of-outbreak>.

White, Alex. 2020. 'Aged care evacuation', *Herald Sun*, 18 July, p. 10.

10

ROBODEBTS AND ROLLERCOASTERS: SOCIAL (IN)SECURITY IN THE 46TH PARLIAMENT

Emma Dawson

Perhaps the most famous refrain of our 30th prime minister was the claim that 'if you have a go, you'll get a go'. Yet the events and policy responses that governed the lives of Australia's most vulnerable citizens in the years between the 2019 and 2022 elections revealed Scott Morrison's favourite slogan to be a hollow rationalisation for callousness, and one utterly without basis in fact. If the 46th Parliament showed us anything, it is that 'the go' in Australia is no longer fair, neither as reward for individual effort nor as return on the social contract established in the years after our last great global upheaval, the Second World War.

The social and economic disruption of the COVID-19 pandemic exposed deep structural problems in Australia's social security system. After three decades in which Australia's gross domestic product and aggregate wealth grew without fault, the first genuine economic crisis in a generation crashed into a welfare state that has suffered decades of misguided, economically rationalist policies that reduced the size of government by cutting essential services and financial support to people in need.

Successive federal administrations, basking in the glow of uninterrupted headline growth over more than a quarter of a century, have steadily immiserated a significant and persistent minority of citizens, leaving Australia's safety net threadbare. Just how inadequate are the provisions of that safety net, and how punishing its administration, were thrown into stark relief with the onset of the pandemic in early 2020, when a record number of Australians were forced to rely on some form of government income support to survive the acute phase of the crisis.

As a result, the systemic and long-term problems besetting Australia's social security system are now evident, not only to experts in social security but also to the population at large. The incapacity of our safety net to provide security to people in a time of almost unprecedented crisis *without urgent, ad hoc and temporary interventions* is indicative of a system that is no longer fit for its purpose: to secure the livelihoods and wellbeing of Australians if, and when, circumstances diminish their capacity for self-reliance.

In fact, the failures and brutalities of Australia's social security system have been obvious for years to anyone paying attention, and especially to those caught up in it, usually through no fault of their own. Yet rather than learn from the natural experiment in policy response to a crisis that threw millions of people out of work in the space of a month, the Morrison Government 'snapped back' to an economic system that disenfranchises a significant proportion of the populace from our common wealth, and then blames and punishes them for misfortune almost entirely beyond their control.

What follows is an assessment of the dispensation of social security in the 46th Australian Parliament. Australia's welfare state arguably (and hopefully) reached its nadir under that administration, whose policy choices have caused avoidable harm to the most vulnerable people in society. There are significant and urgent lessons for the new federal government and subsequent parliaments in the evidence of damage wrought by the rhetorical and actual division of Australia's people into 'lifters and leaners', and the inevitable human costs of an ideological pursuit of the most vulnerable citizens, masquerading as fiscal responsibility.

Not my debt

While it was the sudden and shocking effect of the COVID-19 pandemic on Australia's labour market that threw the social security system into acute crisis, that system's vindictive parsimony was evident well before its onset. The earliest days of the 46th Parliament were marked by the scandal that became known as 'robodebt', arguably the greatest moral transgression of any Australian government in the area of social security.

Formally known as the Income Compliance Program, it was introduced in the 2015–16 federal Budget under the social services minister at the time, Scott Morrison, who described the program as putting '... a strong welfare cop on the beat focusing on deterrence, detection, investigation and prosecution to track down suspected welfare fraud and non-compliance' (Morrison, 2015). The 'welfare cop' was, in fact, an automated process using 'income-averaging' based on data from the Australian Taxation Office (ATO) to assess whether a recipient of income support may have been paid more than they were entitled to. The reliance on automated data matching was a significant departure from previous practice within the then-Department of Human Services, under which such income-averaging had only been used as a last resort after the department had exhausted 'every possible means of obtaining the actual income information through normal channels' – that is, compliance officers would gather information directly from welfare recipients or their employers or, if all relevant information was not available, would manually calculate the debt (Commonwealth Ombudsman, 2017).

From July 2016, this manual process was replaced by automated systems, without human oversight. This enabled the department to process approximately 20 000 'debts' per week – a number that previously would have taken a year (Senate Community Affairs References Committee, 2020). It was this entirely automated process that led to the epithet 'robodebt'. The removal of human oversight and the manual calculation of presumed welfare debts was intended to produce significant savings within the department while returning an estimated $3.5 billion in recovered 'debts' (Morrison, 2015).

Such savings would be made possible only by an extraordinary reversal of the onus of proof under the direction of the social services minister. The department simply raised a debt based on automated income-averaging from ATO data, without checking the information directly with welfare recipients or their employers. This debt was then issued through a notice to the recipient, who was required to prove the absence of the debt by checking their employment records and income statements for up to decades prior.

Given the inherent difficulty involved in obtaining financial records from previous employers and bank accounts, many people issued with a 'robodebt' simply paid up, and this caused significant financial hardship. More damningly, there are at least two credible reports of debt recipients having died by suicide due to the stress of the demand to prove their 'innocence' against the accusation of welfare fraud or to 'repay' money they did not have (McPherson, 2019, Karp, 2020).

Not all those targeted by the robodebt program were intimidated into acquiescence: almost as soon as the first robodebts were issued, activists initiated a fearless community campaign, under the banner 'Not My Debt'. This grassroots movement worked tirelessly to tell the stories of welfare recipients targeted under the program and the harm it was causing to already marginalised and vulnerable people. Using social media, the campaign raised awareness of robodebt among the general public, aided by strong reporting in the mainstream media, especially by *Guardian Australia*'s social affairs reporter, Luke Henriques-Gomes, who was ultimately awarded a Young Walkley for his coverage of the scandal.

After years of grassroots activism against robodebt, a scathing Ombudsman's report in 2017, a 2018 paper by former Administrative Appeals Tribunal member Terry Carney that questioned the legality of the program (Carney, 2018) and a challenge to the lawfulness of automated income-averaging in February 2019 by Victorian Legal Aid (Henriques-Gomes, 2019a), the Labor Opposition finally took up the cause in late 2019.

Declaring that he believed the program to be '… faulty, immoral and quite possibly illegal', the shadow minister for government services at the time, Bill Shorten, announced a class-action lawsuit to be spearheaded by Gordon Legal (Murphy, 2019a). The government settled the lawsuit out of court a day before the trial was to commence, and six months later abandoned the program altogether (Hayne & Doran, 2020).

A subsequent judgment in the Federal Court approved a settlement of at least $1.8 billion to those wrongly pursued by robodebt, with presiding Justice Bernard Murphy issuing a scathing assessment of the program, calling it '… a shameful chapter in the administration of the Commonwealth social security system and a massive failure of public administration' (Turner, 2021).

The report of the Senate Community Affairs Reference Committee Inquiry, released just ahead of the 2022 federal election, quantified the widespread harm robodebt caused to Australians, noting that:

> In total, an estimated $1.73 billion in illegitimate debts were raised against approximately 433,000 Australians. Within this group, approximately 381,000 individuals were pursued, often through private debt collection agencies, to repay almost $752 million to the Commonwealth. (Senate Community Affairs References Committee, 2022)

The government accepted the settlement terms decided by the Federal Court, and the originator of robodebt – and by now prime minister Scott Morrison – offered a grudging apology in parliament in June 2020, following the end of the program in May that year. However, there were no material consequences for those involved in the conception and maladministration of the program, other than the waste of billions of dollars of public funds. None of the responsible ministers were censured or otherwise penalised, and those who were in charge have never accepted formal responsibility for the trauma, distress and alleged loss of life due to the program. This contrasts starkly with the voluntary resignation of the entire Dutch Government in January 2021 after a similar scandal in which the Netherlands Taxation Office wrongly accused some 20 000 families of fraudulently claiming child benefits (Henley, 2021).

Nevertheless, with the change of government on 21 May 2022, and the Australian Labor Party having established a royal commission into the robodebt scandal, a reckoning with the program is inevitable. This program was the starkest demonstration of a political ideology that punishes people for being marginalised by an economic system that requires their disenfranchisement. As long as Australia maintains a monetary policy that relies on a Non-Accelerating Inflation Rate of Unemployment (NAIRU) to maintain price stability in the economy – that is, while it requires a certain percentage of the population to be involuntarily unemployed in order to keep inflation down – it is morally indefensible to target the recipients of working-age income support payments in order to make relatively meagre savings for the federal Budget.

The 47th Parliament would be well advised to learn from the deeper lessons of robodebt before the outcome of the royal commission. Those lessons are not only concerned with the maladministration of government services but go to the broader questions regarding the fundamental purpose of social security in a market-based economy and the obligation of the state to those who are marginalised in its economic and labour-market settings.

To that end, an understanding of the rollercoaster ride that recipients of income support experienced during the COVID-19 pandemic and its aftermath is instructive.

Lifters and leaners

As noted by Michael Klapdor (2022), social policy researcher at the federal Parliamentary Library, in his contribution to the Library's Briefing Book for the incoming 47th Parliament:

> The government response to COVID-19 saw unprecedented levels of income support provided to Australians including increased rates, new payments, and expanded eligibility. The use of ad hoc, temporary changes suggests the design of the social security safety net may need to be reconsidered to ensure it can withstand future economic shocks. Long-standing concerns with the adequacy of some payment rates and eligibility criteria have also re-emerged as COVID-19 supports were withdrawn.

There is no single, agreed poverty line in Australia, but the rate of unemployment payments – now known as JobSeeker – is well below any measure of a living income. Perhaps the most robust measure is the budget standards approach, under which Emeritus Professor Peter Saunders and his colleagues at the University of New South Wales calculate the minimum weekly income required to maintain a basic standard of living (Saunders

& Bedford, 2017). By this measure, the rates of JobSeeker and related payments, such as Youth Allowance and the Disability Support Payment, are significantly below the poverty line for all household categories, from single adults to couples with children.

Social security experts and advocates have long recognised the inadequacy of Australia's working-age income support payment. A decade before the onset of the COVID-19 pandemic, the Henry Tax Review raised concerns about the rate of unemployment benefit, then known as 'Newstart'. In late 2009, Ken Henry's seminal report noted that the Howard Government's 1997 decision to index working-age income support payments to inflation rather than to wages – as is the case with the age pension – would see the rate of Newstart shrink to less than a third of the age pension, which is itself marginally below the poverty line, by 2050. The report called for an immediate increase to Newstart of $50 a week and its indexation to wages (Henry, 2009). Like many of the recommendations of the Henry Review, the government ignored this, but the issue was firmly on the public's radar. Individuals and advocacy groups from across the political spectrum began to call in earnest for a significant increase to the rate of Newstart, with the Australian Senate conducting what would be the first of many inquiries into the adequacy of working-age income support payments in 2012 (Senate Education, Employment and Workplace Relations Committee, 2012).

In its submission to this Inquiry, the Business Council of Australia (BCA) – not an outfit known for its welfare advocacy – strongly supported an increase in the rate of Newstart, stating that '[t]he rate of the ... Allowance for jobseekers no longer meets a reasonable community standard of adequacy and may now be so low as to represent a barrier to employment' (BCA, 2012). It was not long before the atomised calls for a meaningful increase to unemployment benefits coalesced into a concerted campaign, led by the Australian Council of Social Service (ACOSS) to permanently 'Raise the Rate'. Initially, the campaign called for an increase of $75 a week to Newstart and related payments. The campaign gathered steam during the years of the Abbott and Turnbull governments, under which increasingly punitive social-security measures were put before the parliament. Many of the harshest of the government's proposals, such as raising the age of eligibility for Newstart to 25 years and denying the payment to unemployed people aged under 30 years for six months of every year, were blocked by the Senate, to the great relief of social-security advocates. However, the pitiless approach of Coalition governments to welfare recipients was not diminished by these legislative failures, and future changes, such as the creation of robodebt, were enacted through regulation to avoid the countervailing force of the Opposition and crossbenchers in the Upper House.

By the time of the 2019 election, the campaign to raise the rate was supported by the vast majority of civil society organisations, the BCA, Deloitte Access Economics and former prime minister John Howard. Notwithstanding its opposition to many of the government's mooted welfare changes, and the significant support within its caucus for increasing the rate of Newstart, the Labor Party took to the election in May 2019 only a commitment to conduct a review into the rate of Newstart and related payments. The government itself remained implacably opposed to increasing the payment, despite all evidence that it would be beneficial not only to welfare recipients but also to the wider economy (Henriques-Gomes, 2019b).

Upon seizing the prime ministership in late 2018, Scott Morrison had begun regularly to deliver his favoured catchphrase: 'If you have a go, you'll get a go'. This apparently anodyne phrase revealed the ideological position that help should only be given to those who help themselves – a continuation of the 'lifters and leaners' narrative of his predecessor as treasurer, Joe Hockey, and an emphasis of the division between the 'deserving' and 'undeserving' poor.

As noted during the 2019 election campaign by *Guardian Australia*'s political editor Katharine Murphy, the phrase indicated that '… the prime minister of Australia believes the fair go is conditional' – that:

> … some categories of people are inherently more deserving than others; that finding yourself on the bottom rung of the ladder is attributable not to a set of circumstances that governments might look at correcting for the good of society as a whole, but because of a failure of individual imagination and work ethic. (Murphy, 2019b)

Understanding that this ideological position lay at the heart of the Morrison Government is critical to comprehending what happened to welfare payments when the COVID-19 pandemic crashed into Australia's economy in early 2020.

Get me off this rollercoaster

As the full effect of the pandemic became clear, with state governments ordering the immediate closure of non-essential retail and hospitality businesses in mid-March 2020, the federal government was spurred into radical action to prevent hundreds of thousands of households falling into poverty as a result of the looming, inevitable recession. Overnight, it seemed, the Coalition's longstanding opposition to increasing the rate of unemployment payments evaporated: Newstart, rebadged JobSeeker, was effectively doubled and access expanded by waiving the liquid assets test and removing the requirement to attend a Centrelink office to apply for the payment. Morrison described this as a 'supercharging of the safety net [to] … support the most vulnerable to the impact of the crisis' (Henriques-Gomes, 2020).

For six months from 27 April 2020, unemployed Australians receiving JobKeeper were eligible for a maximum fortnightly payment of $1115.70: the previous rate had been $565.70. Welfare advocates were delighted. ACOSS Chief Cassandra Goldie described the increase as a 'huge relief', while Greens Senator Rachel Siewert, arguably the parliament's most steadfast advocate for welfare reform before her retirement in 2021, asserted her belief that it would be 'absolutely untenable to drop people back onto $40 a day' when the crisis passed (Henriques-Gomes, 2020).

The transformation wrought by the increase to the JobSeeker payment was inarguable. Research by the Centre for Social Research and Methods at the Australian National University in August 2020 found that the so-called 'coronavirus supplement' of $550 a fortnight reduced poverty rates among recipients of unemployment payments from 67 per cent to just 7 per cent (Phillips et al, 2020). But Siewert's prediction, if not false, was proven to be highly optimistic. The government was clear from the outset that the $550 per fortnight supplement would be temporary, and it began to reduce the payment, as promised, after six months: initially to $250 per fortnight from 25 September 2020, affecting more than 2 million recipients (Klapdor, 2022), and then to $150 per fortnight from 1 January 2021, before removing it altogether by 31 March that year. Along with the initial reduction in September 2020, the liquid-assets waiting period and the assets test were also reintroduced, reinstating the stringent eligibility requirements that had been waived in the early days of the pandemic.

Despite increasingly strident calls from advocates to keep the full rate of the supplement in place until a permanent and meaningful increase in the base rate was legislated, and more than 30 submissions to a Senate Inquiry supporting the retention of at least the $250 supplement, the government remained impervious to such pleas, and determined to return unemployment benefits to the pre-pandemic rate before the 2021 federal Budget.

Ultimately, due to the relentless community and political pressure, the government introduced legislation to increase the base rate by a meagre $25 a week, or just $3.57 a day, before the supplement was removed. So while Siewert's prediction that the rate would not return to $40 a day was vindicated, with a new permanent rate of just $44 a day and no avenues remaining for a greater increase in line with the evidence of need, the victory was a pyrrhic one.

Welfare recipients and anti-poverty activists were vocal about the effect of their wildly swinging fortunes under the temporary increases to income support over the 12 months from April 2020. A strong streak of outrage, and a sense of bewilderment, coloured much of the commentary from activists and those with lived experience of surviving on unemployment benefits for years. Why, they asked, would the government not reinstate the full rate of the coronavirus supplement, thereby lifting the rate of unemployment payments to 'at least the Henderson poverty line' of around $88 a day? Having proven that it is able to almost eliminate poverty at the stroke of a pen, why did the government insist on returning welfare recipients to a rate half of that provided during the height of the crisis? The obvious, and unwelcome, answer is that the coronavirus supplement was never intended for the long-term recipients of welfare: it was aimed at those people newly, and almost certainly temporarily, thrown out of work by the public health measures implemented at the outset of the pandemic.

Michael Klapdor estimates that the number of people in receipt of unemployment payments increased by more than 5 per cent during that time and that, combined with the number of people on the JobKeeper wage subsidy, '... 38.7% of the population aged 15–64 was receiving government income support in mid-2020' (Klapdoor, 2022).

The queues that appeared outside Centrelink offices in March 2020, which frightened political leaders into drastic action, included many people who had never before relied on income support – people with mortgages, some with small or sole-trader businesses: the so-called 'deserving poor'. The government's largesse was aimed at them, not at the increasing number of people with disabilities and chronic health conditions, and the growing numbers of long-term unemployed, who had relied on welfare payments before the pandemic and continue to do so today. The simple truth is that the coronavirus supplement was intended to support the 'lifters' – to lift them above the level of grinding poverty long deemed acceptable for the 'leaners'. It was never an indication that those with control of the government's purse strings had had a change of heart towards the marginalised citizens who live in a permanent state of income poverty.

By the time the 46th Parliament was prorogued in April 2022, the unemployment rate was at a record low of just 4 per cent, but this was not translating into a commensurate reduction in the number of people relying on JobSeeker: from a peak of over 1 450 000 recipients in August 2020 (Australian Government, 2020), the number had fallen back to just over 816 000, but the proportion of people in receipt of working-age income support payments remained well over 10 per cent – more than triple the rate at the height of the Global Financial Crisis (Australian Bureau of Statistics, 2008). The fact is, welfare reliance deepened under the Coalition's watch. Analysis by *Guardian Australia* before the pandemic found that the number of people on unemployment benefits for more than five years and for more than ten had *more than doubled* since 2014: to 121 700 and 28 444 respectively at March 2019 (Henriques-Gomes, 2019c).

According to research by the Productivity Commission, released six months before the 2019 election (Productivity Commission, 2018), and the Melbourne Institute during the 2022 campaign (Vera-Toscano and Wilkins, 2022), 10–15 per cent of Australians live in permanent and persistent poverty, and the vast majority of these households experience long-term, often intergenerational, unemployment and welfare dependency. Yet the 46th Parliament ended with precious little hope that meaningful action to alleviate this indefensible level of poverty in our wealthy country is on the horizon. While the Labor Party made much of its commitment to support an inflation-matching rise in the minimum wage during the election campaign, rightly identifying this as a significant point of difference between it and the Coalition, neither major party has promised any permanent increase to the rate of working-age income support payments, with Labor dropping its 2019 commitment to review the rate with an intention to lift it above the poverty line.

At the same time, the Greens have adopted a radical agenda to increase all welfare payments, including the age pension and all working-age payments, to a minimum of $88 a day, in line with the more strident calls of anti-poverty activists, and exceeding even the ACOSS campaign's revised call for a rate of $73 per day. The Greens' policy would deliver almost unconditional welfare payments at a rate of $32 120 per annum, costing an eyewatering $44.9 billion per annum, as estimated by the Parliamentary Budget Office (Quiggin, 2022). Effectively a universal basic income set at a rate equivalent to the median part-time income from labour, it is unclear how the Greens policy would interact with Australia's minimum-wage settings, effective marginal tax rates and other labour-force measures. Nor is it obvious where the $88 figure was derived from, other than that it matches almost perfectly the original rate of JobSeeker with the coronavirus supplement, and the Henderson poverty line, established more than 50 years ago but rarely used by social policy experts in discussion of appropriate reform. This policy is much further-reaching than those of the two major parties, neither of which has made commitments that will repair the inadequate social-security system.

After the wild swings and roundabouts welfare recipients experienced during the term of the 46th Parliament, and the clear evidence of government's ability to eliminate persistent poverty and disadvantage through higher income-support payments and better use of technology to target transfers, one thing seems clear: calls for meaningful reform of the social security system will be a constant pressure on the Albanese Labor Government, and a key point of division and debate in the 47th Australian Parliament.

References

Australian Council of Social Services (ACOSS). 'Government urged to make a new start in 2015' (media release), 30 December 2014, <www.acoss.org.au/media_release/government_urged_to_make_a_new_start_in_2015/>.

ACOSS, 'Raise the Rate' Campaign, <raisetherate.org.au/>.

Australian Bureau of Statistics. *Income Support Among People of Working Age*, Commonwealth of Australia, 2008, <www.ausstats.abs.gov.au/ausstats/subscriber.nsf/LookupAttach/4102.0 Publication16.03.106/$File/41020_IncomeSupport.pdf>.

Australian Government. 'JobSeeker Payment and Youth Allowance recipients – monthly profile', 18 September 2020, <data.gov.au/data/dataset/jobseeker-payment-and-youth-allowance-recipients-monthly-profile/resource/93518964-8e7b-4a64-84ee-b1ea54def75d>.

Business Council of Australia (BCA). 'Submission to the Senate Inquiry into the Adequacy of the Allowance Payment System for Jobseekers and Others', 10 August 2012.

Carney, Terry. 'The new digital future for welfare: Debts without legal proofs or moral authority?', *UNSW Law Journal*, 41(3), 2018, <www.unswlawjournal.unsw.edu.au/wp-content/uploads/2018/03/006-Carney.pdf>.

Commonwealth Ombudsman. *Centrelink's Automated Debt Raising and Recovery System*, Report No. 2, April 2017.

Hayne, Jordan and Doran, Matthew. 'Government to pay back $721 million as it scraps Robodebt for Centrelink welfare recipients', *ABC News*, May 2020, <www.abc.net.au/news/2020-05-29/federal-government-refund-robodebt-scheme-repay-debts/12299410>.

Henley, John, 'Dutch government resigns over child benefits scandal', *Guardian*, 16 January 2021, <www.theguardian.com/world/2021/jan/15/dutch-government-resigns-over-child-benefits-scandal>.

Henriques-Gomes, Luke. 'Centrelink cancels 40,000 robodebts, new figures reveal', *Guardian Australia*, 6 February 2019a, <www.theguardian.com/australia-news/2019/feb/06/robodebt-faces-landmark-legal-challenge-over-crude-income-calculations>.

— 'Morrison government defends Newstart amid criticism it is among lowest welfare payments in OECD', *Guardian Australia*, 8 October 2019b, <www.theguardian.com/australia-news/2019/oct/08/morrison-government-defends-newstart-amid-criticism-it-is-among-lowest-welfare-payments-in-oecd>.

— 'Newstart analysis reveals huge leap in amount of time people spend on dole', *Guardian Australia*, 21 October 2019c, <www.theguardian.com/australia-news/2019/oct/21/newstart-analysis-reveals-huge-leap-in-amount-of-time-people-spend-on-dole>.

— 'Australian jobseekers to get $550 payment increase as part of huge coronavirus welfare package', *Guardian*, 22 March 2020, <www.theguardian.com/world/2020/mar/22/australian-jobseekers-to-get-550-increase-as-part-of-huge-coronavirus-welfare-package>.

Henry, Ken. *Australia's Future Tax System: Report to the Treasurer*, Commonwealth of Australia, December 2009.

Karp, Charlotte. 'Grieving mother whose son, 28, killed himself after he was incorrectly billed $28k by Centrelink breaks her silence on PM's move to repay "unlawful debts"', 3 June 2020, <www.dailymail.co.uk/news/article-8383213/Jennifer-Millers-son-killed-received-Centrelink-debt-28-00.html>.

Klapdor, Michael. 'Changes to the COVID-19 social security measures: A brief assessment', Parliamentary Library, Commonwealth of Australia, 30 July 2020. <www.aph.gov.au/

About_Parliament/Parliamentary_Departments/Parliamentary_Library/pubs/rp/rp2021/ChangesCOVID-19SocialSecurity>.

— 'Social security and family assistance', Parliamentary Library Briefing Book, 2022, <www.aph.gov.au/About_Parliament/Parliamentary_Departments/Parliamentary_Library/pubs/BriefingBook47p/SocialSecurityFamilyAssistance>.

McPherson, Emily. 'Queensland man took his own life after learning of Centrelink debt, says mum', 9News, 30 July 2019, <www.9news.com.au/national/centrelink-robodebts-queensland-man-took-his-own-life-over-debt-mum-says-australia-news/e31e6f28-2e4b-4d3f-9095-d8f74e00cbc1>.

Morrison, Scott. 'Welfare integrity, fairness and sustainability for all Australians' (Media Release), 12 May 2015.

Murphy, Katharine. 'Robodebt class action: Shorten unveils "David and Goliath" legal battle into Centrelink scheme', Guardian, 17 September 2019a, <www.theguardian.com/australia-news/2019/sep/17/robodebt-class-action-shorten-unveils-david-and-goliath-legal-battle-into-centrelink-scheme>.

— 'The meaning of Morrison's mantra about getting a fair go is clear. It's conditional', Guardian, 17 April 2019b, <www.theguardian.com/australia-news/2019/apr/17/the-meaning-of-morrisons-mantra-about-getting-a-fair-go-is-clear-its-conditional>.

Phillips, Ben, Matthew Gray and Nicholas Biddle. COVID-19 JobKeeper and JobSeeker Impacts on Poverty and Housing Stress under Current and Alternative Economic and Policy Scenarios, Centre for Social Research and Methods, Australian National University, 29 August 2020.

Productivity Commission. Rising Inequality? A Stocktake of the Evidence, 2018, <www.pc.gov.au/research/completed/rising-inequality>.

Quiggin, John. 'The Greens' liveable income guarantee is a serious idea the major parties won't touch – yet', The Conversation, 21 March 2022, <theconversation.com/the-greens-liveable-income-guarantee-is-a-serious-idea-the-major-parties-wont-touch-yet-179573>.

Saunders, Peter and Megan Bedford. New Minimum Income for Healthy Living Budget Standards for Low-Paid and Unemployed Australians, UNSW, August 2017.

Senate Community Affairs References Committee. Centrelink's Compliance Program: Second Interim Report, September 2020.

Senate Community Affairs References Committee. Accountability and Justice: Why we Need a Royal Commission into Robodebt, Commonwealth of Australia, May 2022.

Senate Education, Employment and Workplace Relations Committee. The Adequacy of the Allowance Payment System for Jobseekers and Others, the Appropriateness of the Allowance Payment System as a Support into Work and the Impact of the Changing Nature of the Labour Market, Commonwealth of Australia, November 29, 2012.

Turner, Rebecca. 'Robodebt condemned as a "shameful chapter" in withering assessment by federal court judge', ABC News, 11 June 2021, <www.abc.net.au/news/2021-06-11/robodebt-condemned-by-federal-court-judge-as-shameful-chapter/100207674>.

Vera-Toscano, Esperanza and Wilkins, Roger. The Dynamics of Income Poverty in Australia: Evidence from the HILDA Survey, 2001 to 2019, The Melbourne Institute, University of Melbourne, April 2022, <melbourneinstitute.unimelb.edu.au/__data/assets/pdf_file/0011/4107629/Breaking-Down-Barriers-Report-4-May-2022.pdf>.

11

HIGHER EDUCATION

Andrew Norton

On election night in May 2019, few expected the returned Morrison Government to pay higher education much attention. Abbott and Turnbull government higher education policies had failed in the Senate. The political case for risking a third attempt seemed weak. Yet through a mix of circumstance and design, the second Morrison Government was the most eventful parliamentary term for higher education in many decades. Border closures, campus closures, job losses, foreign interference laws and the Job-ready Graduates policy all provided drama with long-term consequences.

Closed borders

In 2019 nearly a third of enrolments in Australian higher education were international students, including those studying online or at offshore campuses. On ABS figures they paid $13.1 billion in fees. For the universities – non-university higher education providers are also active in international education – international student fees contributed 27 per cent of their total income in 2019.

International student fees brought significant benefits to Australian universities, especially in funding a research boom. On ABS figures, university research expenditure doubled in real terms between 2004 and 2018. But, as was regularly pointed out before COVID-19, success in international education left universities reliant on an inherently risky market.

Those risks began turning into reality on 1 February 2020, when to limit the spread of COVID-19 the Morrison Government imposed travel restrictions on people coming from China, Australia's most important international student source country. February is usually the busiest month for international student arrivals, including new students and continuing students returning from holidays. For a while, Chinese students could still travel to Australia if they first spent 14 days in a third country. But on 15 March 2020 the borders closed to all international students.

Fortunately for universities, with first semesters typically starting in late February or early March, most international students were already in Australia. Department of Home Affairs figures showed that the student visa holder population in Australia on 31 March 2020 was down 7 per cent on the same date in 2019, but the total would have been slightly up except for the missing Chinese students. The border closures had more widespread consequences from second semester 2020, when the usual commencing cohort could not arrive.

Final international enrolment figures for 2020, counting students who studied online from their home countries, showed an 18.2 per cent fall in commencing students. Due to the preceding boom years, however, the number of continuing students increased. The net effect was a 6.6 per cent fall in international enrolments in 2020 compared to 2019.

A short border closure would have been manageable. But the borders did not re-open for general international student entry until 15 December 2021. This created a negative 'pipeline' effect. Fewer first-year students in 2020 translates into fewer second-year students in 2021, and so on. Although international student numbers began recovering before the Morrison Government left office, arrivals from January to April 2022 were only 34 per cent of 2019 numbers. In the Morrison Government's last week the number of international students present in Australia was only 1000 higher than 12 months previously, as students completing courses offset those commencing courses.

Closed campuses

Whether university campuses remained open or not was formally a matter for state governments and the judgment of university leaders. Through National Cabinet the Morrison Government shared in these decisions, especially during the national lockdown that began in March 2020.

Initially, the National Cabinet was reluctant to close schools and other educational institutions. But restrictions on gatherings made it impossible to run university campuses normally, and by mid-March 2020 universities were transitioning to online education.

Through 2020 and 2021 the frequency and level of COVID-19 restrictions varied around Australia, from least severe in Western Australia to most severe in Victoria. These controls had significant consequences for universities and their students. Universities were concerned that students would, at least temporarily, drop out rather than accept an inferior substitute for on-campus education. Potentially universities were in trouble in both their local and international markets.

Higher education–specific COVID-19 measures

Although the immediate impact of border closures was largely confined to the Chinese market, universities could see the enrolment and financial pipeline consequences of a prolonged border closure and potential weak domestic demand. On 7 April 2020 the Universities Australia lobby group warned that 21 000 jobs could go over the next six months.

To assist universities, Education Minister Dan Tehan announced a modest initial suite of measures on 12 April 2020. Its key element was a domestic student funding guarantee. Universities could keep money allocated to them under the Commonwealth Grant Scheme, the source of tuition subsidies, even if their enrolments fell short of the level required to receive the full amount (a decision that cost the government $82 million). Universities could also keep their previously estimated HELP student loan revenue, paying back over eight years any money received in excess of their entitlements. Some regulatory charges were waived.

The government also announced 'short course' student places at discount student contributions, the fee paid by students in Commonwealth-supported places, aimed at people who had lost work during the COVID-19 labour market downturn. Most short courses were graduate certificates, a well-established six-month postgraduate qualification. The minister also invented a new six-month 'undergraduate certificate'. This new qualification ran across an existing Australian Qualifications Framework (AQF) reform process, the subject of a significant report released in October 2019. A federal minister cannot unilaterally change the AQF but state ministers agreed to temporarily permit undergraduate certificates.

Discount student contributions were a support for students rather than universities. If universities offered additional short courses they had to forgo part of their usual student contribution revenue.

JobKeeper

On 30 March 2020 the government announced its JobKeeper policy, a $1500-per-fortnight wage subsidy for eligible employees of non-government organisations seriously affected by COVID-19. In a tweet, treasurer Josh Frydenberg stated that charities would be eligible for JobKeeper if their revenue decline was 15 per cent, rather than the at least 30 per cent applying to businesses. All universities other than the for-profit Torrens University are registered charities, raising hopes that universities could benefit and reduce job losses.

In the first of a series of disappointments, however, the government clarified that they had in mind charities such as the Salvation Army. Universities, along with private schools, would have to meet the 30 per cent revenue decline threshold, or a 50 per cent decline for the 13 universities with annual revenue exceeding $1 billion. Thirty per cent exceeded total university reliance on international students.

In late April 2020, however, some universities still thought they might receive JobKeeper. The JobKeeper scheme, devised quickly with businesses primarily in mind, used GST turnover to calculate revenue decline. Government grants received by universities are not counted in GST turnover, and so universities could exclude the stable half of their income from the test. A 30 per cent decline in non-government income was more feasible than all their income. But on realising what universities were thinking the government changed the rules to count all university revenue.

University financial and legal advisers did not give up. JobKeeper rules let organisations choose their period of expected revenue decline, which could be monthly or quarterly. The timing of university cash flows created an opportunity. Government grants and student HELP loans are paid in fortnightly instalments through the year, but upfront student fees are paid in lump sums around due dates. There was no chance of a 30 per cent decline in total revenue for any university over 2020, but it might be possible in a single month when international student fees were due. For universities, the government made the revenue decline over a six-month period – except for three private universities. Bond University became the only university to receive JobKeeper directly, although at least 12 public universities received it via subsidiary companies (Norton, 2021c).

Job-ready Graduates

On 19 June 2020 the government announced Job-ready Graduates, a major higher education reform package unrelated to COVID-19. It proposed a radical change to the system of student contributions along with new arrangements for equity funding and encouraging work-integrated learning. Its legislation added new highly bureaucratic processes for assessing student suitability and penalising students who failed too many subjects. Despite widespread criticism of Job-ready Graduates, Dan Tehan succeeded where his education minister predecessors Christopher Pyne in 2014 and Simon Birmingham in 2017 failed. He persuaded the Senate crossbench to support a controversial higher education policy. Job-ready Graduates commenced in January 2021.

Changes to student contributions attracted the most public attention. These supported three Job-ready Graduates policy objectives: growth in student places, adjusting overall funding rates and steering student course preferences.

In an August 2019 speech, Tehan acknowledged that a large birth cohort would reach university age in the mid-2020s, but warned that extra student places had to be delivered in a 'fiscally responsible' way. In 2019 universities were in the second year of a freeze in their total Commonwealth Grant Scheme funding for bachelor degree students. The government had previously promised performance-based incremental increases in funding for 2020 and beyond, but this was unlikely to support much enrolment growth.

Job-ready Graduates provided a solution for delivering more student places without increasing public funding. The average Commonwealth contribution, the discipline-based subsidy paid for student places, would be reduced. The practical consequence would be that universities had to deliver more student places per each $1 million in Commonwealth Grant Scheme funds. To minimise financial consequences for universities, student contributions would be increased.

Two other policy changes affected the final student contributions charged. The government had commissioned Deloitte Access Economics to report on 'teaching and scholarship' costs by field of education. As the existing funding rates were loosely descended from a late 1980s university expenditure study, a review was reasonable. Deloitte found that most existing funding rates (Commonwealth plus student contributions) exceeded average teaching and scholarship costs. One reason was that funding rates included research support above teaching and scholarship costs, particularly in science and engineering. Job-ready Graduates removed the research component by cutting overall funding rates, including by reducing student contributions in some fields. Humanities, business and law were found to be under-resourced. Their move to a higher student contribution level was in part to bring their total resources up to average teaching and scholarship costs in their fields.

The third aspect of student contribution policy was the most controversial. The mix of student contributions was altered to steer student preferences towards courses that led to 'job-ready' qualifications or were deemed 'national priorities'. Nursing, teaching and agriculture were discounted from $6800 to $3950 a year. The Job-ready Graduates discussion paper warned that the 'current funding system could encourage sub-optimal choices for students' and more than doubled humanities student contributions from $6800 to $14500 a year (DESE, 2020, p. 11). Business and law (both formerly $11355 a year) were also allocated to the $14500 a year student contribution band. Discount pricing to attract students had been tried before and abandoned as unsuccessful. Deterrence pricing to steer people away from courses was new. While 2021 enrolment data is not yet available – a faulty new enrolment IT system adding to the sector's problems – applications data is consistent with the new student contributions having little influence on course choices (Norton, 2021a).

Job-ready Graduates introduced contradictory incentives for students and universities. In several courses with lower student contributions, intended to attract enrolments, the total funding rate received by universities was reduced. This might deter universities from increasing enrolments. Conversely, in humanities, business and law increased student contributions to deter students contributed to higher total funding rates, creating a financial reason for universities to enrol more students (see Norton, 2021a).

More higher education–specific COVID-19 measures

By October 2020 Morrison Government decisions had, from a university perspective, dealt them three major blows – the border closure (not questioned, but the most significant), denial of JobKeeper, and Job-ready Graduates. But to the surprise of many the university lobby groups never came out strongly against Job-ready Graduates. A possible reason for holding back became apparent on Budget night, 6 October 2020. After nearly seven months of an apparently unsympathetic reaction to the COVID-19 plight of universities, the government announced $1 billion in additional funding for 2021 under the Research Support Program, doubling payments under this flexible block grant. This partly offset financial losses caused by declining international student revenue and took Commonwealth research support for universities to an all-time high (DISR, 2021). Another $550 million was allocated to additional short course places for domestic students. This time they would be offered at the normal student contributions, which would provide additional income for universities.

Research policy

Over the past 30 years university research has become more applied, a trend promoted by successive governments with direct funding and funding incentives. But the Morrison Government still saw a weak link between research findings and research commercialisation.

With Alan Tudge as education minister, in November 2021 the government announced its 'Trailblazer Universities' initiative, to fund four universities at up to $50 million to develop projects in government manufacturing priority areas to commercialisation stage. Two successful bidders were announced before the May 2022 election. In December 2021, with Stuart Robert now the acting education minister, the government announced that 70 per cent of Australian Research Council Linkage grants, research project funding involving universities and non-university partners, would go to projects related to the manufacturing priority areas. In February 2022 a $1.6 billion Australia's Economic Accelerator program was announced, again aligning university incentives to the manufacturing priority areas. The necessary legislation lapsed with the end of the 46th Parliament, but the program has survived the change of government.

The research decisions of Morrison Government education ministers that provoked most academic outrage were vetoes of research project grants recommended for funding by the Australian Research Council (ARC). After an earlier veto controversy in 2017 the government in 2018 added a national interest test to ARC applications. But this failed to filter out projects at risk of ministerial disapproval. Dan Tehan rejected five recommended projects in 2020. In late 2021 Stuart Robert rejected another six. The vetoed projects were a small percentage of all those recommended for funding by the ARC. But academics saw project funding vetoes as unjustified political interference.

A more far-reaching government move into academic life came from the Morrison Government's policies against 'foreign interference', with China primarily in mind. Among other things, these policies covered international research collaboration and the foreign connections of university staff and students. In 2020 legislation gave the minister for foreign affairs the power to invalidate certain university 'foreign arrangements'. In March 2022 new student visa regulations were introduced, requiring international students to have thesis topic changes approved by the minister for immigration to prevent an 'unwanted transfer of critical technology'.

Academic freedom

Australian Research Council grant, international research collaboration and international student thesis topic vetoes all sat uneasily with the government's academic freedom agenda. In March 2021 a legal definition of academic freedom was inserted into university funding legislation, mainly to give legal authority to a Model Code on Freedom of Speech and Academic Freedom that the government had already pressured universities to adopt. In December 2021 the same definition was inserted into legal rules defining a higher education institution. These changes assumed that threats to academic freedom came from within the universities, rather than from the government itself.

The Morrison Government and higher education

To many of its critics the Morrison Government was hostile to universities (eg Barnett, 2021; Price, 2020). Effectively excluding universities from JobKeeper was key evidence. I have argued elsewhere that few, if any, public universities would have qualified for JobKeeper under rules that made them equivalent to other organisations (Norton, 2021c). Their revenue losses in 2020 were too low; across the sector in 2020 compared to 2019 international student fee revenue was down 7.5 per cent and total income was down 5 per cent. Especially in first semester 2020, when JobKeeper was introduced, revenue losses were limited by international borders only fully closing after the start of first semester.

Higher education was not like other industries forced by lockdowns to temporarily close entirely or offer limited services. Universities still delivered most classes online and their largest customer, the Commonwealth, guaranteed its payments. But unlike the rapid recovery of many other businesses as lockdowns were lifted, universities could not quickly restore previous international enrolment levels. The loss of commencing students in 2020 and 2021 will affect continuing student numbers for several years. Commencing students in 2022 are up on 2021, but with no guarantee of a return to 2019 levels. The global dynamics of international education have changed.

The specific situation of higher education suggested tailored assistance. JobKeeper ended in March 2021 but 2021 and 2022 will be the worst years for international student fee revenue. The 2021 timing of the second COVID-19 support package partly covers that timeframe. Protecting now-redundant international student-related jobs would not have used limited resources efficiently. The second support package instead funded on-going research and domestic student teaching.

The government would, however, have saved itself and the sector grief by ruling out JobKeeper from the start and promising something like the second support package. Job losses of 9000, or nearly 7 per cent of the university permanent and fixed-term contract workforce in the year to 31 March 2021, may have been higher than necessary because universities had already retrenched staff, assuming no new government assistance (Norton, 2022).[1] Medium-term international student fee decline, however, meant that significant job losses were inevitable.

If the second COVID-19 support package was announced too late, Job-ready Graduates was launched too early. Nothing in it was genuinely urgent. Requiring universities to make complex changes to domestic student arrangements while also managing COVID-19 disruptions was unreasonable. The government could have placed fewer burdens on universities and minimised the weaknesses of Job-ready Graduates by delaying change and setting up a policy review.

The Morrison Government also implemented policies in questionable ways. The discount student contribution initiative of the first COVID-19 support package was one of several instances of using university funding agreements in ways that, at best, do not reflect the intention of the funding legislation (Norton, 2021b). While the government eventually provided a statutory basis for its academic freedom policy, this was after it had commissioned an external review of university compliance with a code that at the time had no legal force. ARC grant vetoes were within the minister's legal authority, but exercising it on unclear grounds undermined confidence in what was otherwise a rule-driven process.

The Morrison Government's overall higher education policy stance was less one of outright hostility – the second COVID-19 assistance package is inconsistent with that interpretation – than a very utilitarian valuing of higher education. Its attempts to steer student enrolments towards 'job-ready' fields it chose and research activity towards its manufacturing priorities micro-managed universities into the government's overall economic strategy. On the student side, this departed not just from how the universities thought of their mission but also from previous Coalition policy. In 2017 the Turnbull Government tried to reduce per student public funding rates rather than end a demand-driven system of student funding that supported student and university choices. The Morrison Government wanted more control over which choices students and universities could make.

The Morrison Government's targeted higher education response to COVID-19 would have warranted a good rating if all its eventual policies had been announced in April 2020. It loses marks, however, for delays and mixed messages. The government's non-COVID-19 higher education policies were marred by an overly narrow view of university purposes, excessive intervention in university decisions, poor processes and inconsistency. Job-ready Graduates contains contradictory incentives for students and universities. New interference in academic life undermines academic freedom legislation. For subsequent governments, Labor or Liberal, the Morrison Government provided lessons in how not to do higher education policy.

References

Barnett, Katy. 'Why is the government unwilling to support universities?', *Sydney Morning Herald*, 20 May 2021.

DESE. *Job-ready Graduates: Higher Education Reform Package 2020* (discussion paper), Department of Education, Skills and Employment, 2020.

DISR. *2021–22 Science, Research and Innovation Budget Tables*, Department of Industry, Science and Resources, 2021.

Norton, Andrew. *Submission on the Higher Education Support Amendment (Job-ready Graduates and Supporting Regional and Remote Students) Bill 2020*, Senate Education and Employment Committee.

— 'The first Job-ready Graduates university applications data'. *Andrew Norton: Higher education commentary from Carlton* (blog), 25 October 2021a.

— 'University-Commonwealth funding agreements and the rule of law in higher education', *Andrew Norton: Higher education commentary from Carlton* (blog), 17 March 2021b.

— 'Would universities have received JobKeeper under more favourable rules?', *Andrew Norton: Higher education commentary from Carlton* (blog), 6 July 2021c.

— 'University job losses in the first year of COVID-19', *Andrew Norton: Higher education commentary from Carlton* (blog), 10 February 2022.

Price, Jenna. 'Why has the government waged war on our universities?', the *Canberra Times*, 15 May 2020.

12

FROM 'DAGGY DAD' TO 'WOKE AGENDAS': WOMEN AND EQUALITY

Pia Rowe

The fight for justice and equity for women across our nation is far from over, but this is not just a fight for women; it's a fight for every family. It's a fight for our nation's future productivity, because we know that, when women do well, families do well, and when families do well we create a hopeful, prosperous nation.

Libby Coker MP, 31 March 2022

The 46th Parliament (2019–22) proved to be a tumultuous period for women in Australia, as noted by Labor MP Libby Coker just over a week before Prime Minister Scott Morrison called the federal election. A far cry from the hopeful and prosperous nation underpinned by the principles of gender equity and fairness many had hoped, and continued to advocate for, we instead witnessed an onslaught of upheavals. Australia slipped down further in the international gender-equality rankings, the global COVID-19 pandemic created new and unprecedented challenges for men and women alike, and news of sexual harassment and violence against women became commonplace in much of the mainstream media coverage.

In terms of the cultural attitudes towards women, the period was also often marked – albeit inadvertently – by outdated and sometimes downright contradictory ideas of gender roles in the nation's psyche. As Libby Coker's speech demonstrates, the collective mood for advancing gender equality had become increasingly palpable across the whole society.

And yet, all too often the narratives of women link their roles in society to those of nurturers and caregivers, with their value calculated in terms of the nation's productivity, instead of furthering the human rights of all citizens as the only right thing to do ethically and morally. As the leader of the nation, Morrison himself often branded his identity as the paternalistic father figure, though there was a significant shift from his 'daggy dad' schtick to a more Instagram-friendly leader figure in the lead-up to the 2022 election (Warren, 2021).

Of course, family is important. As I argued in the previous instalment of this series (Rowe, 2019), the Turnbull and Morrison governments had not been able to address the conflict of work and family balance in their own ranks, let alone in the broader society. Instead, under their leadership, several high-profile politicians, including Kelly O'Dwyer, stepped down from their roles, citing 'family reasons' (Rowe, 2019). The current statistics amply demonstrate that women across diverse demographics continue to undertake most of the care in unpaid and paid labour in Australia. These lived realities naturally reflect the ways in which gender equality is often framed and discussed. However, to create a holistic picture of how women fared under the Morrison Government, we must examine a broad range of indicators of gender equality as part of their lives as individual human beings.

Here I focus on the key events pertaining to women and gender equality that took place during the Morrison years. Gender equality in Australia is at a crossroads, and the numerous positive developments – such as reaching equal representation of men and women in the Senate – were often juxtaposed with the darker narratives of rampant, gender-based violence. The most significant global challenge of this period, the COVID-19 pandemic, had gendered effects on women. There were significant moments of gender-based violence in Australia that caught the nation's attention, and the government responded inadequately to these events. This period of government also affected First Nations women and girls, and LGBTIQ+ rights, in ways that warrant close attention. The shortcomings in gender equality were not due to the unprecedented events that transpired during this period, but rather the result of a wilful refusal to listen to the subject-matter experts.

From the beginning of the COVID-19 pandemic in Australia in early 2020, it was clear that its impacts were not gender equal. While the situation was unprecedented and leaders around the globe scrambled to find information and evidence on how to best handle the challenges, it soon became obvious that the governing bodies did not apply a gender lens on the pandemic as it unfolded. Women, in particular, suffered more than they needed to in the COVID-19 economic recession, due to inadequate or ill-directed government response. As argued by Wood, Griffiths and Crowley (2021):

> Policy makers seemed oblivious to the fact that this recession was different to previous crises – women now make up almost half the workforce, and they are overwhelmingly employed in the industries that were hit hardest by the government-imposed lockdowns, such as hospitality, tourism, and higher education.

In the period February to May 2020, the construction sector lost less than 5 per cent of its work hours, whereas the hospitality sector lost more than 47 per cent. And yet, the former received more than $35 billion in government assistance, while the hospitality sector received only $1.3 billion in direct government assistance (Wood et al, 2021).

In another baffling move, the government's response to childcare was also at odds with its stated continuing commitment to improve gender equality at work. The fact that women continue to represent the majority of all carers – from childcare to aged care and disability, paid and unpaid – has long been known by industries, advocates and policymakers alike. The extensive statistics provided by government entities such as the Australian Bureau of Statistics (ABS) and the Workplace Gender Equality Agency (WGEA) highlight the need to address these gendered imbalances in order to improve the persistent workplace inequalities, including the gender pay gap, the reduced earning capacity of women over their whole life cycle and the other subsequent crisis points, such as the increased risk of poverty and homelessness in retirement.

In the context of the pandemic, the COVID-19 recession created a 'triple whammy' for women, who were more likely to lose their jobs, more likely to do additional unpaid labour, and less likely to get government support. Mothers in couples and single parents (80 per cent of whom are women) were more likely to leave the paid workforce, further magnifying the long-term economic impacts on women (Woods et al, 2021). And yet, the childcare sector, 95 per cent of whose employees are women, was the first to be taken off the JobKeeper scheme, and the free childcare arrangement in place during the first set of lockdowns in 2020 was discontinued despite evidence of its crucial role in the economic recovery. Against this backdrop, it is hardly surprising that men and women felt the psychological toll of the pandemic differently. In June 2021, one in four (23 per cent) women reported experiencing high or very high levels of psychological stress, compared with 17 per cent of men (ABS, 2021).

'Well, gee, I bet it felt good to get that out'

While the COVID-19 pandemic arguably presented many extreme challenges to the second Morrison ministry, some other major crisis points were sadly more predictable. Gender-based violence remains one of the darkest spots in Australian society, spanning from home to school, to work and the media. According to Our Watch (2021), one in three Australian women has experienced physical violence since the age of 15; one in five has experienced sexual violence; one in three has experienced physical and/or sexual violence perpetrated by a man since the age of 15; and Australian women are three times more likely than men to experience violence from an intimate partner. Globally, 'home' has been shown to be the most dangerous place for women and children (UNODC, 2019). However, violence in the private and the public spheres also 'complement one another' (Dawson, 2021). Private violence is both facilitated and maintained by women's everyday experiences of misogyny, abuse and violence, which limit their movement. Women and girls are often taught to fear the 'stranger danger' in public spaces, yet home may not be safe either. 'Through their interdependence', argued Professor Dawson (2021), 'these forms of violence maintain the patriarchal social structures that keep women and children "in place" both in the home and in public'.

Over the years, the Morrison Government was provided with ample opportunities to change the course and create a safer society for women and girls. The speed at which it responded, however, can only be described as glacial. In 2019, the Australian Human Rights Commission delivered its landmark Respect@Work report to the government. In March 2020, the report was released to the public. It laid bare the horrendous truth that Australian women are not safe at work – including in the highest echelons of power, in Parliament House, and provided 55 recommendations for the government to address the problems. Initially, there was very little action following the release of the report. Almost a year later, when a federal government staffer, Brittany Higgins, publicly alleged that she had been raped by a colleague in the Parliament House offices, some action finally commenced.

It took until April 2021 for the government to release its response, 'A roadmap for respect: Preventing and addressing sexual harassment in Australian workplaces' (Australian Government, 2021). The government noted that it accepted in full, in part or in principle 46 of the 55 recommendations. Following the release, some scholars argued that the report was light on detail and fell 'significantly short of the commitment to fully implement all 55 recommendations put forth by Jenkins' (Golledge et al, 2021). Of the 12 recommendations for legislative reform, six were included in the Sex Discrimination and Fair Work (Respect at Work) Amendment Bill of 2021.

Meanwhile, the general public's intolerance for the lack of action had become clearly palpable, and grassroots protest movements such as March4Justice saw over 100 000 women and allies taking to the streets to protest against sexual abuse and harassment. The organisers of the Canberra rally presented a petition with over 90 000 signatures to the lawmakers, demanding action on gendered violence. Many other high-profile campaigns and petitions followed, including the harrowing tribute by Melbourne artist Dans Bain to the women and children who have lost their lives. Bain unfurled *The Lost Petition*, a 30-metre-long fabric artwork which lists the names of the 978 victims 'who have been taken from this earth at the hands of a man' outside Parliament House in March 2022.

While concrete action from the Morrison Government was often lacking, unfortunately, symbolic responses from the leaders similarly left a lot to be desired. For example, it's impossible to forget the comment Scott Morrison made to Grace Tame, following her speech on child sexual abuse at the Australian of the Year awards: 'Well, gee, I bet it felt good to get that out' (Hislop, 2021). Well, gee indeed. Rather than this fatherly pat on the head, what she and the rest of the nation needed was urgent action to prevent such horrors from occurring in the future. Grace Tame's experience shows that, far too often, structural change hinges on individuals' willingness and ability to share their trauma with the media and public. To be named as Australian of the Year is notable, but without concrete action to further the work, such accolades only go so far. In the words of Brittany Higgins: 'There is a horrible societal acceptance of sexual violence experienced by women in Australia. My story was on the front page for the sole reason that it was a painful reminder to women that if it can happen in Parliament House, it can truly happen anywhere' (BBC News, 2021).

First Nations women and girls

While no one is immune from gender-based violence in Australia, some groups are more vulnerable than others. The statistics regarding Indigenous women experiencing violence at higher rates than other women in Australia are well documented. For example, Indigenous women are 32 times more likely to be hospitalised because of family violence, and five times more likely to die from homicide than non-Indigenous women. In Western Australia, Aboriginal mothers are 17.5 times more likely to be killed than non-Aboriginal mothers (Carlson, 2021).

Aboriginal and Torres Strait Islander people are subject to disproportionate incarceration rates. While they make up around 3 per cent of the national population, they constitute 27 per cent of the prison population, and Aboriginal and Torres Strait Islander women constitute 34 per cent of the female prison population. To put this in context, the rate of Indigenous women's imprisonment is 464.8 per 100 000, compared to 21.9 per 100 000 for non-Indigenous women, and 291.1 per 100 000 for non-Indigenous men. Violence against Indigenous women extends to government-mandated acts, such as the high rates of removal of children from their families (Family

Matters, 2020). The Morrison Government's fourth action plan to reduce violence against women and their children 2010–2022 claimed supporting Aboriginal and Torres Strait Islander women and their children as one of its priorities. But, as Professor Bronwyn Carlson (2021) notes, this did not lead to any real change.

Gender-based violence aside, Aboriginal and Torres Strait Islander women continue to be underrepresented in the workforce. Research by the UTS Jumbunna Institute for Indigenous Education and Research, the Diversity Council Australia (DCA) and the WGEA highlights that in terms of workplace diversity and inclusion, progress has been patchy at best and cultural barriers continue to affect people differently based on their identity markers such as ethnicity, sexuality or gender identity (WGEA, 2021). The research showed that Indigenous women 'in culturally unsafe workplaces were over 10 times more likely to be often or very often treated unfairly at work than Indigenous women who work in culturally safe businesses; and around 20 times more likely to hear racial or ethnic slurs'. Indigenous women who are also carers face 'triple jeopardy' at work (WGEA, 2021). In essence, they are more likely to feel unsafe at work, more likely to carry extra expectations to make their workplace culturally sensitive and engaged, and less supported when they encounter racism and unfair treatment.

The uncomfortable battle of religion vs 'woke agenda'

Only a few months into the second Morrison ministry (29 May 2019 to 23 May 2022), the government contradicted its supposed commitment to workplace diversity and inclusion, when Scott Morrison waged a public battle against gender-inclusive toilet signs at the Department of Prime Minister and Cabinet (PM&C). Speaking on the radio, he argued that the signage was silly and unnecessary. 'Honestly, this is why we call it the Canberra bubble, it's ridiculous ... it will be sorted out' (ABC News, 2019). In addition to being a strange hill to climb (after all, a gender-inclusive toilet sign did not incur any additional costs to the taxpayers, nor did it negatively affect anyone working at PM&C), the timing of his outburst was rather unfortunate. Just the previous week in his address to the Australian Public Service, Morrison had extolled the value of diversity, noting that it was 'in keeping with the more diverse, pluralistic society Australia has become over many decades' (ABC News, 2019).

It appears that the diversity Morrison was advocating for was not a stable concept bound by societally agreed-upon definitions or ethics, but rather one that was subject to individual opinions and subjectivities. While arguing that 'diversity also meant tolerating people with different opinions' (ABC News, 2019), a position that at least on the surface seems reasonable enough, the ways many LGBTIQ+ issues were handled during his ministry would attest to the dangers of such an approach. Despite the multitudes of urgent issues facing Australians due to the global pandemic, it was an innocent morning tea celebration at the Department of Defence that caught the eye of the then-minister for defence, Peter Dutton. Opposing the idea of people wearing rainbow-coloured clothing to mark the International Day Against Homophobia, Biphobia, Intersexism and Transphobia (IDAHOBIT), Dutton ordered the department to stop these events, and argued that while he would never tolerate discrimination, he 'would not pursue a "woke" agenda' either (Bonyhady & Galloway, 2021).

The attempts to silence or erase the LGBTIQ+ communities at the societal level became even more prominent in 2021, when the Census failed to collect data on sex, sexual orientation and gender diversity. Questions developed in consultation with LBGTIQ+ communities and generally considered best practice had been proposed for inclusion in a submission to the Senate in 2019. Rather oddly, the ABS decided to exclude them on the basis of perceived public backlash, even though the qualitative testing conducted beforehand showed that they performed well with both target and non-target audiences, and were also recommended by multiple federal departments (Stephenson & Hayes, 2021). As noted by Stephenson and Hayes (2021), this was not just a matter of calculating the number of LGBTIQ+ people in Australia. It would have also provided crucial information about their socioeconomic status, health, relationships and lives more broadly, to provide appropriate support and services to already vulnerable populations. In effect, the omission constituted discrimination against LGBTIQ+ communities, despite the government's frequent assurances of their commitment to diversity and tolerance.

Sadly, the government was not above overt discrimination either, as became apparent over the prolonged debate about the now-shelved religious discrimination Bill (for the timeline, see Moore, 2022). The Bill, ostensibly to protect religious people from discrimination following the passing of same-sex marriage laws, at its worst iterations would have instead resulted in the ability of various schools, employers and health providers, including pharmacists and charities, to deny services and medications on religious grounds, and to discriminate against LGBTIQ+ people. The Bill also included a 'statement of belief' clause, which would have allowed people to make discriminatory statements against others on the basis of their faith (Lixinski, nd). As Professor Lixinski has argued, the problem with these proposed 'protections' was their subjectivity, as they hinged on the intention of the speaker, rather than on how the statements were perceived by others. As long as the speaker could find a reference to the topic in a religious text and stated that their intention was to spread the religious message, they would essentially be able to vilify and reject people different to them (Lixinski, nd). In this context, Morrison's earlier claims regarding the need to tolerate differing viewpoints take on a chilling new meaning. Blessed be tolerance and diversity, indeed. 'May the Lord open' (or the government deliver), as we learned from the book and TV series, *The Handmaid's Tale*.

On protests and bullets: The failure to listen?

'Not far from here, such marches, even now, are being met with bullets, but not here in this country. This is a triumph of democracy when we see these things take place.'

If the words uttered by Scott Morrison in the wake of the March4Justice protests were meant to celebrate Australian democracy, the intended message was somewhat lost in their absurdity. It is one thing to publicly consider the fact that women are entitled to speak out loud and be visible in the public sphere as a sign of progress. While a prime example of the deeply embedded patriarchal values of the government, it at least could be seen as coming from the right place. However, to compare the ability of women to exercise their democratic rights with state-sanctioned violence in other countries was not just 'tone deaf', it was also abhorrent. 'Consider yourselves lucky; elsewhere you would be shot', it warned. It was entirely, however, in keeping with his 'daggy dad' persona; his clumsy wording just another example of his 'I'm one of you', a quintessential and ordinary Aussie bloke act.

Other responses from the government also often left a lot to be desired. Morrison's keynote speech at the Women's Safety Summit in September 2021 was a case in point, with many openly criticising the government's 'platitudes and warm sentiments', which didn't match its actions (Murphy, 2021). As with his comments on tolerance for differing opinions with regard to the gender-inclusive toilets at PM&C, Morrison again advocated for unity and respect for one another, though by then he seemed to have developed a greater awareness of the gravity of women's anger. No longer something that could be brushed under the carpet, the time left for him to act before the next federal election was rapidly running out.

So, how did Morrison's government fare when it came to gender equality more broadly? His time in government was marked by many unprecedented challenges. But while the pandemic and its effects on women had no blueprint for action, it would be wholly disingenuous to suggest that there was not enough knowledge available to sidestep the many and varied crisis points detailed in this chapter. The various community and government organisations, academics, industry experts and activists working to advance gender equality have been compiling and generating the evidence base for best practice across the different facets of equality, more broadly, for decades. It was rather unfortunate that the government did not appear to accept this information until it was too late – and even then, its actions failed to meet the expectations of a nation tired of waiting for improvements. As the period showed, it is not enough for a leader to act as though they are listening. The real redemption can only be achieved through a genuine commitment to structural change.

References

ABC News. 'Scott Morrison vows to "sort out" gender-inclusive toilet sign posted at his department', 29 August 2021, <www.abc.net.au/news/2019-08-29/scott-morrison-vows-to-take-down-gender-inclusion-bathroom-sign/11462552>.

ABS, Australian Bureau of Statistics. *Household Impacts of COVID-19 Survey*. Released 14 July 2021, <www.abs.gov.au/statistics/people/people-and-communities/household-impacts-covid-19-survey/jun-2021#emotional-and-mental-wellbeing>.

Australian Government. *A Roadmap for Respect: Preventing and addressing sexual harassment in Australian workplaces*, Commonwealth of Australia, 2021, <www.ag.gov.au/sites/default/files/2021-04/roadmap-respect-preventing-addressing-sexual-harassment-australian-workplaces.pdf>.

BBC News. 'Australia March 4 Justice: Thousands march against sexual assault', 15 March 2021, <www.bbc.com/news/world-australia-56397170>.

Bonyhady, Nick and Anthony Galloway. 'Defence emails reveal staff shame at Dutton's "tone-deaf" IDAHOBIT morning tea ban', *Sydney Morning Herald*, 14 October 2021, <www.smh.com.au/politics/federal/defence-emails-reveal-staff-shame-at-dutton-s-tone-deaf-idahobit-morning-tea-ban-20211013-p58zht.html>.

Carlson, Bronwyn. 'No public outrage, no vigils: Australia's silence at violence against Indigenous women', *The Conversation*, 16 April 2021, <theconversation.com/no-public-outrage-no-vigils-australias-silence-at-violence-against-indigenous-women-158875>.

Coker, Libby. Women: Justice and Equity. Statement, House of Representatives, 31 March 2022, <www.aph.gov.au/Parliamentary_Business/Hansard/Hansard_Display?bid=chamber/hansardr/25472/&sid=0402>.

Dawson, Myrna. '"Home is the most dangerous place for women and girls", but private and public violence are connected', *The Conversation*, 25 November 2021, <theconversation.com/home-is-the-most-dangerous-place-for-women-but-private-and-public-violence-are-connected-171348>.

Family Matters. *The Family Matters Report 2020: Measuring trends to turn the tide on the over-representation of Aboriginal and Torres Strait Islander children in out-of-home care in Australia*, 2020, <www.familymatters.org.au/wp-content/uploads/2020/11/FamilyMattersReport2020_LR.pdf?mc_cid=38b1093983&mc_eid=571fa80e1b>.

Golledge, Emma, Dianne Anagnos, Madeleine Causbrook and Sean Bowes. 'The government's "roadmap" for dealing with sexual harassment falls short. What we need is radical change', *The Conversation*, 8 April 2021, <theconversation.com/the-governments-roadmap-for-dealing-with-sexual-harassment-falls-short-what-we-need-is-radical-change-158431>.

Hislop, Madeline. 'Morrison's tone-deaf response to Grace Tame's speech: "Well, gee, I bet it felt good to get that out"', *Women's Agenda*, 24 May 2021, <womensagenda.com.au/latest/morrisons-tone-deaf-response-to-grace-tames-speech-well-gee-i-bet-it-felt-good-to-get-that-out/>.

Lixinski, Lucas. 'Explainer: What happened to the Religious Discrimination Bill?' (blogpost), Australian Human Rights Institute, nd, <www.humanrights.unsw.edu.au/research/commentary/explainer-what-happened-religious-discrimination-bill>.

Moore, Georgie. 'Timeline of religious discrimination laws' (blogpost), 7news.com.au, 4 February 2022, <7news.com.au/politics/timeline-of-religious-discrimination-laws-c-5564603>.

Murphy, Katharine. 'Platitudes and sentiment at women's safety summit won't cut it: When will PM learn?' *Guardian*, 6 September 2021, <www.theguardian.com/australia-news/2021/sep/06/platitudes-and-sentiment-at-womens-safety-summit-wont-cut-it-when-will-pm-learn>.

Our Watch. Quick Facts, nd, <www.ourwatch.org.au/quick-facts/>.

Rowe, Pia. 'The O'Dwyer case: Don't throw the mother out with the bathwater.' In Mark Evans, Michelle Grattan and Brendan McCaffrie (eds), *From Turnbull to Morrison: The trust divide*, Melbourne University Press, 2019, pp. 199–210.

Stephenson, Elise and Jack Hayes. 'LGBTIQ+ people are being ignored in the census again. Not only is this discriminatory, it's bad public policy', *The Conversation*, 10 August 2021, <theconversation.

com/lgbtiq-people-are-being-ignored-in-the-census-again-not-only-is-this-discriminatory-its-bad-public-policy-165800>.

UNODC, United Nations Office on Drugs and Crime. *Global Study on Homicide: Gender-related killing of women and girls*. Research report, 2019, <www.unodc.org/documents/data-and-analysis/gsh/Booklet_5.pdf>.

Warren, Christopher. 'Reading between the pixels: Morrison makes a social media pivot from daggy dad to Instagram square', *Crikey*, 14 May 2021, <www.crikey.com.au/2021/05/14/reading-between-the-pixels-morrison-makes-a-social-media-pivot-from-daggy-dad-to-instagram-square/>.

WGEA. 'Australian-first research on Indigenous women's working lives reveals Aboriginal and Torres Strait Islander mums and carers most at risk at work' (media release), Workplace Gender Equality Agency, 2021, <www.wgea.gov.au/newsroom/gari-yala-research-released>.

Wood, Danielle, Kate Griffiths and Tom Crowley. *Women's Work: The impact of the COVID crisis on Australian women*. Grattan Institute Report, 2021, <grattan.edu.au/report/womens-work/>.

13

INDIGENOUS PEOPLE AND THE MORRISON GOVERNMENT

Stan Grant

Aboriginal people can laugh; there are few things more joyous for me than hearing Aboriginal people laugh. It is a laugh that defies the pain and struggle and, too often, grief of their daily lives. I recall being at a Reconciliation Week dinner with a group of elders, women from Swan Hill in Victoria. For me, it was like being back home; these women were like the women who raised me, just like my mother or my aunties. They told me stories of their childhood; we mapped our families and found that some of them were indeed related to me.

They told me about their fears for the futures of their children and communities. One woman told me how she cares for her disabled daughter and her husband, sick with diabetes. Another told me how her grandson had broken a window in their house and she couldn't afford to get it fixed. Another told me of her son, who had died outside a nightclub in town the previous year. His body had been left in the street for half a day so that police could carry out their investigations.

These are the people we don't always see; the voices we don't often hear. Each year during Reconciliation Week we hear a lot about truth and truth-telling. Here is the truth for far too many Indigenous people: poverty, sickness, death. They are lives measured in statistics: the lowest life expectancy; the highest imprisonment rate; the worst health, housing, employment and educational outcomes of any Australians.

Of course they laugh; it is a way of surviving.

Sitting with the elders of Swan Hill felt a world away from the politics of Canberra. Scott Morrison had just sworn in his new Cabinet and had made history by appointing Ken Wyatt as the first Aboriginal Minister for Indigenous Australians. I asked the women what they thought about that and was met with a shrug of indifference. 'He will just do what the government tells him to do', they said. It isn't cynicism; it is born of harsh experience.

Even that title, 'Minister for Indigenous Australians', seemed absurd in that context: being Indigenous doesn't feel the same as being Australian. These women are formed out of a long, hard history of exclusion, segregation and discrimination. Most being in their late 70s, they could remember a time when they were told they were anything but Australian.

Ken Wyatt knows this. His story, his family's story, would be all too familiar to the elders of Swan Hill. Wyatt emerged from the Stolen Generations, those Indigenous people forcibly removed from their families at a time when Australia believed that the future for Aboriginal people would be to become 'absorbed into the Commonwealth'; through assimilation they would vanish, disappear, become indistinguishable from other Australians. Culture, kinship, community: gone.

Ken Wyatt came to his new portfolio with the weight of his own history, the burden of expectation and the shrug of indifference. He was a minister without a department, the portfolio of Indigenous affairs remaining under the control of the Department of Prime Minister and Cabinet. Wyatt inherited a legacy of failed policy. He was tasked with closing a gap that seemed as wide as it ever had been and – with only four of 17 targets on track to be met in the next decade – would remain so throughout his term.

The elders of Swan Hill were a reminder of how Indigenous people are born into an inheritance of trauma and intergenerational poverty. This is what the Uluru Statement from the Heart refers to as 'the torment of our powerlessness'.

That's what confronted the incoming Morrison Government in 2019: the torment of Indigenous powerlessness. Scott Morrison had inherited the unfinished business of the Australian settlement. For two centuries, Australia has lived in tension with the sovereignty of the Crown and the never ceded, extant sovereignty of those who call themselves the First Nations of the continent.

Two hundred years of conflict, protest, legal and political activism have tested Australia's legitimacy. A legitimacy still wanting.

From colonial times until Federation, the popular belief was that Aboriginal people would die out. This was captured in the macabre phrase, 'to smooth the dying pillow'.

Policies after Federation included imperatives to segregate, assimilate and integrate. Yet, the Aboriginal voice was not silenced. On Australia Day, 26 January 1938 – the sesquicentenary of the arrival of the First Fleet – a delegation of Aboriginal people gathered at Australia Hall in Sydney to move a resolution:

> WE, representing THE ABORIGINES OF AUSTRALIA,
> assembled in conference at the Australian Hall, Sydney, on the
> 26th day of January, 1938, this being the 150th Anniversary
> of the Whiteman's seizure of our country, HEREBY MAKE
> PROTEST against the callous treatment of our people by the
> whitemen during the past 150 years, AND WE APPEAL to the
> Australian nation of today to make new laws for the education
> and care of Aborigines, we ask for a new policy which will raise
> our people TO FULL CITIZEN STATUS and EQUALITY
> WITHIN THE COMMUNITY.

The first Day of Mourning was inspired by the Australian Aborigines League and the Aborigines Progressive Association. They laid a platform for Aboriginal and Torres Strait Islander activism that reached its zenith with the 1967 Referendum, still the most resounding 'yes' vote in Australian history, which determined that Aboriginal people would now be formally counted in the Australian Census, and conferred power on the federal parliament to make laws for Aboriginal and Torres Strait Islander peoples.

Fifty years later, on 26 May 2017, First Nations delegates released the Uluru Statement from the Heart. It was a call for another referendum to recognise Indigenous peoples in the Australian Constitution. It sought to build on the legacy of 1967. As the Uluru Statement read: 'In 1967 we were counted, in 2017 we seek to be heard'. The Uluru Statement was the culmination of a national consultation by a parliamentary-appointed

Referendum Council with Indigenous communities and leaders. The centrepiece was a recommendation for an Indigenous representative body, a constitutionally enshrined voice, to speak to parliament and advise on government policy. It also advocated for a national truth-telling about our shared history and a Makarrata Commission to formalise agreement-making with the nation-state. The catchcry: 'voice, treaty, truth'.

The Turnbull Government rejected the Uluru Statement, claiming it would effectively constitute a third chamber of parliament. That claim was denounced by Indigenous leaders. It marked yet another low in relations with the Aboriginal and Torres Strait Islander communities. The Uluru Statement loomed over the Morrison Government. The prime minister returned to power with the words of Noel Pearson, lawyer, activist and one of the chief architects of the Uluru Statement, ringing in his ears. In an article published in the December 2017 edition of the *Monthly* magazine, Pearson unloaded on Turnbull, accusing the prime minister of having supported then recanted on the proposal for a Constitutional Voice for Indigenous peoples. Pearson stopped short – barely – of calling him a liar:

> Turnbull supported the Indigenous voice to parliament when he was not prime minister, but then ended up calling it a 'third chamber of parliament' when he was, knowing full well that was a gross untruth.

Pearson further wrote that he had lost faith in the political process, but not in the Australian people. He was seething and determined to maintain the rage:

> Righteous anger at injustice is the fuel for future justice. Otherwise we just retire to lives of relaxation and comfort while anger destroys our people from within. This agenda will not die. It is the agenda for the future.

Scott Morrison was one of those who had opposed the ambition of the Uluru Statement. He sent the entire process back to committee. A new, select group of Indigenous and non-Indigenous Australians, headed by the eminent Indigenous academics, professors Marcia Langton and Tom

Calma, began a new round of consultations before delivering a report that recommended a two-tiered model comprising local and regional voices and an overarching national voice for Indigenous peoples to have a direct say on laws and issues affecting them. The representative body would be legislated, not constitutionally enshrined. The opportunity for a referendum in the life of this parliament was thereby lost.

For steadfast advocates of constitutional enshrinement, the proposed legislation lacked ambition and moral weight. Professor Megan Davis, constitutional lawyer and, like Noel Pearson, a member of the original Referendum Council, continues to argue that only the Constitution can meet Aboriginal demand for full recognition, sovereignty and political representation. She calls the Uluru Statement 'a First Nations roadmap to peace in this country'. As Professor Davis wrote in *The Australian* in 2021:

> As the rule book for the nation, the Constitution determines
> the lines of power in our society, the legitimacy of people and
> institutions, and informs our values and national aspirations ...
> Aboriginal and Torres Strait Islander peoples spoke in the Uluru
> Statement about how the Constitution must be changed. Four years
> later it's time we respected this call ...

Most Australians support the Indigenous Voice proposal. The 2021 Australian Constitutional Values Survey, by Central Queensland and Griffith universities, revealed that 60 per cent of Australians were in favour of a First Nations Voice to Parliament (Deem, Bird and Brown, 2021). The majority of those – 53 per cent – prefer it be constitutionally enshrined. Other polling (Vote Compass, 2022; The Australia Institute, 2022) also indicates broad community support, to varying degrees. Yet, that support is far from unanimous – or even overwhelming. It may also be 'soft'; it may not survive a robust 'no' campaign and meet the threshold for a successful referendum: a majority of votes in a majority of states. This is a formidable bar, given that only eight of 44 nationwide referendums have been carried. Without bipartisan federal political support, history tells us that a referendum on Indigenous recognition could fail.

Even among Indigenous people, the Uluru Statement commands

strong but not unanimous support. Some refuse to co-operate with Australian governments they view as colonisers and oppressors. Many would prefer more explicit recognition of Indigenous peoples as sovereign peoples. Treaty remains a favoured course for many. Indeed, there are treaty negotiations underway in Victoria and the Northern Territory. Supporters of the Uluru Statement also advocate for treaties.

Calls for treaty, constitutional recognition, and/or a legislated Voice all point to a fundamental question that no Australian government has successfully answered: is the Australian liberal democracy capable of incorporating the sovereign demands of First Nations peoples? The Uluru Statement from the Heart offers a new compact with all Australians that would reset our national identity and enhance our political legitimacy.

The Uluru Statement seeks to reconcile two historically divergent, if not hitherto hostile, ideas – Indigenous sovereignty and the sovereignty of the Commonwealth. It asks the nation to embark on a project of moral and political rehabilitation, yet the Australian polity appears generally indifferent to historical introspection. Did the Uluru Statement offer nation-building for a nation that seems content with itself?

It proved an easy target for conservative politicians. The great lie of the Turnbull government – that the Voice to parliament would be a 'third chamber' of parliament – prevailed over Indigenous truth, because to enough ears it sounded right. The appearance of Indigenous people enjoying rights not shared by other Australians was cast as offensive to liberal principles. Indigenous advocates had no simple answer to the bumper-sticker slogan that they were putting race into the Constitution.

The Uluru Statement had been junked, and Australians, apparently generous to the idea of constitutional recognition, barely raised a whimper. They cared but didn't care enough. What could have been a high watermark of Australian liberalism became instead a victim of Australian liberalism. To the existential question about whether the liberal democracy can meet the demands of First Nations peoples: the classical liberals' answer is 'no'. Not if it means privileging group rights over the individual. Indigenous liberals are in a bind: caught between other Indigenous people who share their struggle yet reject their solutions, and liberals with whom they share a political belief but with whom they struggle to find common cause.

Can we untie this Gordian knot? Political philosopher Duncan Ivison (2020) believes so. The Uluru Statement, he argues, presents an opportunity for 'a refounding of Australia'. It was an invitation to re-imagine Australian liberalism around what the profoundly influential US political thinker John Rawls (1996) called 'reasonable pluralism'. Can a liberal state negotiate unavoidable, deep moral and political disagreements without fracturing civic unity?

Take the issues of rights and history: the Scylla and Charybdis of Australian politics. To navigate the straits between them would be a treacherous undertaking, invariably triggering culture wars over who 'owns' the truth. Ivison (2020) argues that if Indigenous people are to accept the legitimacy of the state, then the most important shift liberalism can make is to 'embrace a more historically informed approach to justice'.

Yet liberalism is a progressive idea that seeks to transcend history. There is a persuasive imperative to 'forget': to 'move on' and build a peacefully reconciled nation, free of historic grudges. Some Australians may be interested in learning more about our past, but that interest stops short of national catharsis. The 'great Australian silence' persists. Yes, there is greater revisionist scholarship about our history, and Indigenous voices are increasingly being heard. But that is yet to penetrate the broader Australian imagination or consciousness. It does not correspond to a great Australian reckoning. A 2022 Roy Morgan poll, for instance, indicated growing support for recognition of 26 January as Australia Day and not 'Invasion Day'. Sixty-five per cent of those polled prefer to call it Australia Day, an increase of 6 per cent from a year earlier (Roy Morgan, 2022). Australians generally don't think history is a debt to be repaid. First Nations people are still asked: why can't you just get over it?

Liberalism looks forward, not back.

Symbolic acts of reconciliation, such as apologies to the Stolen Generations and welcomes to Country are okay, but separate rights are not. The pertinent tension here is between group rights and individual rights. Duncan Ivison (2020) concedes that it is a tight fit. It is not beyond the scope of liberal democracies to embrace group rights. Ivison's native Canada incorporates what's been called a 'doctrine of Aboriginal rights': not so Australia. In Canada and the United States, the First Peoples were recognised as the original sovereigns of the land; treaties were signed that remain in force today (albeit contested, challenged and inadequate).

In Aotearoa New Zealand, the Treaty of Waitangi in 1840, between the British Crown and Māori chiefs, gave rise to the very notion of New Zealand's sovereignty. It was, if you like, the 'Big Bang' that created the modern New Zealand state. There are seats reserved in New Zealand's parliament specifically for Māori. In Norway, Finland and Sweden, the Indigenous Sámi people have their own parliament; it coexists with the national parliaments, and Sámi people are fully participating citizens of their countries. In those countries there is an acknowledgment that the nations are founded on the lands of two peoples: the Sámi and the later settlers.

Australia remains the only Commonwealth nation not to have signed a treaty with Indigenous peoples. This is despite Australia being a signatory to the United Nations Declaration on the Rights of Indigenous Peoples, which recognises the legitimacy and necessity of self-determination. Canadian philosopher Will Kymlicka (1995) acknowledges that groups' rights may appear antithetical to 'existing conceptions of representative democracy', but there is also a longstanding practice of drawing the boundaries of local constituencies so as to correspond with 'communities of interest'. In an urban society for instance, rural and agricultural groups may warrant special consideration. Kymlicka, though, concedes that this can become 'a source of major controversy when it involves racial groups'.

Political scientists Nicolas Peterson and Will Sanders (1998), in their book *Citizenship and Indigenous Australians*, ask: 'How is it possible for people from different cultural and historical backgrounds to be members of a common society on equal terms?' They question what is fair and equitable. Whether the citizens of a nation can have different rights, and, if Indigenous people do have distinct rights, they ask, 'what will hold the Australian nation and society together?'

Duncan Ivison has put forward the idea of a 'postcolonial liberalism', based on a 'complex mutual coexistence' (2002). Ivison's quest for a liberal resolution to contested sovereignty raises a fundamental question: do Indigenous claims for justice and distinct recognition place an unsustainable burden on liberalism? Does incorporating those claims deform liberalism itself, to the point at which it becomes unrecognisable, even meaningless?

In the absence of political reform in Australia, the courts have wrestled with the nature of Indigenous belonging. Most notable was the 1992 Mabo High Court ruling, which established the principle of Native Title, even if it did not (as is popularly believed) overturn the doctrine of terra nullius. The judges stopped short of the question of Indigenous sovereignty, lest it disturb what is known as 'the skeleton' of Australian law: that this land was an uncultivated desert and thus free to be claimed by the Crown.

In 2020, the High Court delivered another landmark decision, in *Love v Commonwealth*. The case was brought by lawyers for two Aboriginal men, Brendan Thoms and Daniel Love, both born overseas but having Indigenous heritage. Both men faced potential deportation arising from criminal charges. But this case was about more than just the fates of two individuals. This was about our nation's history: the legacy of dispossession. Where do First Nations people fit within the Commonwealth? What is it to be Australian? Indigenous? Can we be equally one and the same? Can two centuries of imported British law and tradition here extinguish a connection, law and lore that have existed for time immemorial? These questions go to the very heart of the legitimacy of the nation.

The seven-member court found 4–3 that Indigenous people cannot be considered aliens, even if they do not hold Australian citizenship. The judges' opinions make fascinating and inspiring reading. In their determination, they confronted the emotionally and politically loaded questions of race, history, identity and, crucially, sovereignty. In doing so, they widened the horizon of what it is to be Indigenous and to belong to this land. Justice James Edelman captured the strength of the Aboriginal men's claim:

> The sense of identity that ties Aboriginal people to Australia is an underlying fundamental truth that cannot be altered or deemed not to exist by legislation … (Edelman J, 2020)

Justice Virginia Bell argued, too, that an Indigenous person cannot be considered alien, because '… an Aboriginal Australian cannot be said to belong to another place'. Justice Stephen Gagelar rejected the claim, but also acknowledged an Aboriginal connection is 'deep' and 'enduring'. Despite the 'morally and emotionally engaging' argument, Justice Gagelar said it was 'not legally sustainable', that he could 'not be a party' to inserting what he saw as a 'race based constitutional distinction' (Gagelar J, 2020).

Justice Edelman argues that embracing difference is critical to achieving justice:

> To treat differences as though they were alike is not equality. It
> is a denial of community. Any tolerant view of community must
> recognise that community is based upon difference. (Edelman J, 2020)

Most Australians would have paid scant attention to *Love v Commonwealth*, but it was legal dynamite. Justice Gageler belled the cat, writing that the case has 'come perilously close to an assertion of Aboriginal and Torres Strait Islander sovereignty' (Gagelar J, 2020). That is a line no Australian court, to date, has dared cross.

The Morrison Government's response to the High Court ruling was that the judges have 'created a new category of persons' (Caisley, 2020). The ruling represented a profound challenge to the very idea of being Australian. Constitutional law professor and Indigenous woman Megan Davis described the High Court as restating its emphatic position that recognition of Indigenous sovereignty was for the parliament and not the court (Davis, 2020). The unresolved question of Indigenous sovereignty bedevils Australia. First Peoples hold to truths of 60 000 years or more that they say can never be erased. The judgment in *Love v Commonwealth* attests to that. Indigenous leaders say politics has failed us. The lack of treaties, the refusal to acknowledge meaningful Indigenous sovereignty, reveals what sovereign First Nations see as the limits or even contempt of the nation.

Noel Pearson and Megan Davis are among those who have argued that we remain not, as the Constitution says, a nation indissoluble, but a nation incomplete. Yawuru man Peter Yu, reflecting on decades of struggle in a 2018 speech at the Australian National University, said meaningful reconciliation 'no longer exists' (Yu, 2018). It had failed to heal the wounds of our past or to reach a political settlement with First Nations peoples. Reconciliation, Yu says, has 'lost its moral and political gravitas' (Yu, 2018). Tasmanian Aboriginal lawyer and activist Michael Mansell poses pertinent and profound questions: Are we Aboriginal Australians or Australian Aboriginals? Simply: are we a part of the Australian nation or a people apart?

To the Morrison Government, the answer was: we are Australians. To many – if not most – First Nations people, that presents a repugnant idea that sovereignty is to all intents and purposes extinguished. Sovereignty exists in the hearts and minds, the law and lore of First Nations people, but not in the law of the land. This is the existential dilemma of Australia as it has passed from parliament to parliament since Federation.

This parliament ended as it began, with so many Indigenous people feeling estranged from the nation. Not yet fully recognised in the land of their ancestors. The hopes for a Constitutional 'Voice' remained unfulfilled. Yet throughout the Morrison government Indigenous leaders continued to advance the cause of the Voice. Marcia Langton and Tom Calma chaired an Indigenous Voice Co-Design Process. Their report represented a significant public consultation process engaging nearly ten thousand people and organisations. It set out a series of proposals integrating regional and local Indigenous voices with a national Voice.

It has been a long hard journey. First Nations people could be excused for wondering if they should have any faith in political liberalism? To some, at its worst it is a project of imperialism and colonisation inseparable from the tyranny of whiteness. At best, it offers a Rawlsian neutrality – a weightlessness – that is in itself the conceit of the comfortable. It is ahistorical. It cannot hold the claims of those who have faced existential threat. It is undeniable that Australian political liberalism has failed to deliver justice or meaningful political recognition. After two centuries, Australia has refused to embed principles of First Nations self-determination. Native Title and land rights legislation have returned great swathes of land, but the 'torment of powerlessness' remains.

Anthony Albanese came to office promising to take the Voice to a referendum. Australian liberalism will be tested again. Albanese seeks to mollify a scare campaign against Indigenous power over-reach by reassuring Australians that this will be a Voice, 'nothing more, nothing less'. Not a veto. The Voice itself – hopeful and righteous – is a liberal compromise. A pact with a nation built on the invasion and theft of Aboriginal and Torres Strait Islander land. Yet it offers through truth telling and treaty a pathway to peace. A collective reimagining of Australia. A gift of healing to the nation.

For First Nations people engaging with Australian politics can be bruising and disheartening. Yet it is essential. Generations of First Nations leaders have led us to this historic point. There remains for some a view that Constitutional Voice to many First Nations people is the least we deserve, yet may be the best we can expect. It is captured in the words of Greens Senator Lidia Thorpe: 'There is unfinished business in this country that needs to be reconciled'. An advisory body is not enough to provide 'justice for our people in this country.' (Thorpe, quoted in Wahlquist, 2022)

Then there are the words of the Uluru Statement itself: 'We invite you to walk with us in a movement of the Australian people for a better future.'

References

The Australia Institute, *Polling – Voice to Parliament in the Constitution*, The Australia Institute, July 2022, <australiainstitute.org.au/wp-content/uploads/2022/08/Polling-brief-Voice-to-Parliament-in-the-Constitution-Web.pdf>.

Brennan, Bridget and Kirstie Wellauer. 'Vote Compass data finds most Australians support Indigenous Voice to Parliament – and it has grown since the last election', ABC, 4 May 2022.

Caisley, Olivia. 'High Court rules on new status for Indigenous people', *The Australian*, 12 February 2020.

Davis, Megan. 'The High Court and the "aliens" power', *Saturday Paper*, 15 February 2020.

— 'Time to give all people choice on Indigenous Voice', *The Australian*, 29 May 2021.

Deakin, Alfred. 'For a white Australia', speech in the House of Representatives, 12 September 1901.

Deem, Jacob, Susan Bird and AJ Brown. 'Australian Constitutional Values Survey 2021', Central Queensland and Griffith universities, March 2021.

Ivison, Duncan. *Postcolonial Liberalism*, Cambridge University Press, 2002.

— *Can Liberal States Accommodate Indigenous Peoples?*, Polity Press, 2020.

Kymlicka, Will. *Multicultural Citizenship: A liberal theory of minority rights*, Clarendon Press, Oxford, 1995.

Lahn, Julie. 'Aboriginal professionals: Work, class and culture', AEPR Working Paper no. 89, Centre for Aboriginal Economic Policy Research, ANU College of Arts & Social Sciences, 2013.

Langton, Marcia. *The Quiet Revolution: Indigenous people and the resources boom*, Boyer Lectures 2012, HarperCollins Publishers, 2013.

Love v Commonwealth of Australia (2020) 375 ALR 597.

Pearson, Noel. 'Betrayal: The Turnbull government has burned the bridge of bipartisanship', the *Monthly*, December–January, 2017, <www.themonthly.com.au/issue/2017/december/1512046800/noel-pearson/betrayal>.

Peterson, Nicholas and Will Sanders (eds). *Citizenship and Indigenous Australians: Changing Conceptions and Possibilities*, Cambridge University Press, 1998.

Rawls, John. *Political Liberalism*, Columbia University Press, 1996.

Roy Morgan, 'Nearly two-thirds of Australians (65%) say January 26 should be known as "Australia Day" – up 6% points on a year ago', Roy Morgan, 25 January 2022.

Wahlquist, Calla. 'Staunch or stubborn? Lidia Thorpe on the voice, the treaty and real power', *Guardian*, 15 October 2022, <www.theguardian.com/australia-news/2022/oct/15/staunch-or-stubborn-lidia-thorpe-on-the-voice-the-treaty-and-real-power>.

Yu, Peter. 'Reconciliation, Treaty Making and Nation Building', 2018 Reconciliation Lecture, Australian National University, 7 February 2018, <www.anu.edu.au/news/all-news/2018-anu-reconciliation-lecture-full-speech-by-peter-yu>.

14

FOREIGN POLICY

Tony Walker

Foreign policy timeline: Morrison and Albanese governments, 2018–22

August 2018: Scott Morrison replaces Malcom Turnbull as leader of the
Liberal Party and prime minister

January 2019: Australian Chinese democracy activist Yang Hengjun
arrested in China

May 2019: Morrison Government re-elected

September 2019: Morrison makes a state visit to Washington, draws closer
to US President Donald Trump

March 2020: World Health Organisation declares a COVID-19 global
pandemic

March 2020: Morrison closes Australia's international border due to
COVID-19

April 2020: Morrison calls for an independent investigation into the
origins of COVID-19, drawing an angry response from China

May 2020: China slaps 80 per cent tariffs on Australian barley exports,
followed over time by punitive tariffs on wine and other exports

August 2020: Deal to sell Lion Dairy to a Chinese company terminated
on national-interest grounds

August 2020: Australian journalist Cheng Lei detained in Beijing

November 2020: Morrison visits Tokyo on election of a new Japanese
prime minister; signs Defence Pact, angering China

November 2020: Regional Economic Partnership Agreement signed

September 2021: Australia–United Kingdom–United States Partnership
(AUKUS) announced

September 2021: Morrison visits Washington for talks with President
    Biden. Inaugural, face-to-face quadrilateral security dialogue held
May 2022: Albanese Government elected
May 2022: Quad meeting in Tokyo involving US President Biden and
    prime ministers Albanese, Modi (India) and Kishida (Japan)
May 2022: Foreign Minister Penny Wong tours the Pacific in face of
    rising Chinese influence in the region
June 2022: Defence Minister Richard Marles holds first ministerial-level
    talk with Chinese counterpart, signalling a thaw in bilateral relations
June 2022: Albanese visits Indonesia
November 2022: Prime Minister Albanese meets Chinese Premier
    Xi Jinping

Australian foreign policy in the years 2018–22 was scarred by deteriorating relations between Canberra and Beijing, to the point where there was little official contact. No Australian prime minister had visited Beijing since Malcolm Turnbull's visit in April 2016. Contact between Australian ministers and their Chinese counterparts over the years was sparse. These were confined to brief encounters on the margins of multilateral gatherings, including Prime Minister Scott Morrison's exchanges with President Xi Jinping on the sidelines of the G20 conference in Japan in June 2019, and a similar interaction at the East Asia Summit in Thailand in November of that year.

This was the paradox of Australia's relationship with its principal trading partner. China absorbs about one-third of Australia's exports, and yet its officials shunned direct contact with the elected representatives of its main raw materials supplier. That protracted estrangement ended in June 2022, when newly elected Defence Minister Richard Marles held talks with his Chinese counterpart, Wei Fenghe, on the sidelines of the annual Shangri-La Dialogue in Singapore. Over the years, this event, organised by the International Institute for Strategic Studies (IISS), has become one of the more significant global gatherings of defence ministers, officials and security specialists. The Marles–Wei encounter, despite significant differences expressed by both sides, signalled a thaw in relations.

When Scott Morrison assumed the office of prime minister in August 2018, after Turnbull lost the confidence of his parliamentary colleagues, relations with Beijing were already on a downward trend. They did not improve during Morrison's tenure. Relations had been strained by the Turnbull Government's foreign interference legislation aimed at China, and by the government's lobbying among its Five Eyes partners against the Chinese technology giant, Huawei. In August 2018, the same month Morrison became prime minister, Australia banned Huawei from participating in the buildout of its 5G network. Canberra's Five Eyes lobbying efforts in London, Washington, Wellington and Ottawa infuriated Beijing.

This was the background to Morrison's tenure in charge of Australian foreign and security policy, in which China's rise overshadowed all other considerations. Australian governments in the current era are being tested by the most challenging regional security environment since the Second World War. These post-Second World War years encompassed the Korean War, the Malayan Emergency, Indonesia's colonial conflict with the Dutch, the Vietnam War and East Timor's bloody transition to independence. China's astonishing transformation economically, and its growing assertiveness militarily, has presented Australian policymakers with a set of challenges that are both profound and long-lasting.

While an assertive China remained the dominant foreign and security policy issue of the Morrison era, other challenges taxed policymakers in Canberra. These included climate policy in all its dimensions; Australia's role as a reluctant metropolitan power in the south-west Pacific; Canberra's relationship with a populist 'America First' Trump administration; an infectious diseases pandemic whose requirements for income support have exerted enormous pressure on the budget; a war in Ukraine whose economic consequences are playing themselves out in supply chain disruptions and increased energy prices, gas in particular; and perhaps most challenging of all, a need for Australia to take stock of its defence capabilities in a disrupted security environment. Australia's lack of defence equipment preparedness has been exposed. At the heart of all of this is the certain knowledge that US hegemony is fraying, in a contest for power and influence with a rival player whose rapid rise has taken the world by surprise. Here it is worth noting that when the Berlin Wall came down in 1989, followed by the implosion of the former Soviet Union, the United States ruled briefly as the world's hyperpower. Now, the United States neither rules the waves, as it once did, nor is it unchallenged on the new global security frontier of cyberspace. The era of Pax Americana is over.

In the lead-up to Morrison assuming the office of prime minister in August 2018, Canberra was already being put on notice that successive Australian governments would be dealing with a rising power that was putting behind it late paramount leader Deng Xiaoping's advice that China should 'hide your capabilities, bide your time'. This has been interpreted as an instruction from Deng that his successors should not overreach. Another interpretation is that Beijing should disguise its real aims. Whatever Deng's intentions, his advice is being ignored in this latest period.

In the decade since Xi Jinping became General Secretary of the Chinese Communist Party and thus President, China has become steadily more assertive. This has involved upgrading defence 'features' on remote atolls in the South China Sea, investing heavily in what is now the world's largest naval capability, including its biggest submarine fleet, and conducting a policy of intimidation and harassment against Taiwan by sending clusters of fighter aircraft into that country's defence space. While China's 'on the books' defence expenditures (as opposed to those that are disguised) are dwarfed by those of the United States, the fact is that it is engaging in an escalating militarisation process that risks fuelling an arms race in the Indo-Pacific. Japan, for example, is easing restrictions on postwar constitutional constraints on its abilities to re-arm and project its own military power.

Australian political leaders would have difficulty arguing they were not forewarned about the emergence of a more aggressive China. However, Canberra's responses have been inconsistent and inadequate. A botched submarine-acquisition process that will end up costing the taxpayer around $4 billion, including compensation to France for a cancelled contract, is but one example of a mishandled defence procurement program. What is not in question is that Australia has under-invested in its defence capability, and one that is fit for purpose, under successive Labor and

Coalition administrations. Any government in the future, including the newly elected Labor Party, will have no choice but to ramp up defence expenditures beyond the 2 per cent of gross domestic product regarded as a benchmark for maintaining an adequate defence preparedness.

In the calendars of a national security establishment that had come to dominate foreign policymaking during the Turnbull and Morrison administrations, the date of October 2017 should be etched. This was the moment when it should have been clear that President Xi Jinping was emerging as his country's most dominant leader since Deng Xiaoping and, possibly, Mao Zedong himself. In that month, Chinese Communist Party leaders, at a meeting held in Beijing ahead of the party's 19th quinquennial National Party Congress, bestowed the title of Core Leader on President Xi. That was followed, in early 2018, by the country's rubber-stamp parliament, the National People's Congress (NPC), changing China's constitution to remove term limits on the position of president of the Republic. Such positions had been restricted to two terms under legislation enacted during the Deng era, to guard against dictatorial rule. President Xi has ruled China effectively since 2012 when he became General Secretary of the Central Committee of the Chinese Communist Party. His grip on power was further strengthened at China's 20th National Party Congress late in 2022 when he was confirmed as party leader for a further five years. Xi is now, to all intents and purposes, leader for life, or until such time as ill health or internal party conflict brings his rule to an end.

These are important developments for Australian policymakers, since there is little likelihood of respite from a more assertive and nationalistic Chinese foreign and security policy under President Xi. This means that issues – such as the future of Taiwan, Chinese assertiveness in the South China Sea and the Pacific, its human rights violations, including the jailing of citizens of countries with whom it is at odds and its ruthless suppression of dissent in Hong Kong – will continue to bedevil relations into the future. Concerning, given the situation in Ukraine, is Beijing's alignment with Moscow. A China–Russia axis of autocrats is an affront to a rules-based international order that is now in danger of fragmenting. Managing all those challenges constructively, in a way that contrasts with the Morrison Government's heavy-handed approach to relations with

China, will not be the least of hurdles for the incoming Labor Government. Perhaps the prime example of this heavy-handedness came when Morrison took it upon himself to advocate an international inquiry into the origins of the COVID-19 outbreak in China. Needless to say this further poisoned relations.

In the face of China's surging power and influence in the Indo-Pacific, Australia has been at the forefront of efforts to create a regional architecture as a hedge against pressures from Beijing. These efforts have included a revitalisation of the Quadrilateral Security Dialogue, first established as a loose partnership at the time of the 2004 Indian Ocean tsunami as a vehicle for four countries – the United States, Japan, Australia and India – to provide humanitarian and disaster relief. The so-called Quad was formalised in 2007 by then-Japanese Prime Minister Shinzo Abe. It then fell into abeyance for a decade, as the Australian Government of Kevin Rudd, elected in 2007, regarded the Quad as an unnecessary irritant to relations with Beijing. The Quad was revived in 2017 under the Turnbull Government, in collaboration with the Trump administration. However, it was not until the advent of the Biden White House that Quad leaders held their inaugural 'in person' summit. This was convened in Washington on 24 September 2021, hosted by President Biden and attended by prime ministers Morrison, Modi (India) and Suga (Japan). In March 2022, Morrison engaged in a virtual summit with Quad leaders to discuss the ongoing conflict and humanitarian crisis in Ukraine. On his election as Prime Minister, Anthony Albanese travelled to Tokyo for his first Quad gathering with President Biden, and prime ministers Modi and Keshida. This was the second 'in-person' encounter of Quad leaders and it reflected growing concerns about China's rise. In remarks after the Quad session, Albanese (2022a) emphasised new climate change targets as a policy priority for his Labor Government. He described climate change as a security issue in the context of China seeking greater influence in the Pacific. The Department of Foreign Affairs and Trade defines the Quad as a 'network of countries committed to supporting a free and open Indo-Pacific that is inclusive and resilient, and one that complements our other bilateral, regional and multilateral cooperation, including with ASEAN member states and Pacific partners' (Department of Foreign Affairs and Trade, nda).

DFAT's emphasis on collaboration with ASEAN member states and Pacific partners is important, since among criticisms of the Morrison Government's foreign policy was its lack of initiative in Australia's immediate region, and particularly in the south-west Pacific. Pacific Island states had become distant from Australia on the issue of climate, and their leaders were critical of Australia's reticence on global targets. China has, in recent years, sought to extend its influence in the Pacific. This has included a recent proposal for a region-wide economic and security pact among all Pacific Island states. China's security pact idea has been pushed aside for the time being, but it is clear that Beijing is making a long-term investment in a south-west Pacific presence as it extends its reach across the entire Indo-Pacific. Foreign Minister Penny Wong's several visits to the region soon after the election in May 2022 are testament to Australia's concerns about growing Chinese influence in its own backyard. Wong appears to have established a useful working relationship with Pacific leaders. Albanese's visit to Jakarta, two weeks after the 21 May election, for what has become an obligatory first mission for Australian prime ministers to Australia's largest neighbour and growing economic power was designed to underscore Canberra's commitment to closer ties (Albanese, 2022b). The Prime Minister was accompanied by Foreign Minister Wong. Albanese appears to have been well received by his Indonesian hosts. Minister Wong's ability to speak fluent Bahasa Indonesian will have done no harm to bilateral relations.

In the Morrison era, from August 2018 to May 2022, a period of four years, no single initiative will likely prove to be as substantial as the Australia–United Kingdom–United States partnership (AUKUS), unveiled on 15 September 2021 (White House, 2022). This agreement, which lacks the treaty obligations of the ANZUS Treaty of 1951, whose Article I requires signatories to consult in the event of a security threat to one or the other, represents, nevertheless, a landmark moment in the evolution of Australian security policy. Whether AUKUS lives up to ambitions held for it by Canberra will depend on circumstance, but on the face of it, the partnership draws Australia and the United States into a landmark security embrace. Central to AUKUS is an undertaking by the nuclear-capable United States and United Kingdom to 'provide Australia with a conventionally armed nuclear power submarine capability at the earliest possible date' (White House, 2022). AUKUS also obliges the partners to collaborate in the exchange of 'advanced military capabilities to promote security and stability in the Indo-Pacific region' (White House, 2022). This element of AUKUS comprises a long list of cooperative projects in the areas of undersea capabilities, quantum technologies, artificial intelligence, advanced cyber technologies, hypersonic and counter-hypersonic capabilities, electronic war and innovation in the defence space. In these comprehensive terms, the partnership represents a significant leap forward in military interoperability between Australia and its principal allies. At this early stage, it is not clear when, or how, Australia might acquire nuclear submarines. Among options is for Canberra to buy, or lease, US or British versions. A further option would be to build the submarines in Australian shipyards. The latter would require extremely long lead times. This would further expose a capability gap between Australia's existing submarine fleet of ageing Collins Class subs, already due for retirement, and the commissioning of Australian-built, nuclear-propelled vessels. Another option would be for the government to buy off-the-shelf conventional submarines, possibly from Germany, to bridge the gap between the decommissioning of the Collins Class and the arrival of nuclear-powered submarines. Whichever solution is decided upon to overcome a problem exacerbated by years of waste and indecision in the country's submarine program will prove expensive and complex.

The convergence of security priorities in response to China's rise ushered in a period when relations between Canberra and Washington were aligned more closely than they had been for many years. Morrison was, among world leaders, one of those closest to Trump. This was underscored in 2019 by Morrison becoming only the second world leader to that point – the other was President Emmanuel Macron of France – to be granted a state visit to Washington, with all the pomp and circumstance that accompany such occasions. Remarks by Trump and Morrison (2019) at a Rose Garden State Dinner were fulsome in praise of each other. In speeches to various audiences on his September 2019 visit to the United States, Morrison echoed prevalent Trump themes, such as a suspicion of 'globalism' – the idea that supra-national bodies such as the United Nations were seeking to usurp national sovereignty.

At the UN, Morrison rejected criticism of Australia's efforts to mitigate climate change. 'Australia is doing our bit on climate change and we reject any suggestion to the contrary', he told the General Assembly. This was not necessarily how the world saw Australia's contributions to the fight against global warming, nor, for that matter, was this the view of the Biden administration, which came to office in January 2021. Officials in the new administration expressed frustrations over Australia's reluctance to embrace more ambitious emissions-reduction targets. Nonetheless, Morrison's visit to Washington in September 2021 for bilateral meetings with Biden and for a Quad summit proved fruitful. This will have owed much to the initialling of the AUKUS agreement in the previous week. History provided a useful context for the Morrison mission. It coincided with the 70th anniversary year of the initialling of the ANZUS Treaty, a cornerstone of Australian security. In a White House readout of Biden's meeting with Morrison, the two leaders 'reaffirmed their commitment to a free and open Indo-Pacific region ... to defend against threats to the international rules based order' (White House, 2021). China was firmly in their sights.

After adjusting his own sights in accordance with a change of management in Washington, from the populism of Trump to a traditional Democratic administration, Morrison's next hurdle was to prove more problematic. Preparations for his participation in the COP26 Glasgow climate summit in November 2021 were overshadowed by a lingering debate within the National Party about whether it would support a net-zero emissions target by 2050. In the end, compromise was reached among Nationals MPs that enabled the Morrison Government to announce a Long Term Emissions Reduction Plan. However, with an election pending, the issue was awkward for the prime minister, since it left the impression the Liberal Party was being held hostage by its junior Coalition partner. In its announcement of the new emissions reduction plan, the Morrison Government insisted that technology would provide a 'credible pathway' to net zero by 2050. In Glasgow, where host prime minister Boris Johnson had urged global emitters, like Australia, to pledge more, Morrison was left on the defensive. Australia re-emphasised its commitment to net zero by 2050, but resisted pressure to increase its 2030 commitment.

Morrison told the summit that Australia was sticking to an earlier goal of a 26–28 per cent reduction in emissions based on 2005 levels, but noted that on present indications emissions would fall by 35 per cent. The United States, for example, has a 50–52 per cent target. Immediately after the Glasgow summit, the Labor Opposition committed to a 43 per cent reduction target by 2030.

Glasgow proved to be a disappointment for those who had hoped for bolder initiatives. In the end, Australia signed on to a watered-down suite of commitments that did not require an obligation to transition from investment in fossil-fuel production. Canberra did not join an effort to curb emissions of methane by 30 per cent by 2030, but it did sign up to an agreement to combat deforestation. On the face of it, politically Glasgow could have been worse for Morrison, but an impression was left, nevertheless, that Australia remained a laggard on climate action. This was not helpful in Liberal progressive heartland seats in Sydney, Melbourne, Adelaide and Perth in the Federal Election of 2022. The Coalition under Morrison was punished severely in these seats on issues of climate and integrity.

In the four years since Morrison became prime minister in 2018, one area of achievement that tends to be overlooked is trade (Department of Foreign Affairs and Trade, ndb). In that period, Australian foreign and trade policy has been active. Trade Minister Dan Tehan, installed after Morrison became prime minister in May 2018, continued to build on the foundation of bilateral agreements that have become a feature of Australian trade policy for several decades. These include the Australia–United States Free Trade Agreement (AUSFTA), which came into force on 1 January 2005; the Korea–Australia Free Trade Agreement of 2014 (KAFTA); the Japan–Australia Economic Partnership Agreement of 2015 (JAEPA); the China–Australia Free Trade Agreement of 2015 (CHAFTA); and the Comprehensive and Progressive Agreement for Trans Pacific Partnership of 2018 (CPTPP). China has expressed interest in participating.

In the Morrison term, two other significant initiatives were concluded. These were the Indonesia–Australia Comprehensive Economic Partnership of 2020 (IA-CEPA) and the Regional Comprehensive Economic Partnership Agreement (RCEP) of 2020. This latter agreement came into effect in 2022. China's decision in 2021 to join the grouping adds significantly to its weight. Other members, among 15 signatories, are Australia, Brunei, Cambodia, Japan, Indonesia, Laos, Malaysia, Myanmar, New Zealand, Republic of Korea, Philippines, Singapore, Thailand and Vietnam. The grouping accounts for 30 per cent of global trade. The RCEP does not have the same trade-liberalising components as the CPTPP, but it does represent a further step, nevertheless, towards a wider Asia-Pacific free trade zone.

The new Labor Government will have much on its plate in the trade arena, with agreements under negotiation including, principally, the Australia–European Union Free Trade Agreement and the Australia–India Economic Cooperation and Trade Agreement (AI-ECTA). In the case of the former, negotiations were hampered by ill-will between Australia and France over Canberra's abrupt decision to cancel the French submarine contract. Other significant trade agreements pending include that with the Gulf Cooperation Council. An Australia–United Kingdom Free Trade Agreement, initialled in 2021 and enabled by Britain's withdrawal from the European Union, is due to come into effect in 2023.

Any assessment of the Morrison Government's foreign policy tenure presents a mixed picture. Successes, as outlined above, include an activist trade policy. Collaborative trade agreements in the region aimed at liberalising Indo-Pacific trade represent an important contribution to regional peace and stability. A centrepiece of the Morrison era's tenure is the AUKUS agreement of September 2021. This[1] represents a down payment on a more muscular Australian response to China's rise and the security challenges involved. However, the initiative is not without its risks, if one of its consequences is a more belligerent regional environment. It may well be the case that an Indo-Pacific arms race is unavoidable, given China's accelerating militarisation and its apparent determination to assert itself more widely. In all of this, the Taiwan issue remains a potential hair-trigger to a wider regional conflict. Risks posed by a miscalculation in the Taiwan Strait, in a potentially volatile military environment, are real. An incident at sea or in the air involving Australia or its allies in conflict with the Chinese military, and leading to a wider conflagration, cannot be discounted. In the absence of regional security arrangements, such as those that prevailed in Europe during the Cold War under the Helsinki Accords, the security environment in the Indo-Pacific will remain unpredictable. A rising China is bumping up against a status quo power. North Korea's nuclear ambitions and Pyongyang's propensity to engage in the sort of nuclear brinkmanship that unsettles the region are other causes for concern. Whether AUKUS will live up to expectations as a strategic hedge against Chinese assertiveness remains to be seen. AUKUS is a bold initiative, and one that will define the Morrison era. Morrison himself articulated this approach in an interview by Paul Kelly for his book, *Morrison's Mission: How a beginner reshaped Australian foreign policy* (2022). 'Our interests are inextricably linked … to a strategic balance in the region that favors freedom and allows us to be what we are: a vibrant liberal democracy, an outward-looking open economy, a free people determined to shape our own destiny.'

These aims are unexceptional in the circumstances and could be uttered by a prime minister from the left or right, but any judgment of the Morrison era will involve these central questions: Did Morrison make Australia more or less secure? Did a policy of 'standing up to China', as opposed to managing the relationship less confrontationally, yield the foreign policy benefits that might have been achieved otherwise? Will the policy of drawing Australia ever closer into a US security embrace prove to be the best course of action, given uncertainties associated with a corrosive domestic political environment in the United States? Will Australia get its defence procurement act together? Will the Trump presidency prove to be an aberration, or has it signalled a different United States from the one to which, under Morrison, Australia has mortgaged its future? Can Australia continue to rely on a traditional cornerstone ally whose internal politics are so toxic the United States may simply cease to be a reliable ally? Will Trump return to the White House in 2024, thereby consigning the United States to the state of chaos that prevailed under his leadership? Will China respect a rules-based international order, or will it continue to disrespect its guard rails? Will the rise of the autocrats usher in a new international order?

On all these questions, as Zhou Enlai, the first premier of the People's Republic, might have said: it is too early to say.

References

Albanese, Anthony. Opening remarks of the Quad Leaders' meeting, 24 May 2022a, <www.pm.gov.au/media/opening-remarks-quad-leaders-meeting>.

— 'Press Conference: Jakarta', 6 June 2022b, <www.pm.gov.au/media/press-conference-jakarta>.

Department of Foreign Affairs and Trade. 'Quad' (nda), <www.dfat.gov.au/international-relations/regional-architecture/quad>.

Department of Foreign Affairs and Trade. Australia's free trade agreements (ndb), <www.dfat.gov.au/trade/agreements/trade-agreements>.

Kelly, Paul. *Morrison's Mission: How a beginner reshaped Australian foreign policy*, 1 February 2022, <www.lowyinstitute.org/publications/morrison-mission-how-beginner-reshaped-australian-foreign-policy>.

Trump, Donald and Scott Morrison. 'Remarks by President Trump and Prime Minister Morrison of Australia at State Dinner', *US Embassy and Consulates in Australia*, 20 September 2019, <au.usembassy.gov/remarks-by-president-trump-and-prime-minister-morrison-of-australia-at-state-dinner/>.

White House, The. 'Readout of President Joseph R. Biden Jr's meeting with Prime Minister Scott Morrison of Australia', 21 September 2021, <www.whitehouse.gov/briefing-room/statements-releases/2021/09/21/readout-of-president-joseph-r-biden-jr-s-meeting-with-prime-minister-scott-morrison-of-australia/>.

White House, The. 'Fact Sheet: Implementation of the Australia–United Kingdom–United States Partnership (AUKUS)', 5 April 2022, <www.whitehouse.gov/briefing-room/statements-releases/2022/04/05/fact-sheet-implementation-of-the-australia-united-kingdom-united-states-partnership-aukus/>.

15

COMMUNICATIONS POLICY

Julianne Schultz

Paul Keating, whose term as prime minister ended in a landslide loss in 1996, lost no time rubbing salt into Scott Morrison's wounds when his term ended in a similarly humiliating fashion. 'The point about the Morrison Government', Keating declared, pausing for dramatic emphasis before brandishing his verbal sword, 'was there was no point to it'.

Keating was not the first, from any side of politics, to argue that the Morrison Government had lacked an agenda, a clear set of policy objectives or a raison d'etre. It was a government that lived, and eventually died, by events (largely) beyond its control. Faced with extraordinary challenges, its responses were at best opportunistic and generous, at worst tone deaf, profligate, verging on excessive, and counterproductive.

Strikingly, the government was led by a man who had actively rejected the notion of leaving a legacy. Power was its own reward. He told *Sydney Morning Herald* associate editor Deborah Snow, in January 2022, that he had given no thought to his legacy: 'When prime ministers think about their legacies, they stop thinking about what they have to do now' (Snow, 2022).

It is tempting to apply these two insights – no point, no legacy ambition – to the ways in which communications policy was implemented during the 1367 days that Scott Morrison was Australia's 30th prime minister. On one reading, nothing much happened, apart from the government responding to events. On another, the power of the oligopoly that long dominated the communications sector saw its positions entrenched, with government support, despite operating in an increasingly complex and globalised environment. Under the cover of pandemic relief, the oligopoly won concessions that were plausibly urgent and necessary, and others it had quietly coveted and hoped to see permanently extended. The final months of the Morrison Government were a last-minute dash. The auction of low-band 5G spectrum licences in 2021 brought in nearly $3 billion in revenue, more than $2 billion in December alone. A month before the writs were issued for the 2022 election, a nearly $5 billion investment in the National Broadband Network (NBN) was announced to significantly upgrade the service offered to 8 million households. Three days before the prime minister travelled to Government House, the Future of Broadcasting Working Group met for the first time to consider possible structural reforms to free-to-air television.

This was, arguably, the point of the Morrison Government. It was not without purpose. Its point was to entrench the power of the prevailing status quo and hold challengers at bay.

Herald of power

Communications policy, particularly broadcasting policy, has long been the canary in the mine of corporate–government influence. Media and communications companies have been accustomed to exercising political power for generations, and the expectation of influence lingered in the organisational DNA long after the ultimate head offices moved offshore to New York, Luxembourg or London. Unlike other businesses that depended on government decisions, the media companies had a megaphone they were sometimes willing to use to achieve corporate benefits (Schultz, 1998). Prime ministers frequently complained. Robert Menzies had felt that that the press had been 'out to kill' him, and therefore was reluctant to stand up to the media proprietors (Young, 2019). Malcolm Turnbull declared that he had been brought down as prime minister by an insurgency backed by 'powerful voices in the media' (Schultz, 2021). Kevin Rudd was convinced that Murdoch's News Corporation had undermined Australian democracy, 'abusing his monopoly to bully' (Hirst, 2021).

The newspapers, radio, television stations and the content on other platforms owned by the media companies provide the 'feedback mechanism of democratic system management' (Kunczik, 1989). This has delivered quasi-institutional power to these commercial enterprises and has caused communications policy in a small, interconnected political system to become particularly fraught. For decades, the real and imagined power kept media ownership close and local. The global digital age challenged concentration of power and influence to its core, and even the media companies where family ownership still prevailed looked more like any other business.

By the time Scott Morrison became prime minister, the ability to do political deals to ensure the local media companies flourished was under unprecedented threat. But it was not completely a thing of the past, and the expectation of special influence lingered. The singular legislative achievement of the previous Turnbull Government – removing the cross-media ownership restrictions that had reshaped the industry over three decades, the caps on the reach of free-to-air television, licensing fees – played out during the Morrison Prime Ministership (House of Representatives, 2017). Major companies merged, smaller companies were acquired, and the concentration of ownership reached peaks not seen for decades. Local ownership was no longer privileged, and the Australian Communications and Media Authority (2020) declared that ownership was no longer an appropriate measure of media diversity.

During the Morrison years, Rupert Murdoch's News Corp, with its 140 print and online newspapers and interests in pay television, radio and publishing, was, as always, poised to assert its interests and, through its editorial approach, help mould the political ecosystem (RMIT ABC Fact Check, 2021). Nine Entertainment acquired the 188-year-old Fairfax newspaper company in 2018, with the majority of the shares owned by Luxembourg-based CVC Capital, its local board headed by former Liberal treasurer Peter Costello, who also chaired the Commonwealth-owned Future Fund. Kerry Stokes's Seven West, owner of the Seven Network, the *West Australian* and other regional newspapers, acquired Prime Media in 2021 without any regulatory objection, and although aged in his 80s, Stokes remained an influential power broker and chair of the Australian War Memorial. As if to prove that the old family connections were not sufficient to take advantage of legislative change, Lachlan Murdoch's attempt to acquire the Channel Ten Network, which had had a storied connection with the family's business of many decades, failed and

Ten became a subsidiary of CBS, its largest creditor, and later part of ViacomCBS's international division, which also owned Britain's Channel Five (Burrowes, 2021).

Communications and media policy have always been shaped by outsized personalities ready to charm but also willing to flex their muscles; a pattern that continued even as the former family businesses became more corporatised. This reality made it hard even for the digital behemoths – Google and Facebook (now Meta) – which had remade the global communications sector in their own image, to bend the policy environment to their liking. Over the previous decade, the business models of the old oligopoly had been existentially challenged. The digital newcomers were operating with almost no regulatory constraints and were reshaping the economics of the cultural milieu. In one exercise of communications policy brinkmanship, the Morrison Government stared down the newcomers, which had decimated the local industry by drawing the nation's eyeballs and taking most advertising, and in the process decimating thousands of jobs in journalism; for decades, they had enjoyed eyewatering profitability. The News Media Bargaining Code developed by the Australian Competition and Consumer Commission (ACCC) resulted in a transfer of an estimated $200 million from Google and Facebook to local media companies. The digital operators resisted the move, fearful that it might establish a precedent requiring them to pay for local content globally, but as media commentator Tim Burrowes (2021) wrote, the government had delivered for the locals 'a grubby, imperfect deal that had involved the Australian government running a shakedown on big tech'.

The Turnbull Government had recognised the threat to local industry and the public interest journalism that was integral to the political system. In December 2017, Treasurer Scott Morrison had commissioned the ACCC to investigate 'whether [the digital] platforms are exercising market power in commercial dealings to the detriment of consumers, media content creators and advertisers' (Schultz, 2019). The inquiry had been given a tight timeline and an expansive brief. It was conducted as global concern about the corrosive effects of the enormously profitable digital platforms on democratic systems engaged politicians, policy makers and civil society groups in Australia and around the world.

The ACCC delivered its 623-page *Digital Platforms Inquiry* to Treasurer Josh Frydenberg in June 2019. It documented the economy-wide effects of the digitised information services of the two leading digital platforms and the extent of their disruption and market dominance. In 2019 alone, Facebook had earned revenues of $674 million in Australia and had paid just $13.5 million in local tax, while Google had earned $5.2 billion and had paid $49 million in tax (Chenoweth, 2020). In addition to the transformative services the platforms were providing, they had also enabled the proliferation of misinformation and disinformation. The ACCC found that the loss of readers and advertising revenue for the traditional media companies had also contributed to a significant reduction in public-interest journalism. The ACCC has traditionally been reluctant to regulate 'content' issues, but in this report it stepped beyond the commercial effects of the digital disruption, concluding that:

> While public interest journalism contributes to a healthy democracy, disinformation and misinformation does the opposite. To the degree that online consumption makes it harder for public interest journalism to reach audiences, but easier for disinformation and misinformation to do so, this is clearly a significant public policy concern. (ACCC, 2019)

The following April, the ACCC was directed by Ministers Fletcher and Frydenberg to:

> … develop a mandatory code to address commercial arrangements between digital platforms and news media businesses. Among the elements the code will cover include the sharing of data, ranking and display of news content and the monetisation and the sharing of revenue generated from news. The mandatory code will also establish appropriate enforcement, penalty and binding dispute resolution mechanisms. (Fletcher & Frydenberg, 2020)

The aim was to compensate media companies for the loss of audience and revenue in the aggregation of their content on third-party platforms, which was promoted by search engines and shared on social media. The business model of these platforms assumed that they would not pay for the content they located and enabled users to share. The ACCC's News Media Bargaining Code, released in February 2021, was designed to force the platform operators to reach an agreement with the media companies that had originated much of this news content.

The threat of creating an international precedent motivated the fierce opposition by Google and Facebook. But Google eventually agreed to negotiate; it offered financial support to publishers, in a move dressed up as a new product, Google Showcase. In February 2021 the first deal was signed between Google and Seven West, for an estimated $30 million a year. Other substantial deals soon followed with Nine Entertainment, News Corp, the *Guardian*, the Australian Broadcasting Corporation (ABC) and other major publishers – as well as with a dozen smaller enterprises. In the statements welcoming the agreements, the publishers made it clear that the hand of cards the government held had forced the deal. Kerry Stokes described the government's role as 'instrumental in the ground-breaking agreement' (Burrowes, 2021).

Facebook continued to resist the code. The day after Nine Entertainment signed a letter of intent with Google, on 17 February 2021, Facebook removed from its platform all content from every Australian news source. Any Facebook user attempting to share a link to a news item received an error message. Rather than advancing its case, Facebook was now seen as a bully, locally and abroad. Within a week, following direct negotiations between Treasurer Josh Frydenberg and Facebook's founder Mark Zuckerberg, an agreement was reached. The period for negotiation was extended and the likelihood of mandatory arbitration reduced. As Tim Burrowes (2021) reports, 'in little more than a month Google and Facebook had agreed to spend something like $250 million per year subsidising Australian news'. Robert Thomson, CEO of News Corp, was effusive in his praise for the treasurer, who had come to the rescue of Rupert and Lachlan Murdoch in their 'quixotic quest' to enhance journalism and society (Schultz, 2022).

All the agreements were confidential. There was no monitoring of the nature and scale of the journalism facilitated by the code, no tally of jobs created nor any assessment of a resulting increase in public-interest journalism. When announcing News Corps' annual results, Robert Thomson said that the negotiations would add a nine-figure sum to the corporation's balance sheet. Critics complained that it was a politically enforced gift to the major media companies, but the advocates argued that it had bolstered the standing of an important industry, despite the Special Broadcasting Service (SBS), *The Conversation* and some other smaller organisations being excluded from the code (Sims, 2022).

There is no doubt that the media companies play a significant institutional role in Australia's political and cultural systems, but the protection of the status quo embodied in this policy was striking.

Making of a minister

Paul Fletcher, who had lost to Morrison in the Liberal Party's contest for preselection for the southern Sydney seat of Cook in 2007, was in many ways the communications minister from central casting. Fittingly for a minister also responsible for the arts, he is married to a jewellery designer. The Member for Bradfield since 2009 had joined the Young Liberals at age 16 and had commenced an active life in politics while studying at the University of Sydney, when the neoliberal agenda had begun to challenge the status quo. This made sense to the outstanding student of law and economics. Fletcher had served as a senior adviser to the Coalition's most forceful communications ministers and later to High Commissioner to London and Liberal Party president, Richard Alston. Fletcher is the author of two books about the challenges of the internet age and has worked as head of corporate and regulatory affairs at the Singapore Telecommunications-owned Optus, the telecommunications company that grew to challenge the Telstra monopoly after the national carrier was privatised. By the time he became Minister for Communications, the department once again had oversight of the arts, as well as added responsibility for cybersecurity, urban infrastructure, and cities.

Alston was Communications Minister from 1996 to 2003. Under his administration, Telstra was privatised, digital television broadcasting commenced and, despite two attempts, the laws that restricted what media companies could own were not revoked (*The Age*, 2003). Under Alston's leadership in the Howard Government, the biggest cuts in the ABC's history were meted out, editorial complaints from the government proliferated and became an art form, and the ABC's Board came to resemble what one director once described to me as 'a dysfunctional Liberal Party branch'. Privatisation of the ABC was politically untenable, but as party president Alston was quick to question the purpose of public broadcasting. In 2018, the Liberal Party Council voted overwhelmingly to support the privatisation of the national public broadcaster, leaving ministers to scramble and assert that the party's policy was not shared by the government (Crowe, 2018).

Under Alston's stewardship of the portfolio, digital broadcasting was introduced, and the analogue spectrum sold. There were no surprises: the model of digital broadcasting legislated at the time entrenched the power of the major television companies. At the beginning of the century, the families that had dominated the industry for generations had remained active, ready to charm and bully to achieve their desired outcomes, so the seamless transfer of the digital spectrum was expected. It was contested by those who had missed out, including Foxtel and News Corp, which at the time were restricted by the legislative restrictions on cross-media ownership from owning free-to-air television, but the status quo was maintained.

Two decades on, when Alston's former chief of staff became the minister, the communications policy environment had profoundly changed. The uncertainty about what the emerging digital environment might look like at the beginning of the century had given way to a new reality, one in which the digital platforms reached into every area of citizens' lives, broadband connectivity was an essential, no longer a luxury, traditional sources of news were under threat, the number of secure jobs in journalism and other creative sectors had diminished, and the NBN, which the Coalition had once opposed, had become integral to national life and the communications ecosystem. During the pandemic, when people worked from home, saw their doctors by telehealth and home-schooled their children, fast and reliable broadband became an essential service.

Paul Fletcher's agenda had its roots in the old order of communications policy. In February 2019, in an attempt to signal a less-combative relationship with the national broadcaster, Prime Minister Morrison appointed Ita Buttrose as the Chair of the ABC. In doing this he exercised the traditional authority of the prime minister to appoint a chair to the ABC's Board and ignored the men who had been recommended by an independent expert panel. It was a classic Morrison play. He had a closer eye on the symbolism of appointing an icon of Australian journalism and public life to the coveted role than on the substance of her hardwired commitment to ABC independence.

Although the relationship between the ABC and Canberra was not as combative as it had been under previous Liberal governments, it was not without tensions. In a lesson that could, for instance, have been drawn from the Richard Alston playbook, Fletcher launched a heated complaint about the ABC program *Four Corners*. On 1 December 2020, Fletcher published on Twitter a long letter demanding that the ABC Board answer 15 questions about a November *Four Corners* program that had focused on sexually inappropriate behaviour by two fellow Cabinet ministers, Christian Porter and Alan Tudge (ABC, 2020). Ita Buttrose, as Chair of the ABC, reacted strongly and made it clear that she expected the courtesy of confidentiality to be respected. As it transpired, the *Four Corners* program was a bellwether for an issue that would dog the government for the rest of its term.

In some ways, the questions raised by the *Four Corners* program and in other forums about the treatment of women in parliament and beyond was an unlikely subject to define the Morrison Government. The overwhelming issue, one that shook society to its bones, was the COVID-19 pandemic and the government's response to it. Only months after it first became clear that the virus, which had started its migration in central China and soon winged its way around the world, had lethal potential, the Morrison Government began to adopt unprecedented measures to keep people at home, support businesses and close national borders.

On 15 April 2020, Paul Fletcher announced a substantial support package to 'help sustain Australian media businesses as they do their vital work of keeping the community informed during the pandemic' (Fletcher, 2020). This included waiving the spectrum tax for commercial radio and television broadcasters for a year, saving them more than $43 million dollars in 'red tape relief', which translated into suspension of Australian content quotas for drama and children's television; an additional $13.4 million to bring regional news content funding up to $50 million; an additional $50 million to take to $300 million funding for film production; $400 million in local incentives for international screen producers (announced as jobs for carpenters and other tradies rather than as an investment in cultural creation); $150 million for the NBN; an additional $10 million for Foxtel to increase its coverage of women's sport; $50 million in tax offsets for computer games; and over two years more than $120 million in JobKeeper support for the ASX-listed media companies alone – of which only $15 million was repaid, substantially by Nine Entertainment.

This level of support for the media sector was not unique, but it highlighted the areas of greatest political sensitivity – notably the level of licence fees charged to the broadcasters for use of the public spectrum, at the same time that other parts of the spectrum were being auctioned for limited time frames for billions of dollars. The broadcasters were always ready to argue that they should not be charged what had been restyled as a spectrum and transmission tax, that as a free service they were a public good and one that was no longer able to recoup costs from advertising to the same degree as in the past (although the business still depended on the use of a public resource). The minister signalled that he had recognised this when relaxing the local-content rules, arguing that the broadcasters were now forced to compete with unregulated, paid subscription television platforms, including Netflix, Amazon Prime, Paramount Plus and others. Scarcity was no longer the organising principle of broadcasting content regulation, but the danger of national cultural identity – Australian stories – being swamped by international producers was one close to the hearts of many.

The impact on children's television after the new standards came into force in January 2021 was most dramatic. Its demise was a marked departure from past policy where children's television sat at the heart of local content guidelines, designed to ensure that Australian children had access to recognisable local stories, and to support the local production industry. According to Screen Australia, in 2021/22 only 39 hours of children's television were produced compared with 182 hours three years earlier. Over the year the free-to-air commercial broadcasters transmitted less than 100 hours of children's programs, whereas under the previous guidelines they had been required to annually broadcast 260 hours, half original local content, and at least 130 hours of pre-school programming. The loss was not compensated by the streaming companies, which have no local content requirements (Meade, 2022).

In recognition of this changed context, a Green Paper investigating the future of broadcasting regulation began its slow process through the bureaucracy in 2020. This paper considered local-content obligations, the prospect of compression technologies to release more of the broadcast spectrum for sale to telecommunications and other operators, and mandatory access to free-to-air networks on smart televisions, simplifying broadcasting legislation and licensing fees, among other issues. When the Green Paper was released in early 2022, the major broadcasters were scathing in their criticism, but by the time the Future of Broadcasting Working Group met in April they were more conciliatory. Three days later, the writs for the federal election were issued and the Green Paper process came to a halt. The status quo was maintained, and with it the point of the Morrison Government.

References

ABC (Australian Broadcasting Corporation). 'Inside the Canberra Bubble', *4 Corners*, 9 November 2020.

ACCC (Australian Competition and Consumer Commission). *Digital Platforms Inquiry*, June 2019, <www.accc.gov.au/system/files/Digital%20platforms%20inquiry%20-%20final%20report.pdf>.

ACMA (Australian Communications and Media Authority), *News in Australia: Diversity and Localism*, December 2020, pp. 3–4.

Age, The. 'A momentous decision made for family reasons', 13 September 2003.

Burrowes, Tim. *Media Unmade*, Hardie Grant, 2021.

Chenoweth, Neil. 'Google Facebook $6 billion tax break', *Australian Financial Review*, 4 September 2020, <www.afr.com/companies/media-and-marketing/google-facebook-s-6b-tax-break-20200904-p55sc3>.

Crowe, David. 'Liberal party council votes to sell off ABC', *Sydney Morning Herald*, 16 June 2018.

Fletcher, Paul. 'Immediate COVID-19 relief for Australian media as harmonisation reform process also kicks off' (media release), 15 April 2020, <www.paulfletcher.com.au/media-releases/media-relase-immediate-covid-19-relief-for-australian-media-as-harmonisation-reform>.

Fletcher, Paul and Josh Frydenberg. Joint Media Release ACCC Mandatory Code, 20 April 2020, <www.paulfletcher.com.au/media-releases/joint-media-release-accc-mandatory-code-of-conduct-to-govern-the-commercial>.

Hirst, Daniel. 'Kevin Rudd says Australian politicians "frightened" of "Murdoch media beast" in Senate inquiry', *Guardian*, 19 February 2021, <www.theguardian.com/australia-news/2021/feb/19/kevin-rudd-says-australian-politicians-frightened-of-murdoch-media-beast-in-senate-inquiry>.

House of Representatives. Broadcasting Legislation Amendment (Broadcasting Reform) Bill, 2017, <www.aph.gov.au/Parliamentary_Business/Bills_Legislation/Bills_Search_Results/Result?bId=r5907#:~:text=Introduced%20with%20the%20Commercial%20Broadcasting,per%20cent%20of%20the%20Australian>.

Kunczik, Michael. *Concepts of Journalism*, FES, Bonn, 1989.

Meade, Amanda. 'Australian-made children's TV all but gone from commercial free-to-air networks', *Guardian*, 22 August 2022, <www.theguardian.com/media/2022/aug/22/australian-made-childrens-tv-all-but-gone-on-commercial-free-to-air-networks>.

RMIT ABC Fact Check. 'How large is Rupert Murdoch's reach through News Corp in Australian media, old and new?', *ABC News*, 14 April 2021, <www.abc.net.au/news/2021-04-14/fact-file-rupert-murdoch-media-reach-in-australia/100056660>.

Schultz, Julianne. *Reviving the Fourth Estate*, Cambridge University Press, 1998.

— 'Move very fast and break things', in *Griffith Review* 64, ed Ashley Hay, *The New Disruptors*, ed Ashley Hay, 2019, pp. 11–27.

— 'Disrupting Media and Politics', in *Oxford Handbook to Australian Politics*, ed Jenny M Lewis and Anne Tiernan, Oxford University Press, 2021, pp. 356–376.

— *Idea of Australia*, Allen & Unwin, 2022.

Screen Australia, Australian Children's TV Drama Report, 2022, <www.screenaustralia.gov.au/fact-finders/production-trends/tv-drama-production/childrens-tv-drama>.

Sims, Rod. *Instruments and Objectives: Explaining the News Media Bargaining Code*, Judith Neilson Institute, 2022.

Snow, Deborah. 'Nothing off limits: Scott Morrison on his bruising years as Prime Minister', *Sydney Morning Herald*, 15 January 2022, <www.smh.com.au/national/nothing-off-limits-scott-morrison-on-his-bruising-years-as-prime-minister-20220112-p59nr1.html>.

Young, Sally. *Paper Emperors*, UNSW Press, 2019.

16

THE ARTS AND CULTURE SECTOR UNDER THE 46TH PARLIAMENT: CRISIS AFTER CRISIS

Tully Barnett, Julian Meyrick
and Justin O'Connor

The 46th Parliament saw yet another difficult election cycle for the arts. The COVID-19 pandemic affected this, but successive weakening of the sector through defunding, efficiency dividends and the undermining of the formal and informal structures of the principles of cultural provision meant that the sector was less able to withstand or respond to government decisions.

Scott Morrison served as prime minister for the last nine months of the 45th Parliament, with Mitch Fifield serving as minister for the arts. Morrison had replaced Malcolm Turnbull, whose record on the arts, while not as antagonistic as Tony Abbott's, did not undo the damage to the cultural sector already inflicted in the Abbott years. At the outset of the 46th Parliament, Paul Fletcher was given the role of minister for communications, cybersafety and the arts. Before that first year was out, the government had signalled its real view of the arts: a reshuffle in December 2019 saw the ministry merged into a Department of Infrastructure, Transport, Regional Development and Communications, the portfolio becoming the Office for the Arts in a new mega-department. The demotion did not go unnoticed in the sector (McIllroy, 2019). The relationship between the arts minister, the Office for the Arts and the Australia Council came under scrutiny as the pattern of successive funding cuts to the operational budget of the Australia Council and that of the Australian Broadcasting Corporation continued.

Less than a year into the 46th Parliament, the COVID-19 pandemic began. It would be easy to confuse the ongoing problems the arts sector faced during the Morrison Government's tenure with the fallout from the pandemic that began in early 2020. Certainly, the health crisis had an immeasurable effect on arts sectors around the world, which were especially vulnerable to the pandemic, being the first to close and the last to reopen. Media commentary and academic research on the effects of COVID-19 have come to overshadow almost everything else that happened to the arts in this period (Caust, 2020). This will most likely continue for some time.

Yet it is important not to underestimate the deteriorated state of the sector when the pandemic occurred, the policy decisions that had caused or failed to halt that deterioration, and the weakening of the sector's capacity to withstand the shock of repeated lockdowns. The federal government's relentless disparagement of the sector from the 44th Parliament onwards, the lack of coherent national cultural policy initiatives, the undermining of the role and capacity of the Australia Council and the politicisation of arts governance and the distribution of funding – in addition to the net reduction in funding – meant that when the health crisis hit, the consequences were all the more damaging.

Some backstory

Fletcher took over as minister for the arts in 2019 (Fletcher, 2019). Like George Brandis, who held the role in the 44th Parliament, Fletcher had a very modest arts background, having tried his hand at theatre during his university days with collaborators who went on to senior roles in film and television. 'Lapsed playwright in charge' ran the headline (Hunter & Samios, 2020). Still reeling from Brandis's cuts to the arts budget and damage to the principle of arms-length funding in 2014 and 2015, and from Mitch Fifield's antipathy ('no time to attend arts events'), the sector saw Fletcher as a better option. But still no substantial policy was forthcoming. The sector remained neglected until the government's pandemic response through the Restart Investment to Sustain and Expand (RISE) funding scheme in 2020, which had a positive effect despite numerous problems in its framing and rollout. The 2019 Budget, which was released as Morrison's first as prime minister, a month before the 2019 election, had largely ignored the arts. The next Budget was delayed because of COVID-19, until October 2020. It was described as 'thumb[ing] its nose at Australia's arts and creative industries' (Dow, 2020). After nearly 20 years, the Australian Major Performing Arts Group (AMPAG), the umbrella group representing 28 companies given 'major performing arts company' status and supported as such, was abolished. How the new National Performing Arts Partnership Framework (NPAPF), launched in 2019, will play out is unknown. Replacing the Major Performing Arts (MPA) Framework, it has undertaken to expand the number of companies supported through the Australia Council's ever-diminishing annual allocation.

Artists and the JobKeeper scheme

While some artists were supported by the JobKeeper scheme as it was originally designed, a large percentage was ineligible, as portfolio and gig-economy careers were becoming the main means of organising labour in the cultural sector:

> JobKeeper ... offered eligible applicants a fortnightly payment of $1500 (AUD) to support businesses and their employees during the initial shutdown of May 2020 to March 2021 ... To qualify for the payment, individuals needed to be employed in full-time or casual work; casual workers needed to be employed for a minimum of twelve months by a single employer, while business owners (who were to pass the payment on to workers) had to demonstrate an economic downturn of thirty per cent or more. Sole traders could apply as a registered business if they met the relevant criteria. People employed on short-term contracts (less than twelve months) or freelancers who perform piecemeal work or earn an income through numerous employers were ineligible for the scheme. (Nelligan & Nelligan, 2021)

In May 2020, the main union for the sector, the Media, Entertainment and Arts Alliance (MEAA), suggested that 35 per cent of the sector had been cut adrift (Morrow & Long, 2020). Though governments worldwide had failed to adequately address the needs of the cultural sector, the Morrison Government repeatedly refused to amend the JobKeeper scheme, giving rise to suspicions – as with the university sector – that this was less an oversight than a deliberate choice (Pacella et al, 2021).

In June 2020, the Morrison Government announced the RISE fund: a relief package for the arts and culture sector of $250 million. It was launched by the prime minister, who claimed the scheme was designed to 'help restart the creative economy and get the entertainment, arts and screen sectors back to work' (Morrison & Fletcher, 2020). A joint media release by Morrison and Fletcher included the now much picked-over words: 'This package is as much about supporting the tradies who build stage sets or computer specialists who create the latest special effects, as it is about supporting actors and performers in major productions' (Morrison & Fletcher, 2020). Even while acknowledging that the sector 'was one of the first sectors to be impacted by COVID-19 and will be one of the last to come out of hibernation as social distancing restrictions are eased', the case had to be made that funding for the arts was not really about supporting artists. RISE included seed investment, loans, insurance support, direct funding for 'sector-significant organisations' and the establishment of the Creative Economy Taskforce to 'partner with the Government and the Australia Council to implement the JobMaker plan for the creative economy'. While the announcement of the program received positive responses from the sector, its rollout did not match the fancy launch, which included singer Guy Sebastian speaking alongside the prime minister and Minister Fletcher at Rooty Hill. By the time the delayed Budget was handed down in October, the government had yet to release any of the funds, and a year later Sebastian reported that he was 'embarrassed' about having been 'used as a prop for the government', with his requests for updates on the promised initiative remaining unfulfilled (Brewster, 2021).

In the last months of the 46th Parliament, in March 2022, the seventh round of RISE funding was announced. The media release said, 'Today's announcement takes to $200 million the funding that has been committed under RISE'. As Eltham and Pennington (2021) have written, the funding was slow to get through to its intended target (a common critique of the Morrison Government):

> Announced in June 2020, almost none of the so-called 'emergency' funding was spent until November, and the first batch of RISE funding contracts were not distributed until December. The first Temporary Interruption Fund projects were not funded until September. $35 million provided for the Australia Council's Arts Sustainability Fund was particularly slow to flow – only $16 million had been allocated by May 2021.

In the lead-up to the 2022 election, Fletcher reflected on the effect of RISE funding to date: 'So far, $200 million has been committed under RISE', he wrote in *Limelight* magazine. 'It has gone to 541 projects, creating more than 213 000 jobs across Australia, to be seen by a total audience of 55 million people' (Robertson, 2021). Fletcher pointed to the Arts Sustainability Fund, which was aimed at the major organisations or, as he put it, the 'systemically important arts organisations' and to the Temporary Interruption Fund for film and television production, the Location Incentive Fund and the recurring funding to Australia Council and Screen Australia. To justify this support, Fletcher underscored first the economic importance of the cultural sector, followed by its 'intrinsic' value.

Parliamentary Inquiry into the arts

In August 2020, Minister Paul Fletcher asked the House of Representatives Standing Committee on Communications and the Arts to initiate an inquiry into Australia's creative and cultural industries and institutions. The terms of reference for the inquiry were:

- The direct and indirect economic benefits and employment opportunities of creative and cultural industries and how to recognise, measure and grow them;

- The non-economic benefits that enhance community, social wellbeing and promoting Australia's national identity, and how to recognise, measure and grow them;
- The best mechanism for ensuring cooperation and delivery of policy between layers of government;
- The impact of COVID-19 on the creative and cultural industries; and
- Avenues for increasing access and opportunities for Australia's creative and cultural industries through innovation and the digital environment (House of Representatives Standing Committee on Communications and the Arts, 2021).

Only one reference dealt specifically with the COVID-19 pandemic, indicating awareness that the sector's distress went beyond the pandemic. In fact, most of the inquiry's recommendations involved repairing the effects of years of neglect on the sector and restoring some measure of recognition within public policy, such as explicitly naming the arts in the department's title.

The inquiry received 352 submissions from artists, arts organisations, state government agencies, local government, academics and interested individuals, and representing all art forms. The submissions reveal the sector's complex reaction to both the COVID-19 crisis and three antagonistic Coalition governments. Four hearings were held, from November 2020 to February 2021, with detailed testimonies from a representative selection of the sector. The standing committee conducting the inquiry included members from the Liberal Party, National Party and Labor Party. The inquiry's 227-page report, *Sculpting a National Cultural Plan: Igniting a post-COVID Economy for the Arts* was handed down in October 2021 (House of Representatives Standing Committee on Communications and the Arts, 2021).

The report made 22 recommendations, including the development of a 'national cultural plan' and that the role of growing the cultural and creative industries should work at all levels of government as well as in rural, regional and remote areas. Recommendations were made for a national centre for Indigenous arts and culture co-designed by stakeholders with Office for the Arts support, quotas for Australian content and for local children's content, and internships for the cultural sector in cooperation with the tertiary sector and the Department of Education, Skills and Employment. There was also support for ensuring the Australian Curriculum contains a minimum threshold of Australian authors. Support for digitisation in the National Archives and the National Film and Sound Archive was sought. The standing committee recommended that the arts be listed as a fourth cross-curriculum priority in the Education Ministers Meeting (a meeting of the national, state and territory education ministers and departments). Similarly, the need for access to music education and access to instrument hire was highlighted. Recommendation 15 sought the return in capacity of the Australian Bureau of Statistics to undertake analysis of the Cultural and Creative Satellite Account to provide data on the cultural sector. Recommendation 4 sought to return the term 'Arts' to the department's name. Funding for the ABC and the Australia Council was noticeable only by its absence from the report (noted, however, in Labor's minority report).

There was also a recommendation for a Productivity Commission inquiry to consider 'arrangements which govern funding of artistic programs'. Buried deep in the inquiry's recommendations, it shows how deeply conflicted and confused arts policy is in Australia. On the one hand, it is promoted as an economic sector, vaguely lumped into a shape-shifting entity called 'cultural and creative industries' and, on the other, as something with 'intrinsic' value that could only be elusive to the market-first principles of the Productivity Commission, and which the report could only name negatively as 'non-economic' (Meyrick & O'Connor, 2021).

Business as usual

During this term, the Morrison Government also undermined the arts and culture sector through the Job-ready Graduates Package, which requires tertiary students to pay more to undertake creative arts degrees than degrees in other disciplines. This, too, was purportedly based on the economic value of such degrees, both to the individual recipient and to the 'economy' writ large (Meyrick, 2021).

On the other hand, much was made of First Nations arts, with the 46th Parliament including a 'Consultation Paper on Growing the Indigenous

Visual Arts Industry', and the Australia Council report *Protocols for Using First Nations Cultural and Intellectual Property in the Arts* also announced in 2020. Alongside these, around $50 million over four years was allocated to the 250th anniversary of Captain Cook's voyage. A budget contributed to over successive Coalition governments may be forgotten because of the ephemeral nature of the programming, but the Australian War Memorial, that other controversial marker, will leave a permanent reminder of the lack of balance in arts and cultural funding. Although they imposed successive efficiency dividends on the national cultural and collecting institutions, Coalition governments nevertheless allocated an eyewatering $498 million over ten years for the major expansion of the Australian War Memorial. As late as March 2022, the Morrison Government found an extra $50 million for the project, to meet rising construction and management costs. It's the rest of the sector that has funded this additional cost.

While the final budget of the 46th Parliament announced another round of RISE money, the cuts to the arts were deep. The Arts and Cultural Development Program fund was reduced from $159 million to $20 million (with the forward estimates cutting it to $2.4 million); regional arts were cut from $18 million to $7 million; Screen Australia's funding was cut from $39 million to $27 million (in the 2022–23 financial year, before falling to $11.6 million in 2023–24); and Australian Music funding was cut from $6 million to $0 in the forward estimates. Ben Eltham called the budget 'grinding austerity baked into the next three or four years' (Dow, 2022).

Perhaps the most damage, ultimately, has been to the relationship between the arts sector and the Office for the Arts, which occurred over the term of the Morrison Government. The sidelining of the Australia Council in the RISE funding process and the shift to funding more commercial projects was also worrying. In the overall context, this direct government patronage and general 'pork barrelling' look set to further undermine those intermediary organisations that are central to democratic governance, and to marginalise artists who are seen to be critical of the government.

Despite the attention attracted by the RISE funding, and especially a new round of the scheme as the Coalition Government entered a difficult election period, the March 2022 Budget showed the Morrison Government's true attitude to the arts. Support for many sections of the cultural sector was slashed, community development and regional arts in particular, with an increased emphasis on commercial projects and major organisations, and a preference for loan schemes over grant schemes. The crises of the past three years – bushfires, floods, pandemic – showed the arts sector stepping up, time and again, to assist Australians in situations of dire need: providing moral, cultural and financial support. To this contribution, the Morrison Government was, like its two predecessor governments, mostly indifferent.

Recent international comparisons of arts funding show Australia in the lowly ranking of 23 out of 34 OECD countries in support for the sector (Fielding & Trembath, 2022). In the term of the 46th Parliament, the sector was devalued further, literally and figuratively. Immediately after the election of May 2022, incoming arts Minister Tony Burke announced a consultation process for a new National Cultural Policy on a short timeline. The outcomes of this are for the future, but the submissions themselves tell the story of the Coalition Government's disastrous years of cultural policy. The ideological and political reasons for that antipathy to the arts are still not clear, and need further work, but what is clear is that, on current showing, the Liberal–National Coalition is unlikely to change this approach any time soon.

References

Brewster, Will. 'Guy Sebastian admits he was "used as a prop" by the Federal Government in bungled arts package rollout', *The Music Network*, 22 July 2021, <themusicnetwork.com/guy-sebastian-arts-package-criticism/>.

Caust, Jo. 'Coronovirus: 3 in 4 Australians employed in the creative and performing arts could lose their jobs', *The Conversation*, 20 April 2020, <theconversation.com/coronavirus-3-in-4-australians-employed-in-the-creative-and-performing-arts-could-lose-their-jobs-136505>.

Dow, Steve. 'Arts ignored in 2020–21 Federal Budget', *Limelight*, 7 October 2020, <limelightmagazine.com.au/news/arts-ignored-in-2020-2021-federal-budget/>.

— 'Budget 2022: Arts left reeling as funding slashed', *Limelight*, 30 March 2022, <limelightmagazine.com.au/news/budget-2022-arts-left-reeling-as-funding-slashed/>.

Eltham, Ben and Alison Pennington. *Creativity in Crisis: Rebooting Australia's Arts and Entertainment Sector After COVID*, Centre for Future Work, Australia Institute, 2021, <australiainstitute.org.au/report/creativity-in-crisis-rebooting-australias-arts-and-entertainment-sector-after-covid/>.

Fielding, Kate and Jodie Trembath. *The Big Picture 2: Public Expenditure on Artistic, Cultural and Creative Activity in Australia in 2007–08 to 2019–20*, Insight Report no. 2022–01, A New Approach, 2022, <newapproach.org.au/insight-reports/the-big-picture-2/>.

Fletcher, Paul. 'Fletcher "deeply honoured" to be appointed Minister for Communications, Cybersafety and the Arts' (media release), 26 May 2019, <www.paulfletcher.com.au/media-releases/media-release-fletcher-deeply-honoured-to-be-appointed-minister-for-communications>.

Hunter, Fergus and Zoe Samios. *Brisbane Times*, 1 March 2020, <www.brisbanetimes.com.au/politics/federal/a-nerd-in-charge-the-lapsed-playwright-shaping-australia-s-online-future-20200228-p545hx.html>.

House of Representatives Standing Committee on Communications and the Arts. *Sculpting a National Cultural Plan: Igniting a post-COVID Economy for the Arts*, Parliament of Australia, 2021, <www.aph.gov.au/Parliamentary_Business/Committees/House/Communications/Arts/Report>.

McIlroy, Tom. '"Arts ceases to exist": top billing lost in public service shake-up', *Australian Financial Review*, 5 December 2019, <www.afr.com/politics/federal/departments-slashed-but-even-more-public-service-changes-coming-20191205-p53h7v>.

Meyrick, Julian and Justin O'Connor. 'Slippery definitions and alarming silences: A parliamentary inquiry into the creative industries gives us a plan for a plan', *The Conversation*, 3 November 2021, <theconversation.com/slippery-definitions-and-alarming-silences-a-parliamentary-inquiry-into-the-creative-industries-gives-us-a-plan-for-a-plan-170963>.

Morrison, Scott and Paul Fletcher. '$250 million jobmaker plan to restart Australia's creative economy' (joint media release), 25 June 2020, <parlinfo.aph.gov.au/parlInfo/download/media/pressrel/7415188/upload_binary/7415188.pdf>.

Morrow, Guy and Brian Long. 'The government says artists should be able to access JobKeeper payments. It's not that simple', *The Conversation*, 26 May 2020, <theconversation.com/the-government-says-artists-should-be-able-to-access-jobkeeper-payments-its-not-that-simple-138530>.

Nelligan, Kat and Pariece Nelligan. '"It was hard before and it's even harder now": The impact of COVID-19 on Australia's live music and arts entertainment industries', *Perfect Beat*, 21(2), 2021, pp. 144–58.

Pacella, Jess, Susan Luckman and Justin O'Connor. 'Fire, pestilence and the extractive economy: Cultural policy after cultural policy', *Cultural Trends*, 30(1), 2021, pp. 40–51.

Robertson, Hugh. (2021) 'Fifth round of RISE funding sees $20 million shared by 63 organisations', *Limelight*, 7 September 2021, <limelightmagazine.com.au/news/fifth-round-of-rise-funding-sees-20-million-shared-by-63-organisations/>.

17

THE BATTLE FOR A FEDERAL INTEGRITY COMMISSION

Geoffrey Watson

It is remarkable that it has been necessary to fight to bring in a federal integrity commission. In a decent world you would think politicians would, and should, be the first to welcome the introduction of an agency that could assist in improving standards of governance and removing corruption from political decision-making. An anti-corruption body should not be an enemy of good government – it should be its ally.

Yet, experience has shown that is not the case: governments tend to resist the creation of such bodies, except in three circumstances, each a little different.

The first and most dramatic follows an eruption of corruption, requiring catharsis. The sorry story of systemic corruption in Queensland, mainly at police level but also at the political level, resulted in the Fitzgerald Inquiry and the creation of the Criminal Justice Commission in 1989. The exposure of widespread police corruption in New South Wales during the Wood Royal Commission led to the creation of the Police Integrity Commission in 1996. The exposure of organised corruption at a high political level in Western Australia – which became known as 'WA Inc.' – resulted in the creation of the Corruption and Crime Commission in 2004. These were significant events: governments fell and political leaders and police chiefs were jailed.

The second circumstance is more political, maybe even a little vengeful. It usually follows when one party has been in power for a long time. When one party has been in power too long, rumours begin to swirl and opposing parties take advantage, making campaign promises to 'clean up politics' by appointing an anti-corruption agency. There are two examples of this: the creation of the Independent Commission Against Corruption (ICAC) in New South Wales in 1988 and, to a lesser extent, the creation of the Independent Broad-based Anti-corruption Commission (IBAC) in Victoria in 2012.

The third is deeply cynical. It occurs when the integrity of a long-serving government is under question and it is at risk of losing a forthcoming election. That government then creates an agency – usually a very weak one – to fend off further criticism. The South Australian IBAC is the best example of this. There is a double benefit because history has shown that, if a new government does come in, it is unlikely to amplify those weak watchdog powers. This point is especially pertinent in this discussion.

Here I tell the story behind the politics and social pressures that have led to Australia finally getting a federal integrity commission, tracing the build-up of momentum and the growth of support. I also examine the opposition to a federal integrity commission – and how the entire proposal nearly went badly off the rails. This is not an academic or historical study; it is more a memoir from someone fortunate to have been present during most of the critical events, first as an agitator trying to build momentum, then by advising politicians of all persuasions eager to progress the issue. Nor is this a neutral account: it commences from the premise that creating a federal integrity commission is an essential step towards improving how we are governed and in restoring trust in the government.

The need for a federal anti-corruption agency

The need for a federal anti-corruption agency is not a purely domestic issue; it derives from our international obligations. In 2005, Australia became a party to the United Nations Convention against Corruption, thereby obliging us to create an independent anti-corruption agency. The continuing absence of a specialist federal agency left Australia in breach of that obligation. The World Economic Forum says corruption makes up 5 per cent of global gross domestic product (GDP) and 25 per cent of GDP on the African continent. The cost is not just economic: the World Bank estimates that between 20 per cent and 40 per cent of all development assistance to the developing world is stolen, costing thousands of human lives per day through the inability to prevent or treat simple illnesses. Some of that money passes through Australia; we should do something about it. Australia has a positive role to play in the international anti-corruption network.

Australia does have a patchwork of accountability organisations – examples include the (excellent) Australian National Audit Office (ANAO) and the (not-so-excellent) Australian Commission for Law Enforcement Integrity. But these agencies do not cover the field; they are sometimes of questionable effectiveness within their own specialty. These agencies have proved utterly ineffective in bringing politicians and the senior bureaucracy to heel. The ANAO, for example, has no enforcement powers and thus its valuable work is left to rot on a shelf. Without a federal ICAC, the only way to investigate politicians and bureaucrats is by referral to a police agency – which will never work.

Police agencies are simply not geared up to deal with this kind of crime. Public-sector corruption is, by its nature, carefully concealed. Most often it is a 'victimless' crime, in the sense that no member of the public can point to a specific harm and no member of the public is able to identify graft in defence contracts. Unpicking the crime requires knowledge of the systems and rules of federal government. Those committing the crimes know the systems and rules only too well – often they were the authors of them. To be effective, an organisation investigating public-sector corruption needs the skills and powers of compulsion that police agencies lack. An effective federal anti-corruption agency needs the kinds of powers routinely provided to a Royal Commission or to a standing commission like the National Crimes Authority. This has been known for decades and has been proved to be so on countless occasions, both here and overseas.

It is simply silly to dismiss the possibility of corruption at a federal level. In 2016, 4 per cent of federal public servants reported witnessing other public servants engaged in corrupt conduct – that means over 6000 public servants witnessed acts of corruption in a single year. Given the nature of corruption, this is likely a gross understatement of the true level of crime. Meanwhile, Transparency International (2021) shows that Australia is in a decade-long slide in perceived corruption, down from seventh lowest in the world in 2012 to 18th lowest in 2021. Polling demonstrates that only 15 per cent of us trust our politicians and 85 per cent believe there is some corruption at the federal level. We need a federal agency to help turn these perceptions around.

The pressure builds for a federal commission

All of that is a prelude to recounting the recent history leading to the creation of a federal integrity commission under the Albanese Government.

There were calls to create a federal agency for decades, at least since the creation of an ICAC in New South Wales in 1988. At first, such calls were weak and rare, but they grew stronger after the various agencies – especially those in New South Wales, Queensland and Western Australia – began to prove effective in exposing corruption. There was new dynamism when David Ipp took control of the New South Wales ICAC in 2009 – high-level government corruption was exposed and heads began to roll. The prosecution of those involved in corruption, often senior people, assisted in getting public support. In a strange sense, Brian Burke, Jack Herbert, (Sir) Terry Lewis and Eddie Obeid did each eventually provide a service to the public.

Pressure also began to build after it was identified that well-designed Royal Commissions could expose problems, find the truth and call the rich and powerful to answer for their crimes. The Royal Commission into Institutional Child Abuse (2013) is the most obvious example – it publicly aired dirty secrets; brought justice to ordinary Australians; and developed a plan to prevent these horrors happening again. The Banking Royal Commission was similarly effective and similarly devastating. The public could see and feel the positive effect of an open investigation and inquiry.

All of these matters were important around Australia, yet it was an inquiry overseas that proved the most influential. In 2011, the British Government appointed the Leveson Inquiry to investigate how news organisations had been 'hacking' private telephone accounts belonging to ordinary people, including victims of serious crimes. It was then discovered that one news organisation was stealing private information from some of Britain's most public persons.

During the Leveson Inquiry, the most powerful and wealthy in Britain were compelled to give public evidence. The effect was amplified because the proceedings were televised – proving that the more open the inquiry, the more powerful its effect. Lords and Ladies and four former prime ministers gave evidence. But the key witness was the head of the offending news organisation – Rupert Murdoch. It was compelling television: Murdoch said out loud: 'This is the most humble day of my life'.

It was powerful to watch a class of persons, many of whom thought they were above or beyond the reach of the law, brought to heel; a demonstration of the power of these kinds of investigative bodies. It may also have given Murdoch a distaste for such inquiries, because, ever since, his media outlets have been the loudest and most consistent opponents of creating a federal integrity commission in Australia.

Hesitation and opposition

Although publicly popular, it proved difficult to persuade politicians of the desirability of creating a federal integrity commission. Some were all for the idea – in the House of Representatives there were independents like Victorian MP Cathy McGowan and her successor, Helen Haines, and Andrew Wilkie from Tasmania. In the Senate there was strong support from Jacqui Lambie from Tasmania and Rex Patrick from South Australia. All of the Greens *demanded* a federal ICAC. But a few right-minded crossbenchers cannot push legislation through the parliament. It was necessary to gain the attention of at least one of the major parties.

The position within the Labor Party was complex. There was an abiding scepticism in Labor. Various members reflected upon the use of similar powers adversely with respect to Kevin Rudd in the Pink Batts Royal Commission, and the attacks on Julia Gillard and Bill Shorten during the Building Royal Commission. With some justification, Labor thought that each of those royal commissions had only been appointed to achieve political payback. There were also dark memories of the Murdoch press tailing and portraying Greg Combet and George Campbell in an adverse light, even though the two had only been witnesses at a New South Wales ICAC inquiry and had not been alleged to have engaged in any misconduct.

Over time, the federal Labor party came around, with Mark Dreyfus QC playing a crucial role. Dreyfus had been attorney-general in the previous Labor government, and shadow attorney after that. He had been a powerful legal figure before entering politics; a Queen's Counsel who had appeared in numerous serious cases, including in the High Court. During repeated meetings with leading Labor figures, Dreyfus put the case for an agency with the skills of a forceful advocate.

Another crucial event occurred in 2017, when a major conference in Canberra called for the creation of a federal agency. The occasion was well attended by politicians, bureaucrats and anti-corruption experts from around Australia. Dreyfus was one of the keynote speakers. The result was unanimous: everyone wanted a federal commission. Supporters included the Law Council of Australia and the Council for Civil Liberties. To say that all speakers supported the creation of a federal agency, it should be qualified that it was difficult to find a spokesperson willing to state the opposing view in a public forum. The conference received widespread coverage on television, radio and in the newspapers.

Since 2017, the idea of a federal anti-corruption agency has *always* been in the news. Polling undertaken from then until now has consistently shown that the creation of a federal agency is popular: results repeatedly demonstrated that more than 80 per cent of those polled wanted one – a proportion comparable to the support for gun controls after the Port Arthur tragedy. The creation of such an agency had become a national issue.

Labor came around to supporting the establishment of a federal commission. There was a crucial meeting in late 2017 involving several experts and the leader of the opposition, Bill Shorten. I was not present, but the meeting has become part of the folklore. Shorten expressed his hesitation, scarred as he was from his own experience. At this stage, David Ipp was unleashed. He had retired from the New South Wales ICAC, had a powerful personality and was at his most emphatic and demanding that day. By the end of the meeting Shorten announced that he had been persuaded there was a need for a strong and independent federal agency.

In January 2018, Shorten committed Labor to a federal integrity commission if the party won the following federal election. In a speech to the National Press Club, he described restoring public confidence in governance as 'bigger than me versus Malcolm [Turnbull], bigger than Labor versus Liberal'.

Turnbull may have agreed with Shorten, but we will never know because Turnbull was deposed as prime minister in August 2018 and replaced by a pragmatic political journeyman, Scott Morrison. The Coalition's position on a federal integrity commission remained confusing and unsteady.

The principal opponent – the Murdoch press

While the Coalition dithered over the integrity commission, one powerful body clearly staked its implacable opposition – the Murdoch press.

From about 2012 the Murdoch press waged a concerted campaign to oppose integrity investigations, mainly directed at the New South Wales ICAC. It began when the ICAC examined matters involving the former minister Eddie Obeid, and it heated up when the ICAC investigated election funding malpractices in the Liberal Party. Several Murdoch commentators took a common line, rehearsing precisely the same arguments. There were also puff-piece interviews with Eddie Obeid and his family, and wealthy businessmen (ultimately found to have conducted themselves corruptly) were described as 'victims'. The ICAC was repeatedly called a 'Star Chamber' (the comparison with the historical Star Chamber was laughably inapt; the principal complaint about the Star Chamber was that it had conducted its hearings in secret) or a 'kangaroo court'. There were countless references to 'the Greiner affair', which were embarrassingly misleading.[1] The campaign was highly repetitive, week after week, boring and a little unhinged.

The attacks were not principled: they were personally abusive. When, in 2020, a group of eminent retired judges called for the creation of an effective national integrity commission they were labelled by *The Australian* as a 'gaggle of disgraceful extremists'. More recently, when another group of eminent judges expressed support for such a commission, it was suggested in *The Australian* that they had only done so because they were seeking post-retirement appointments from an incoming Labor government. Some of these 'disgraceful extremists' were former High Court judges.

The Murdoch press probably had little public impact. Very few Australians were reading these attacks in the Murdoch press (some of the articles abused the author of this chapter, who found them so repetitive and boring that even he could not finish them). But the Murdoch stance did have two effects. The first was that it provided talking points for Coalition politicians opposed to the creation of a federal agency. The second was that, given the close connection between the Coalition and the Murdoch press, it probably cowed some Coalition politicians from taking an independent view.

It is difficult to identify a motive for the opposition from the Murdoch press, although it is hard to resist recalling that day in 2011 which Rupert Murdoch said was the 'most humble' of his life.

Battle lines are erased – the promises made in 2019

Polling demonstrated that Labor's promise, if elected, to introduce a federal integrity commission, was popular. The position adopted by the Coalition, and even within the Coalition parties, was confused. Initially, in response to Labor's policy, the response was implacably negative, then mildly negative, then genuinely ambiguous, until the Coalition made its own election promise with the same intent. The Coalition's position resembled the Kübler-Ross five stages of grief: first denial, then anger, bargaining, depression and, finally, acceptance.

The denial phase was long held but might best be reflected in the rather naïve statement in 2014 by then-prime minister Tony Abbott, who dismissed the need for a federal ICAC because he thought Canberra was 'a pretty clean polity'. I say naïve because no serious thinker could imagine that corruption somehow declines to cross borders. In any event, this was not the only basis for Abbott saying a federal ICAC was unnecessary. He also said that it would be far too costly – which is odd, given that at the time he had just ploughed a considerable sum of money into creating an Independent Scientific Committee on Wind Turbines and a National Wind Farm Commissioner.

The other stages can be traced through Morrison's contortions before the 2019 election. The anger stage was reflected in Morrison's rejection of the need for a federal ICAC; he pointed to the experience of the state bodies, describing those organisations as 'kangaroo courts'. He said they had become forums for 'self-serving mudslinging', and that their investigations involved 'the pursuit of personal, corporate and political vendettas'. Morrison, who only ever had a shaky hold of history, might not have been so emphatic had he known that nearly all the agencies around Australia had been established by Liberal governments.

Although he did not like it, in the face of polling showing the popularity of an integrity commission, it was inevitable that Morrison would need to introduce a federal body. That was when he started his bargaining. Kübler-Ross's final stage – acceptance – came in December 2018, when Morrison cracked: he changed completely and promised a 'serious new commission with teeth'. He apparently realised that what he had described as 'mudslinging' was, in fact, essential to good government. So the battlelines in the 2019 election were erased – each of the principal contenders was entering the election campaign with a similar policy, promising the introduction of a powerful federal integrity commission.

Contrary to expectation, the Coalition won the 2019 federal election. The issue then became whether Morrison would deliver on his promise in respect of a federal ICAC. He did not. I had never believed he would.

Christian Porter's National Integrity Commission Bill

In 2017, in a Cabinet reshuffle, Turnbull appointed Christian Porter as attorney-general. Porter was an ambitious, up-and-coming political powerbroker from Western Australia. Porter kept his position as attorney under Morrison and was re-appointed following the 2019 election victory. One of his tasks in the new parliament was, presumably, to fulfil the election promise to create a federal anti-corruption agency body. He did not – but what he attempted was worse than inaction.

Only in November 2020 – 18 months after the election – did Porter front a media conference and present his exposure draft of his Commonwealth Integrity Commission Bill (Porter's Bill). Given that the commission Porter's Bill envisioned was designed to encourage and enhance openness and transparency in government, it was a curious plot twist that, during the media conference, although Porter held a copy of the Bill in his hands, he declined to make it publicly available.

Eventually, when the exposure draft was published, it was a disaster. Porter's Bill made a mockery of the expert advice he had received about designing a federal ICAC. The defects were so obvious and so numerous they cannot all be recounted here. Suffice it to say that Porter's Bill made it almost impossible to refer a politician or senior bureaucrat for investigation. Remarkably, it prohibited an examination of any events that had occurred before the commission commenced operations – thus protecting the Coalition from having any of the various misadventures of its nine-year term in government investigated. Worse still, rather than enhancing openness, it created an impenetrable cloak of secrecy. No politicians or senior bureaucrats could be called to a public hearing, and the fact that they were being investigated was to remain secret. Even if a report concluded that there had been corruption, the report would remain secret. The proposal was much worse than having no integrity commission at all – the terms of Porter's Bill could, in practice, protect corrupt politicians and bureaucrats from exposure.

Porter's Bill was roundly criticised. Every respected expert condemned the Bill – judges, academics, practitioners. There was a price to pay for criticising Porter's efforts because those providing criticism were personally abused, including by Porter under the privilege of parliament. There was only one commentator who supported the Bill and he did so warmly – in the pages of *The Australian*.

Here we come to the third circumstance in which an integrity agency is created: as a defence mechanism by a smelly government. As a corollary, an advantage might accrue from a weak agency which, if put in place, might protect the government from investigation of past misdeeds. It is difficult now to interpret Porter's Bill in any other way. If Porter's Bill had passed through the parliament, it would have allowed Coalition politicians to say (without justification, but nevertheless) that they had fulfilled an election promise and were engaged in fighting corruption. More significantly, if Porter's Bill had passed through the parliament it would have had the appalling effect of immunising the Coalition from any investigation into any past misdeeds.

It was not just the judges, the academics and the practitioners warning against Porter's Bill; the public began grumbling as well. It quickly became evident that Porter's proposal was having a negative public effect, and it was withdrawn for a further period of 'consultation'.

The need for a catharsis

To return to an earlier point: sometimes it is necessary to purge corruption – a catharsis, if you like. During the 2019 term of the Coalition, matters had reached that point.

A remarkable set of scandals emerged from Canberra. This is not the place to examine the rights or wrongs of any of these allegations, but it is appropriate to identify these as matters which, leading up to the 2022 election, had focused the public's attention on a *need* for a federal commission. From a potentially very long list, here are seven such matters:

- Why was $444 million given to the Great Barrier Reef Foundation without a tender process?
- Why was a large part of a $660 million Commuter Car Parks fund allocated into seats targeted by the Coalition, contrary to independent advice?
- Why was $33 million paid for a property in the Leppington Triangle valued at $3 million, even though the property had not been essential to the project?
- Why did Peter Dutton reallocate the Safer Communities Fund, contrary to independent advice and toward Coalition targeted seats?
- Why did Barnaby Joyce pay $80 million to a company related to Angus Taylor to buy water when the water was valued at $1.4 million?
- Why were contracts worth $423 million to provide security on Manus Island awarded in a closed tender process to Paladin – a company with a registered office in a shed on Kangaroo Island?
- Why was Canstruct – a company with no assets – awarded, without a tender, a contract for $385 million to provide security services on

Nauru? That arrangement has been allowed to roll over so that the contract now totals $1.6 billion.

No satisfactory explanation was provided for any of these instances. It could well be that there were explanations; we simply do not know. Whenever efforts were made to get to the bottom of these matters they have been rebuffed – politicians routinely evaded questions from the press; applications for documents under the *Freedom of Information Act* were bluntly rejected. To the extent that the Auditor-General has commented adversely, those criticisms have been ignored. To the extent the police have investigated, they have received no co-operation.

The 2022 election – the parties present their promises

In the months leading to the 2022 election, the issue of a federal integrity commission intensified greatly. It was no longer simply a policy designed to assist good governance; it was perceived to have become a need. With that background, the creation of a federal agency had become an important election issue.

The new Labor leader, Anthony Albanese, supported Dreyfus. Under Dreyfus's guidance the Labor policy remained clear, coherent and consistent. The promise was for an agency that would have the appropriate attributes to make it independent and powerful.

The Coalition's policy was precisely the opposite. It remains unclear, even after the election, what the Coalition had had in mind. Speaking – presumably on behalf of the government – Morrison made a series of hypercritical remarks, disparaging and even ridiculing the need for a federal agency. His language was aggressive. For example, under pressure in parliament in November 2021, Morrison described New South Wales ICAC as a 'kangaroo court' and an 'absolute disgrace'.

Concurrently – presumably speaking on behalf of the Coalition – the deputy prime minister, Barnaby Joyce, was characteristically flamboyant. He was totally opposed to a federal integrity agency, which he likened to recreating the 'Spanish Inquisition'. He complained that if such a body was appointed it would cause politicians to be 'terrified to do their job'.

The reader might wonder what they felt their job was if they were 'terrified' of an anti-corruption body.

Morrison then made a series of statements that the Coalition had fulfilled its 2019 election promise by providing an exposure draft of Porter's Bill. He repeatedly made assertions that Porter's Bill was sound and (despite having been withdrawn for further consultation) remained the government's model. On a few occasions he even claimed that Labor blocking the Bill was the only reason Australia was denied a federal integrity agency.

So, the Coalition's policy on a federal integrity agency for the 2022 election involved two conflicting premises. The first was that the Coalition had promised *not* to introduce a federal integrity agency because to do so would be to create a disgraceful kangaroo court and disrupt politicians from executing their duties. The second was that the Coalition had promised to introduce a federal integrity agency because it was always a good thing to do and would already be in place if it had not been stopped by Labor.

The upside of the Coalition policy was that it was always going to honour at least one of those promises. It does not seem unfair to observe that the confusion revealed on this policy was emblematic of the dying days of the Morrison Government.

References

Transparency International, *Corruption Perceptions Index*, 2021, <transparency.org.au/global-ranking/>.
World Bank, The, *Stolen Asset Recovery Initiative: Challenges, Opportunities, and Action Plan*, 2007.
World Economic Forum, *Global Future Council on Transparency and Anti-corruption*, 2022.

18

NAVIGATING CUMULATIVE DISASTER: DROUGHT, BUSHFIRE, FLOOD AND PANDEMIC

Jacki Schirmer and Lain Dare

Australia is known for its natural disasters, and all its governments have had to respond to multiple challenges during their time in power. However, the scale and number of climate-related disasters the Morrison Government faced were often described as unprecedented (eg Bromfield et al, 2021). In response to the multiple natural disasters Australia endured, there was a growing sense of urgency from many parts of Australian society for greater action to grow resilience to disasters, and critique of the Morrison Government's response to widespread drought, months-long bushfires and multiple major flood events. The Morrison Government fared poorly in navigating its role in disaster prevention, preparedness, response and recovery, in the face of rapidly growing incidence of natural hazards.

Disaster as the 'new normal'

In the period 2018 to 2022, Australia experienced rapid growth in the frequency, scale and intensity of climate-related disasters, something that had long been predicted to occur as a consequence of human-induced global climate change (IPCC, 2014). In 2018, much of Australia was affected by one of the most severe and widespread droughts since European colonisation. The drought culminated in 2019 with Australia's driest (and hottest) year since records began (Binskin et al, 2020), and with the 2019–20 Black Summer bushfires. Starting in September 2019 in Queensland and New South Wales, by November fires were active in multiple states with the area impacted by bushfires expanding through December.

The scale and longevity of the bushfires were more significant than in any previous bushfire event, and widely described as Australia's worst bushfire season on record (Jetten et al, 2021). Thousands of people had to evacuate their homes – not once, but multiple times over a period of weeks or months; the volunteer rural firefighting brigades that form the backbone of the country's firefighting response were stretched to their limits; and extensive smoke pollution affected Melbourne, Sydney and Canberra for weeks. The Black Summer fires caused billions of dollars of damage, destroyed and damaged several thousand homes and directly caused 33 deaths (Binskin et al, 2020) as well as hundreds of indirect deaths due to health problems associated with factors such as smoke pollution (Jetten et al, 2021). Bushfires were followed by flooding rains, with multiple flood events occurring during 2020, 2021 and 2022 across several states and territories. In addition, the incidence of severe storms causing significant damage in localised areas increased, with storms causing blackouts lasting weeks for some residents in major cities, including Melbourne and Canberra.

The number and severity of climate-related disasters occurring during the Morrison Government's term were greater than those experienced by previous governments. The growing frequency, severity and longevity of many 'natural' disaster events are widely agreed to be in large part consequences of the effects of global greenhouse emissions on the climate, which are resulting in greater frequency of a range of extreme weather events (IPCC, 2014). These disasters also occurred alongside the COVID-19 pandemic, meaning that the government was designing and implementing its disaster policy alongside policies that sought to reduce the effects of pandemic lockdowns. This combination of challenges meant the Morrison Government was responding to a unique set of circumstances that Australian disaster governance arrangements – across all levels of governments – had not been designed to respond to.

Disaster governance in Australia

The Morrison Government inherited a disaster governance framework whose disaster response role was focused on coordination, support and the encouraging of shared responsibility (Hunt, 2020). In 2011, the Gillard Government adopted the National Strategy for Disaster Resilience (NSDR); it enshrined the idea of 'shared responsibility' as underpinning Australian policy on preparing for, responding to and recovering from disasters. This approach places strong emphasis on taking responsibility to act to identify and to reduce risk before disasters occur (Australian Institute for Disaster Resilience (AIDR), 2019; Atkinson & Curnin, 2020). Shared responsibility refers to the understanding that all parts of Australian society have roles and responsibilities in disaster prevention, preparedness, response and recovery. This includes all levels of government, business and industry, non-government organisations, community and volunteer groups, and individual communities, households and people (AIDR, 2019). While shared responsibility is seen as essential to meeting the growing demands resulting from increasingly frequent severe disasters (Lukasiewicz et al, 2017), some argue that it may be used as a way of giving responsibility to others without also providing resources and support. This represents a rise of 'responsibilisation', or the shifting of responsibility from organisations to individuals (Atkinson & Curnin 2020; Crosweller & Tschakert, 2021a), particularly those at risk of harm in disasters (Crosweller & Tschakert 2021b). This has resulted in a situation in which, some argue, 'Governments seem to be willing to educate, plan and support in varying levels, however, when it comes to clarifying, coordination, and helping their citizens, they seem less inclined to assume the responsibility' (Atkinson & Curnin 2020, p. 7). For example, in Australia the importance of obtaining insurance coverage is commonly promoted as being a personal responsibility; however, multiple governments have implemented little action to address growing problems of people living in areas that have become uninsurable after they moved there (Lucas & Young, 2022).

Alongside the NSDR, the Australian Government is a signatory to several international disaster agreements and frameworks that guide disaster governance. Most significantly for the Morrison Government, this includes the Sendai Framework for Disaster Risk Reduction 2015–30, endorsed by Australia in 2015. The Sendai Framework guided development of Australia's 2019 National Disaster Risk Reduction Framework (NDRRF), which was adopted by all levels of government and provides a strategic national focus and coordination for disaster response. Disaster policy settings in Australia's federated system of government mean that the Australian Government's role is not to be the 'first responder' to disasters, something that is primarily a state and territory government function. Instead, the Australian Government focuses on coordination, information sharing and supporting disaster prevention, disaster risk reduction, and disaster recovery. In addition, the Australian Defence Force (ADF) has been activated to assist in disaster response in a growing number of disaster events, meaning the Australian Government is contributing to initial disaster response in some circumstances.

Despite rhetoric emphasising risk reduction and prevention as the centre of Australian disaster policy (Hunt, 2020), the amount of funding committed to it has historically been – and remained during the Morrison Government – significantly lower than that committed to post-disaster recovery. This lack of attention was notable during the Morrison Government: from 2020 onwards, public frustration regarding perceived inaction on climate change, a key contributor to the frequency and magnitude of natural disasters in contemporary times, boiled over into anger at the government's apparent lack of responsiveness in supporting disaster response efforts.

Disaster policy under the Morrison Government

The Morrison Government's time in office was characterised by regular public calls for systemic and widespread policy change to implement fit-for-purpose policy for climate-related disaster preparation, response and recovery, while also acting to reduce the impacts of climate change (Jetten et al, 2021; McDonald, 2021). The government largely met these calls with incremental policy changes (discussed later in this chapter), which while widely criticised reflected an adherence to, and continuation of, the complex systems of federated disaster governance in place prior to the Morrison Government. Similarly, these minimal changes reflected a lack of investment – and possibly interest – in expending the political capital required to negotiate significant changes that would require buy-in across state and territory governments.

The Morrison Government inherited the legacy of many years of polarisation regarding climate change action. The Abbott Government had dismantled many climate change–related initiatives, and the Morrison Government continued in this vein and minimised investment in disaster preparedness and response initiatives, despite the growing frequency, intensity and severity of climate-related disasters and strong evidence that this growth would continue into the future due to human-induced climate change (Climate Council, 2019; Grattan, 2019; Jetten et al, 2021). This unwillingness to act on climate change, combined with the complex disaster governance system, created a situation in which significant leadership would be required to enact substantive change – leadership which the Morrison Government did not provide.

The Black Summer bushfires opened what Jetten and colleagues (2021) argue was a window of opportunity for strong leadership from the Morrison Government to reset Australian disaster policy and move beyond incremental policy change. Their sheer scale and significance, following widespread intense drought, created an opening, 'at which departure from the previous policy not only became possible but was widely supported – and in some quarters demanded – by the general public'. The Morrison Government largely ignored this opportunity to fundamentally transform policy related to climate change, disaster response and recovery, and instead went down the path of what Jetten and colleagues (2021) describe as 'a post-disaster state of paralysis'.

Disaster policy under the Morrison Government did make some changes that went beyond the incremental, despite operating in a context in which repeated large-scale disasters focused attention on immediate disaster response and recovery needs. This included the establishment of the National Resilience and Recovery Agency (NRRA) and 'future funds' intended to support investment in building long-term resilience to disasters. However, the government often enacted these changes as a response to external compelling drivers, such as the recommendations of the 2020 Royal Commission into National Natural Disaster Arrangements, rather than actively leading and arguing for them.

(Lack of) leadership and blame-shifting

A lack of willingness to lead and an attitude of blame-shifting were recurrent themes in the Morrison Government's public response to disasters. When called on to increase Australian Government support to disaster-affected areas, one of Prime Minister Morrison's common responses was to argue that responsibility for disaster response lay with state and territory governments and not the Australian Government. A cycle of blame-shifting to state and territory governments, delay and reluctant 'coming to the table' with Australian Government support was repeated in response to multiple climate-related disasters, from the Black Summer fires to the major flooding affecting many areas in autumn 2021, and then again in 2022 (eg Lewis, 2022). This came to be characterised as the 'I don't hold a hose, mate' approach to disaster leadership, after the response Scott Morrison famously gave when asked why he had gone on holiday to another country during the Black Summer bushfires. In this approach, the Australian Government's first public responses – the prime minister's, in particular – often focused on emphasising that the states and territories were responsible for disaster response (Bromfield et al, 2021), despite clear and existing policy frameworks in place that also provided a role for the Australian Government through actions including disaster declaration, national coordination, enabling support from the ADF, and provision of emergency disaster relief.

The Royal Commission into National Natural Disaster Arrangements (Binskin et al, 2020), established after the Black Summer bushfires, recommended the Australian Government take a strong leadership role in disaster arrangements, while recognising that state and territory governments should retain primary responsibility for emergency management. Despite these calls and the 'window of opportunity' created by the scale of disasters, the Morrison Government was reluctant to assert authority and lead on disaster reduction, response and recovery, notwithstanding the fact that 'technically the federal government does have the legal power to take a strong leadership role in implementation of disaster policy' (Hunt, 2020, p. 69).

The 'I don't hold a hose' approach contributed to widespread loss of public support for the Morrison Government; this, combined with a lack of willingness to lead on policy reform and an inclination to blame-shift to state and territory governments, meant opportunity for meaningful reform was often lost (Jetten et al, 2021). When significant policy action was taken, it was commonly perceived as being in response to public demands, rather than as active leadership by the government.

The failure of symbolic action

The disaster policies the Morrison Government implemented in response to the rapidly accumulating series of climate-related disasters ranged from the largely symbolic to the practical. Many of the symbolic actions attracted widespread public criticism, such as the 2018 appointment of Nationals leader Barnaby Joyce as a Special Envoy for Drought Assistance and Recovery, an appointment that resulted in no clear action or documented advice to the Australian Government. Other symbolic actions attracting widespread criticism included visits to bushfire-affected areas by the prime minister, which were used to protest against the perceived insufficient response by his government to the fires, and the establishment of the Royal Commission into the Black Summer Bushfires (referred to from this point as the 2020 Royal Commission), which was criticised as repeating the same process undertaken in multiple previous royal commissions into major bushfires (Jetten et al, 2021). Perhaps the best-known symbolic failure was the prime minister's decision to take a holiday outside Australia in the midst of the Black Summer bushfires, which for many characterised his lack of political responsibility, leadership and responsiveness to climate-change insecurity and risk (Bromfield et al, 2021).

This failure of symbolic action under the Morrison Government is significant and, some argue, represented an inauthenticity and unwilling-ness to act for public, rather than for personal benefit (Komesaroff & Kerridge, 2020). Historically, the prime minister, together with state and territory leaders, has a highly visible role in publicly recognising and acknowledging the impacts of disaster, displaying empathy and providing reassurance to those affected. Attempts to enact this symbolic role, particularly by Morrison, became the focus of protest and anger rather than being seen as acts that united the nation, particularly around the Morrison Government's perceived inaction on climate change. Here, rather than leading the symbolic messaging around disaster, the Morrison Government became the focus of symbolism driven by its critics, with a dominance of strongly negative social media messages criticising its disaster response, and typically linked to concerns about its inaction on climate (Willson et al, 2021).

Incremental change in disaster governance

The Morrison Government largely continued the existing federated disaster-governance arrangements while making incremental change to some. Multiple reviews into disaster-governance arrangements in Australia, most recently the 2020 Royal Commission, have called for 'greater cooperation and coordination across governments and agencies' and 'a greater sharing of resources across jurisdictions' (Binskin et al, 2020). In response, the Morrison Government completed and signed on to the NDRRF, which enables the sharing of resources. Multiple smaller-scale initiatives were continued that involved collaboration and progress on information sharing and the provision of critical communications resources. Most of these initiatives began prior to the Morrison Government, which then only marginally adjusted them. In part, this incrementalism reflected the high demand on the government to use existing governance arrangements in responding to disasters: arguably, the time for significant reform is not when a government is in a continuing state of response to large-scale disasters. However, there will never be an ideal time for making such changes, and the 2020 Royal Commission's findings criticised the incrementalist approach:

> We are concerned that national policy development will continue to be put 'on hold' as priorities shift to operations … to … preparing for, and delivering, immediate response and relief. (Binskin et al 2020)

This incrementalist approach was arguably not 'fit for purpose', given the rapidly growing scale and scope of Australian disasters. For example, the repeated deployment of the ADF to assist in disaster response and recovery was criticised for not being accompanied by investment into the ADF to better enable it to contribute to this role (McDonald, 2021). Legislation introduced to enable the declaration of a National Emergency (the National Emergency Declaration Bill 2020), a response to the 2020 Royal Commission (Commonwealth of Australia, 2020), was largely symbolic, with little meaningful change in access to resources, or cooperation or coordination across jurisdictions.

An increasing number of reports and investigations during the Morrison Government's tenure identified serious shortcomings with exist-ing governance arrangements, including historical reliance on the principle of subsidiarity, short-term funding arrangements following disasters and a complex range of organisations across multiple scales and sectors. For example, local communities have multiple critical roles in disaster recovery, yet government support for these community-based activities is typically limited to short-term emergency funding; this short-termism erodes capacity and effectiveness (Dare & Schirmer, 2021). A diverse range of local, regional, national, and even international, organisations typically work in communities to support disaster response and recovery: this is encouraged by the principle of shared responsibility. However, as identified by the Royal Commission and others, it is common for a lack of communication and coordination across these agencies and organisations to slow disaster recovery, to result in ineffective use of limited resources, and to contribute to high rates of burnout and turnover among disaster-agency staff and volunteers who are traditionally the backbone of disaster response and recovery efforts (Dare & Schirmer, 2021).

These challenges and criticisms demonstrate a need for longer-term, consistent availability of resources to support recovery efforts across multiple disasters, rather than the disaster-by-disaster responses for which current governance arrangements are largely designed. Despite multiple evidence-based calls for change, through continuing incrementalism the Morrison Government missed a key opportunity to critically assess the extent to which existing arrangements are fit for purpose in the Anthropocene epoch.

The National Resilience and Recovery Agency

One of the major disaster policy actions the Morrison Government implemented was to establish the NRRA in 2021. NRRA was formed following two previous disaster-response agencies this government implemented: the National Drought and North Queensland Flood Response and Recovery Agency, and the National Bushfire Recovery Agency. Both these agencies sought to provide a coordinated response to disaster; their merger into the NRRA enabled an agency with a remit that went beyond that of single disasters to a focus on supporting recovery and building resilience from multiple and diverse disasters. However, rather than the Morrison Government conceiving of and driving this initiative, this was done largely in response to the 2020 Royal Commission recommendations.

The growing role of 'future funds'

The Morrison Government's early symbolic reactions to disaster – such as appointing Barnaby Joyce as a Special Envoy – were followed by substantive action with the announcement of the $5 billion Drought Future Fund (DFF) in October 2018. Initially, $3.9 billion was allocated as an investment to grow to $5 billion intended to provide continuous funding for investment into drought resilience, risk reduction and preparedness (Department of Agriculture, 2019). The DFF concept is important, providing a mechanism for investing in longer-term preparedness and resilience-building. A key challenge of such funds is ensuring they are invested in actions that will be effective for their intended purpose. The effectiveness of the DFF cannot be evaluated at the end of the Morrison Government, as the actions it invested in are intended to provide benefits in future years and decades. Notably, however, the DFF is designed to be responsive to changing understandings of what works to build drought resilience, with an independent panel advising on direction. This provides a governance mechanism with potential to achieve positive results if used wisely.

The DFF was followed by the establishment of the Emergency Response Fund (ERF) in 2019, a fund credited initially with $3.9 billion (representing the uncommitted balance of the Education Investment Fund) and intended to grow to $5 billion. The Australian Government is permitted under the *Emergency Response Act* 2019 (Cth) to draw up to $200 million from the ERF in any given financial year, so as to provide funding above and beyond that available through other disaster-funding arrangements. Of this, $50 million is to be used to build resilience to prepare for, or reduce the risk of, future disasters, while $150 million can be used to fund emergency response-and-recovery actions following significant or catastrophic disasters (NRRA, nd). However, the ERF became the focus of widespread anger in 2022 as the Morrison Government expressed its reluctance to access the fund to provide support for those affected by widespread flooding in eastern Australia, then altered its stance and provided access. This highlights that the fund on its own is not sufficient to provide better outcomes: shared agreement on when and how it should be used are critical in ensuring the ERF is used in ways that help reduce trauma associated with disaster, rather than becoming a focal point for it.

Legacy for future governments

The unprecedented disasters the Morrison Government faced demonstrated the limitations of preceding complex disaster-governance arrangements, and provided opportunities for significant change – opportunities that were, for the most part, missed due to a combination of cascading demands related to both disaster and the COVID-19 pandemic, lack of leadership and lack of political will. With disasters rapidly following each other, the government focused on utilising existing disaster-governance systems and implementing mostly incremental change to policy, despite growing demand for bigger, bolder change that recognised and responded to the challenges of climate change. Failures in leadership and symbolic action from Prime Minister Morrison placed further scrutiny and pressure on the government. However, despite the widespread appearance of little change, it did make some significant investments that have potential, if used well, to support future change in ways that can go beyond the incremental, particularly through establishing an agency that can work across multiple disasters and future funds for building resilience. Future governments may be able to leverage and build on these, but only if they are willing to invest in genuine leadership and advocacy for systemwide change in how all levels of government prepare for, respond to and recover from disaster.

References

AIDR (Australian Institute for Disaster Resilience). *Australian Emergency Management Arrangements* 3rd edn. AIDR and Department of Home Affairs, 2019.

Atkinson, Cameron and Steven Curnin. 'Sharing responsibility in disaster management policy', *Progress in Disaster Science*, 7, 2020, pp. 100–122.

Binskin, Mark, Annabelle Bennett and Andrew Macintosh, A. *Royal Commission into National Natural Disaster Arrangements*. Commonwealth of Australia, 2020.

Bromfield, Nicholas, Alexander Page and Kurt Sengul. 'Rhetoric, culture, and climate wars: A discursive analysis of Australian political leaders' responses to the Black Summer bushfire crisis', in *When Politicians Talk*, Springer, 2021, pp. 149–67.

Climate Council. *Climate Policies of Major Australian Political Parties*, 2019, <www.climatecouncil.org.au/wp-content/uploads/2019/05/climate-policies-of-major-australian-political-parties-v2.pdf>.

Commonwealth of Australia. *A National Approach to Disasters: The Commonwealth Government Response to the Royal Commission into National Natural Disaster Arrangements*, 2020.

Crosweller, Mark and Petra Tschakert. 'Disaster management leadership and policy making: A critical examination of communitarian and individualistic understandings of resilience and vulnerability', *Climate Policy*, 21(2), 2021a, pp. 203–21.

— 'Disaster management and the need for a reinstated social contract of shared responsibility', *International Journal of Disaster Risk Reduction*, 63, 2021b, 102440.

Dare, Lain and Jacki Schirmer. *Community Resilience, Wellbeing and Recovery Project: Research Report*. Mental Health Commission of NSW, NSW Council of Social Service and University of Canberra, 2021, <www.nswmentalhealthcommission.com.au/advocacy-work/community-resilience-wellbeing-and-recovery-project-resources>.

Department of Agriculture. *Australian Government Drought Response, Resilience and Preparedness Plan*, Commonwealth of Australia, 2019.

Grattan, Michelle. 'Grattan on Friday: When the firies call him out on climate change, Scott Morrison should listen', *The Conversation*, 15 November 2019, <theconversation.com/grattan-on-friday-when-the-firies-call-him-out-on-climate-change-scott-morrison-should-listen-127049>.

Hunt, Susan. Implementing Disaster Resilience Policy in the Australian Federation, Doctoral dissertation, the Australian National University, 2020.

IPCC (Intergovernmental Panel on Climate Change). *Climate Change 2014: Impacts, Adaptation and Vulnerability*, Cambridge University Press, 2014.

Jetten, Jolanda, Kelly S Fielding, Charlie R Crimston, Frank Mols and S Alexander Haslam. 'Responding to climate change disaster: The case of the 2019/2020 bushfires in Australia', *European Psychologist*, 26(3), 2021, p. 161.

Komesaroff, Paul and Ian Kerridge. 'A continent aflame: Ethical lessons from the Australian bushfire disaster', *Journal of Bioethical Inquiry*, 17(1), 2020, pp. 11–14.

Lewis, Peter. 'The floods seamlessly tied together all of Scott Morrison's biggest failures into one giant catastrophe', *Guardian*, 22 March 2022, <www.theguardian.com/australia-news/commentisfree/2022/mar/22/the-floods-seamlessly-tied-together-all-of-scott-morrisons-biggest-failures-into-one-giant-catastrophe>.

Lucas, Chloe and Travis Young. 'After the flood: Diverse discourses of resilience in the United States and Australia', in Kate Booth, Chloe Lucas and Shaun French (eds), *Climate, Society and Elemental Insurance*, Routledge, 2022, pp. 70–82.

Lukasiewicz, Anna, Stephen Dovers and Michael Eburn. 'Shared responsibility: The who, what and how', *Environmental Hazards*, 16(4), 2017, pp. 291–313.

McDonald, Matt. 'After the fires? Climate change and security in Australia', *Australian Journal of Political Science*, 56(1), 2021, 1–18.

NRRA (National Resilience and Recovery Agency). *Emergency Response Fund*, nd, <recovery.gov.au/emergency-response-fund>.

Willson, Gregory, Violetta Wilk, Ruth Sibson and Ashlee Morgan. 'Twitter content analysis of the Australian bushfires disaster 2019–2020: Futures implications', *Journal of Tourism Futures*, 7(3), 2021, pp. 350–55.

19

WEEKENDS AND WARS: THE STALLING OF CLIMATE CHANGE POLICY

Darren Sinclair and Jo Mummery

In the lead-up to the 2019 election, the prime minister, Scott Morrison, claimed the opposition leader, Bill Shorten:

> … wants to end the weekend when it comes to his policy on electric vehicles where you've got Australians who love being out there in their four-wheel drives (Remeikis, 2019).

This demonstrated a clear intent to politicise policy on electric vehicles (EV) to use it is a weapon in the continuing 'climate wars' by wedging the Labor Party through a blunt election scare campaign. The fact that the claims had no factual basis and were indeed contrary to the Coalition's own EV policy was emblematic of the Morrison Government's approach to climate change.

This memorable statement also proved to be prescient as to how the Morrison Government would engage on climate change over the course of its term, with the primacy of politics over policy coming at the expense of sensible, coherent, market-based and workable mechanisms for an orderly transition to a low-carbon economy. Perhaps not surprisingly, given that the previous prime minister, Malcolm Turnbull, was removed following his failure to steer the proposed National Energy Guarantee through the Coalition Party Room, the Morrison Government's 'end the weekend' opener to the election campaign was bookended by its abject failure to adequately prepare Australia's energy system for the international and domestic shocks that arose by the end of Morrison's tenure.

2019 election commitments

While it is not possible to cover the full suite of climate-related actions and 'inactions' of the Morrison Government in a single chapter, we endeavour to identify and discuss its signature policy milestones in rough chronological order. We begin with the commitments announced in the lead-up to the 2019 election. For context, it should be noted that much of eastern Australia was in the grip of a severe drought at this time and, politically, the polls were predicting a Shorten Labor majority government.

Undaunted, Morrison embarked on a presidential-style election campaign that weaponised Labor's climate change policy as an instrument of fear and division. This was punctuated during the election campaign by the Bob Brown-led 'climate caravan', which Morrison used to portray Labor and the Greens' climate change policies as an attack on 'blue-collar' workers, to polarise urban and regional communities, and to claim they would threaten Australia's economic prosperity and traditional lifestyle (hence, the 'war on the weekend' claims).

In terms of policy announcements, the Coalition went to the 2019 election with a focus on funding 'climate solutions', notably a commitment to inject $2 billion into the Direct Action/Emissions Reduction Fund (ERF) over a 10-year period. The Coalition also supported pumped hydro, honouring the Turnbull Government's Snowy 2.0, and committing $56 million to assess the feasibility of a second interconnector from northern Tasmania to the mainland.

These policy commitments were characterised by a lack of ambition (as evidenced by a continuation of the Abbott Government's meagre 2030 emissions-reduction target, and no 2050 target); limited scope (with many sectors ignored); no overarching policy framework; little integration with energy policies being adopted at the state/territory level; and an avoidance of market-based policies that could in any way be perceived as putting a price on carbon. Further, there was no consideration of international developments, including the climate policies Australia's major trading partners were adopting, nor of developments in our region. There was also no policy seeking to address the phasing out of Australia's ageing coal-fired power stations; only dismissive political rhetoric on a transition to EVs (and rejecting more stringent emissions standards for petrol and diesel vehicles), and no consideration of reducing existing fossil-fuel subsidies (such as the diesel fuel rebate). Finally, there were no adaptation measures to prepare communities and the economy for negative climate change impacts, such as those posed by more extreme weather events. In summary, the Morrison Government won the election with arguably the least ambitious climate policy agenda in two decades (rivalled only by the Abbott Government's 'axe the tax' three-word slogan approach to policy).

The King Review

In October 2019, the Morrison Government, to little fanfare and tepid enthusiasm, commissioned Grant King, the former CEO of Origin Energy, and president of the Business Council of Australia (BCA), to examine additional sources of low-cost abatement. The King Review included on its panel a long-time advocate for the Australian fossil-fuel sector, chief executive of the Australian Industry Greenhouse Network Susie Smith, and David Parker, CEO of the Clean Energy Regulator, which manages the ERF. A short time afterwards, in November 2019, the Morrison Government released its National Hydrogen Strategy (NHS), which was based on Alan Finkel's 2018 Hydrogen Strategy Report. The NHS retained the support of major Coalition political constituencies, particularly the mining and fossil-fuel sectors, for three reasons: first, it maintained the fossil-fuel industry's existing business paradigm by using hydrogen, mostly generated from natural gas, as a 'drop-in replacement' for fossil fuels; second, it involved providing substantial subsidies to the business sector; and third, it is sufficiently 'of the future' so as not to impose any real commitments in the short term.

The King Review released its findings in May 2020, which included recommendations to incentivise voluntary emissions reductions by industry (King et al, 2020). Crucially, the King Review recommended that the government expand the remit of the Australian Renewable Energy

Agency (ARENA) and the Clean Energy Finance Corporation (CEFC) to be technology-neutral; in other words, to enable their programs to fund heavy emitters, and even fossil-fuel projects. The Morrison Government supported most of the King Review's recommendations, and announced inclusions of carbon capture and storage (CCS), and abatement permits to major industrial sources of greenhouse gas emissions (below a baseline set under the Safeguard Mechanism) in the ERF. These measures represented a profound shift in emission-reduction programs under ARENA and the CEFC, away from supporting renewable energy, and were, not surprisingly, highly contested at the time. They were, however, consistent with the Morrison Government's strategy to preference the status quo over a substantive transition to a low-carbon economy. Meanwhile, in March 2020, the Morrison Government announced a 'gas-led recovery' in response to the economic downturn following the COVID-19 pandemic.

In September of 2020, the Morrison Government, informed by the King Review, announced further low-emissions policy commitments. First 'cab off the rank' was a Low Emissions Technology Statement (as part of a Low Emissions Technology Roadmap), which identified technologies to be prioritised, namely hydrogen, CCS, soil carbon, storage options and production of 'low-carbon' steel and aluminium. This was followed by a $1.9 billion commitment to a new energy-technologies investment package, with funding for CCS, an expanded remit of ARENA and CEFC beyond renewables, and for soil carbon. This approach was consistent with the Morrison Government's preference for technologies favoured by fossil-fuel industries (such as hydrogen), which were largely discredited, or at least highly contested (such as CCS), and favoured subsidies to the Coalition's constituency (such as soil carbon by farmers). Consequently, it is difficult to escape the conclusion that the Morrison Government was 'bending over backwards' to avoid providing further support for the most obvious climate change policy solution: greater investment in renewable energy, and something the energy industry and broader business communities were asking for.

As a consequence of AGL Energy's August 2019 announcement that it would commence closure of the Liddell coal-fired power station from April 2022, seven years earlier than expected, the Morrison Government warned that taxpayers would step in if the private sector did not commit to building at least 1000 megawatts of gas power to replace Liddell by 2023 (Clarke, 2020). Again, the government's automatic response was to privilege conventional, fossil fuel–based solutions, rather than to explore innovative, renewable options, or even to allow the market to decide. In this case, joint owner of Atlassian, Mike Cannon-Brookes, proposed renewable generation combined with storage alternatives rather than a gas-fired power plant as a source of dispatchable power, consistent with a market-based approach, but this went unheeded by the Morrison Government.

Subsequently, in May 2021, the Morrison Government announced additional funding for 'clean' energy projects, with up to $600 million allocated to building a new, gas-fired power plant (initially powered by diesel, and to run at 2 per cent capacity to fill peak demand gaps) in the New South Wales Hunter Valley (the Kurri Kurri plant) – this was despite energy experts warning that such an investment made little commercial sense. Another $83 million in Commonwealth and New South Wales government funding was allocated to the Tallawarra B gas–hydrogen plant, which has the capacity to include hydrogen fuel, even though none is currently available, and the most likely short- to medium-term source is from gas reformation. It was claimed the two plants formed part of the Morrison Government's 'gas-fired recovery' and were needed to avoid price hikes when the Liddell coal-fired generator closed in 2023. Finally, they also provided an additional $539 million for more hydrogen production hubs and for CCS – again, premised on the use of gas to produce hydrogen. What was not included in the announcement was any investment in renewable energy or storage, the latter of which is able to provide dispatchable power much faster – in microseconds – than gas-fired plants.

Extreme weather events

A key feature of the Morrison Government's term was the national experience of extreme weather events. Starting with widespread drought in 2019, large swathes of Australia were subjected to devastating bushfires in the summer of 2019–20, only to be followed by massive flooding in 2021 and 2022. Arguably, it was the tone-deaf response of Morrison to these natural disasters, including the infamous Hawai'i holiday and the 'I don't hold a hose' quip, that most defined the inadequacy of the Morrison Government's climate change responses.

Irrespective of whether any single event can be definitively linked to climate change, there was a widespread and growing community perception that climate change was at least in part responsible for these tragic and unsettling natural disasters. The Morrison Government did respond, reactively, by introducing major funding and policy commitments, including the Future Drought Fund (September 2019: $5 billion), Climate Services for Agriculture (2021), the National Bushfire Recovery Agency (announced during the 2019–20 bushfires: $2 billion over two years), the National Recovery and Resilience Agency ($600 million) and the March 2022 flood-recovery payments. These investments reflect, predominantly, an operational recovery agenda, as distinct from preparation for long-term climate change adaptation. In October 2021, the government announced a National Climate Resilience and Adaptation Strategy (NCRAS).

Despite some potentially worthwhile initiatives, the government was hamstrung by not having a comprehensive, integrated climate change policy framework that included resilience and adaptation. It is difficult to escape the conclusion that as the opposition claimed, the Morrison Government was always 'a day late and a dollar short' on climate change policy (Bowen, 2022). For example, the NCRAS reflected a narrow interpretation of the role of government, meeting the minimal requirement of the Paris Agreement for a plan rather than generating any substantial national ambition. The perceived inadequacy of the government's responses to natural disasters often spilled into overt and dramatic community hostility, as was the case when Morrison visited bushfire-affected communities, and in the criticism directed at the government regarding perceptions of bias in the allocation of flood-relief payments to localities with Coalition constituencies (which, strikingly, also included sharp criticism from the Coalition New South Wales State Government).

Glasgow 2021

By mid-2021, the political environment on climate change had heated up. Voter concerns over the devastating impacts of recent fires and floods accentuated frustration within many electorates about the lack of climate action. The Federal Court's decision in May that the water trigger of national environment legislation should have applied to the Adani coal mine, a case won by environmental non-government organisations (NGOs) and supported by community groups associated with the campaign and hashtag #StopAdani, combined with the four big Australian banks and all the big Chinese banks refusing to fund it, failed to prevent the Morrison Government from pushing ahead with the project. Concurrently, strong international pressure was applied to Australia to commit to a net-zero emissions target before the Glasgow climate change Conference of the Parties (COP), including by the United States at the September 2021 security meeting of the Quad (United States, India, Australia and Japan) and diplomatic 'nudging' from the United Kingdom as host of the COP. There were also growing domestic concerns that Australia could be penalised by international measures (such as the European Union's Carbon Border Adjustment Mechanism) if it did not have an equivalent target. Big business, traditionally aligned with more conservative positions on climate change, feared costly catch-ups from further inaction. This culminated in October 2021 when the BCA called for a net-zero target. State governments, including Coalition states such as New South Wales, also disagreed with the Morrison Government's climate change position, having set much more ambitious targets, including plans for the retirement of state-owned, coal-fired power stations.

As the Glasgow COP neared, deep divisions within the Morrison Government were exposed. A small band of influential National Party MPs, including resources minister Keith Pitt and senators from resource-rich Queensland, strongly opposed a 2050 net-zero target. Their views contributed to a change in party leadership in June, from the more pragmatic Michael McCormack, back to Barnaby Joyce, who opposed a net-zero commitment. More moderate National Party members publicly acknowledged that mainstream regional interests included stronger action on climate change, and that many in the party would accept a 2050 target. This aligned with the National Farmers' Federation, who, since August 2020, had supported an economy-wide net-zero 2050 target, creating a division between the traditional National Party constituency of farmers and its more recently embraced regional mining communities.

A speech by Treasurer Josh Frydenberg to business leaders in September 2021, articulating the economic case for net-zero emissions, fuelled the discontent of National Party MPs in the Morrison Government. Concerns were also growing in the Liberal Party, with MPs in marginal and metropolitan seats frustrated that the National Party was setting Australia's climate change policy agenda, and worried that Morrison might not be able to negotiate a credible policy position. An upsurge of community support for climate action, illustrated by the Climate 200 movement raising some $6.5 million in four months to December 2021, raised the prospect of many urban Liberal Party MPs facing independent or Greens challenges in the 2022 election.

Just days before commencement of the Glasgow COP, following secret negotiations between the Liberal and National parties, Morrison announced a net-zero 2050 target. This was taken to Glasgow with a new Long-Term Emissions Reduction Plan (LTERP). Following years of exploiting loopholes in targets that minimised obligations for substantive emissions reduction action, which go back as far as the Kyoto Protocol negotiations under the Howard Government and the infamous 'Australia clause', the marketing gloss of the new LTERP did little to enhance Australia's international reputation on climate change. The 'Australian Way' LTERP is based on the key principles of 'technology not taxes' and 'expand choices, not mandates', and is notable for its lack of detail and a reliance on undefined future technologies. To meet a net-zero target, the LTERP claims 20 per cent emissions reductions have already been achieved in keeping with Australia's commitments to the Paris Agreement (largely achieved from the carryover of credits from reduced land clearing in the 1990s), 10–20 per cent from carbon offsets and 60–70 per cent from future technologies, including from global trends and unknown further technology breakthroughs. Of note, the LTERP fails to mandate any reduction in the burning of fossil fuels, defending a continuing role for fossil-fuel energy in Australia and the export of emissions-intensive coal and gas. It also embeds technologies identified in the 2020 Low Emissions Technology Statement – clean hydrogen, low-emission steel and aluminium, CCS, soil carbon and energy storage.

Scepticism about the LTERP's capacity to deliver emissions reductions grew quickly, assisted by the Morrison Government's initial refusal to release the modelling that underpinned the technology claims. Despite having spent around $3.5 billion on CCS since 2003, there is remarkably little to show for it, and numerous domestic and international reports were beginning to show that the technology has not lived up to expectations (Climate Council, 2021). Nevertheless, a further six such projects were handpicked by the Australian Government for funding support in June 2021. A review by the Climate Change Authority in late 2020, which included commissioned research by the CSIRO, found high levels of risk associated with the storage and maintenance of carbon in agricultural soils (Roxburgh et al, 2020). Together with further independent research and modelling, major questions emerged about the integrity of the land-sector Australian Carbon Credit Units, which comprise 75 per cent of units allocated under the ERF. To compound matters, the NCCC gas-led recovery for Australia after the COVID-19 pandemic also failed, with reports showing that gas did not contribute to an economic recovery, with jobs in the oil and gas industry being cut by around 10 per cent between November 2019 and December 2020 (Ogge, 2021).

Australia's international status as a pariah, including being ranked last for climate action in a July 2021 United Nations report, was further cemented at the Glasgow COP (31 October to 12 November 2021). Prominent at the front of Australia's pavilion was a model of a carbon capture project by oil and gas giant Santos, supported by the Morrison Government's ERF. The symbolism of maintenance of the status quo by having a fossil-fuel company's logo displayed next to Australia's name at the COP was also reflected in the positions of Australia's negotiators. Australia supported Saudi Arabia, Russia and India in blocking a line in the COP's draft statement: to accelerate the phasing out of coal and subsidies for fossil fuels. Australia was 'missing in action' on key pledges led by the United States and Europe to cut methane emissions, and

Australia allied with the United States to resist a new fund for loss and damage to support the most climate-vulnerable countries. During the COP, GermanWatch ranked Australia last on climate policy with a score of zero (Doyle, 2021).

At the same time as the COP, the Morrison Government performed a striking policy pivot in releasing a 'policy lite' strategy for increasing EV take-up in November 2021. When journalists questioned Morrison about how he could honestly make a case for EVs after claiming in the lead-up to the 2019 election that they would 'end the weekend' and require apartment-dwellers to dangle extension cords out of their windows, he said 'that's a Labor lie' (Butler, 2021). However, as with the Morrison Government's net-zero commitment and the LTERP, the EV strategy had little content to show for its years in the making. It contained some $178 million of funding for infrastructure, but no new policies. The strategy was heavily criticised for not including the two measures viewed by experts as the most important in promoting EVs: vehicle emissions standards and market signals to incentivise take-up.

2022 election

Unsurprisingly, climate change was a central theme during campaigning in the lead-up to the 2022 election. Labor's pitch to voters was deliberately modest, and clearly differentiated from its ambitious 2019 election campaign. Labor's policies were carefully designed to constrain the political risk of a Morrison Government scare campaign, while further supporting the rollout of electorally popular renewable energy, reducing the cost of EVs and flagging gradual approaches to reducing emissions from major industries. Importantly, Labor's 2030 emissions target of a 43 per cent reduction in emissions on 2005 levels is substantially stronger than the Morrison Government's unchanged commitment of a target of 26 to 28 per cent reduction in emissions and is consistent with the 2 degrees Celsius global warming goal of the Paris Agreement. In contrast, the Greens actively campaigned for a 74 per cent 2030 emissions reduction target, and the 23 or so candidates challenging urban Coalition MPs on platforms of climate action and greater integrity, who became known as the 'teal' independents, rallied around the Steggall Climate Bill, which contained a target reduction of 60 per cent in emissions by 2030.

While the polls consistently predicted that the Morrison Government would likely fall in the 2022 election, the significance of the climate change impact on the result was surprising. Voters who would normally have voted for a moderate Liberal candidate, but who would have been unlikely to vote for Labor or the Greens, were given a viable choice with the advent of the 'teals'. With a decline in primary votes to both major parties, the 2022 election saw the rise of community-driven and climate-committed independents, often with Climate 200 support. Consequently, the crossbench doubled in size and obtained a strong focus on climate change. Further, the Greens secured four House of Representatives seats based on a strong climate-change platform, including winning two seats in Queensland from the Coalition, and one from Labor. The Greens' strong showing in the Senate, together with the Climate 200–aligned David Pocock, means that the balance of power in the Senate is held by parties supporting stronger action on climate.

Overall, the Morrison Government's approach to climate change policy was characterised by denial, marginalisation, reactivity and politicisation. Denial, in terms of ignoring both the immediacy and severity of the negative consequences of climate change and the potential economic, employment, environmental and national security benefits derived from the transition to a low-carbon economy. Marginalisation, in terms of viewing climate change policy (and the scientific evidence underpinning the need for action) as something on the periphery both of its core policy agenda and the perceived interests of the Australian community (or at least those parts that have traditionally voted for the Coalition). Reactivity, in terms of not anticipating or adequately preparing to address either the impacts of, or opportunities arising from, climate change, instead only doing so reluctantly and without a full commitment when its hand was forced by external circumstances, and often after the fact. And politicisation, in terms of preferencing the exploitation of perceived short-term political advantage by creating division over climate change issues rather than seeking to build consensus for a policy platform that would deliver substantial long-term benefits to the nation.

With the election of the Albanese Government, and the Greens and climate-focused crossbenchers, the centre of political debate on climate may finally have shifted away from an unrelenting, misleading and ultimately destructive focus on the costs of action, to instead acknowledging the costs of inaction and embracing the enormous economic, social, strategic and environmental benefits that a transition to a low-carbon economy can bring. To achieve this, the Albanese Government will need support in the Senate to pass any legislation opposed by the Coalition. Within the Coalition, the election shockwaves are still reverberating, with remaining moderate Liberal MPs calling for more ambitious climate policies, while the National MPs warn they could break the LNP alliance and abandon their commitment to the net-zero emissions target. It cannot be assumed, then, that the 'climate wars' are over – it may, sadly, be merely a temporary ceasefire.

References

Bowen, Chris. 'Remarks to Bioenergy 2030: Unlocking Austraia's Renewable Energy Giant', Chris Bowen, MP, personal website, 16 February 2022, <chrisbowen.net/media/transcripts-speeches/remarks-to-bioenergy-2030-unlocking-australia-s-renewable-energy-giant/>.

Butler, Josh. 'From "war on the weekend" to "key building block": Scott Morrison denies EV backflip', New Daily, 9 November 2021, <thenewdaily.com.au/news/2021/11/09/morrison-denies-ev-backflip/>.

Clarke, Melissa. 'Federal government threatens to build gas plant if electricity sector doesn't replace retiring coal-fired power stations', ABC News, 14 September 2020, <www.abc.net.au/news/2020-09-14/government-unveils-gas-fired-coronavirus-recovery-plan/12663214>.

Climate Council. 'What is carbon capture and storage?' Climate Council blog, 20 July 2021, <www.climatecouncil.org.au/resources/what-is-carbon-capture-and-storage/>.

Doyle, Michael. 'Australia scores zero on climate policy in latest Climate Change Performance Index', ABC News, 10 November 2021, <www.abc.net.au/news/2021-11-10/australia-scores-zero-on-climate-policy-in-latest-report/100608026>.

King, Grant, Susie Smith, David Parker and Andrew Macintosh. Report of the Expert Panel Examining Additional Sources of Low Cost Abatement, Commonwealth of Australia, 2020.

Ogge, Mark. Wrong Way, Go Back: Why the gas-fired recovery plan will fail to reduce energy prices or create jobs but will increase emissions, the Australia Institute, 2021, <australiainstitute.org.au/report/wrong-way-go-back/>.

Remeikis, Amy. '"Shorten wants to end the weekend": Morrison attacks Labor's electric vehicle policy', Guardian, 7 April 2019. <www.theguardian.com/australia-news/2019/apr/07/shorten-wants-to-end-the-weekend-morrison-attacks-labors-electric-vehicle-policy>.

Roxburgh, Stephen, Keryn Paul and Libby Pinkard. Technical Review of Physical Risks to Carbon Sequestration under the Emissions Reduction Fund (ERF): Final Report to the Climate Change Authority, CSIRO, 2020.

Leadership

20

EXPERTS AND DEMOCRACY IN AUSTRALIA: THE CASE OF COVID-19

Mark Evans and Michelle Grattan

Coping with crises has become a new normal. Terrorist attacks, floods, drought, bushfires and pandemics – all of these natural and people-made events are now an integral part of the 21st-century experience of democratic governance. Indeed, the political management of the COVID-19 pandemic has provided the most sustained experience of crisis management since the Second World War. Responding to the crisis created by COVID-19 has led to interventions in social and economic life, more disruptive and radical than anything that has normally been part of political decision-making within peacetime. So, how did the Morrison Government and Australian democracy fare in the pandemic context?[1]

There are reasons to think that some of the practices of democracy are more difficult in a crisis. Firstly, the normal, time-consuming nature of democratic decision-making does not always fit comfortably when rapid decisions in an uncertain environment are required. Executive decision-making may take precedence, reducing oversight and input from more reflective and representative elements of democracy (Merkel, 2020).

Secondly, in crises citizens face fear, and to relieve that psychological pressure they may be more willing to trust, follow or support political leaders without engaging in the scrutiny and challenge that would normally be integral in democratic oversight.

Thirdly, responding to a crisis may involve value calls (where to put resources, how to weigh different risks), which are the normal business of democracy. But meeting the demands of a crisis can also involve greater need for expertise or knowledge. During the COVID-19 crisis the demand for expertise was expressed through repeated calls for decision-makers to 'follow the science'. Some democratic theorists are nervous that experts claim too much authority and squeeze out other voices in decision-making (see Edis, 2020). Such concerns expose what can be a difficult relationship between expertise and democracy, and can lead us to ask how that relationship could be effectively managed.

In looking at the issues of experts and the pandemic in Australia, we draw on interviews the authors conducted with key protagonists within and outside the COVID-19 epistemic community, as well as public opinion surveys conducted for the Democracy 2025 project at the Museum of Australian Democracy.

What does the pre-COVID-19 evidence tell us about the role of expertise in Australian public policy? Public attitudes towards the management of COVID-19 are worth reviewing, as are key issues of contestation between experts, to highlight the dominant ideas informing government policy. And what role should expertise play in liberal democracies?

The role of experts in liberal democracies

As James March and Johan Olsen (1995) observe, 'the relation between democracy and expert knowledge is troubled'. If democracy is defined as the opportunity for citizens to decide together what they want to do collectively, then experts appear as a threat to democracy rather than an enhancement. In this light, experts might not automatically be seen as part of the mechanisms necessary to help save democracy. But we believe that one of the key reforms necessary is to find a way of making expertise and evidence central to collective democratic decision-making.

There are strong forces that would appear to question that commitment. On the one hand, there is the growth of a form of right-wing populist movement that encourages distrust of expertise and more generally of scientific institutions (Edis, 2020). On the other hand, there are progressive democratic reformers who express considerable distrust of experts (Lightbody & Roberts, 2019). There are at least four lines of critique. Experts present their evidence as though it was unchallengeable when that is not the case; experts claim to be value-free in their advice, and that position often hides their political motives; the language and style of argument used by experts are exclusionary at best, and may even be designed to confuse others; and finally, how experts reach their advice or recommendations often lacks transparency and accountability.

There is some validity in each of these areas of critique. But we offer an alternative position. Democracy is valued for the opportunity for citizens to have their say (input legitimacy), but also because it delivers effective collective action to tackle social and economic problems (output legitimacy). Experts bring something essential to achieving output legitimacy in three ways (Bertsou & Caramani, 2020). First, and most importantly, they have specialist knowledge to aid the understanding of the issues. Second, they can often be valued because they are not tied to special interests, affording them a perceived integrity that others in the policy process can lack. While not neglecting the observation that experts can be funded by businesses, campaigners or governments, there are relatively strong protocols and matching cultures in place to declare any conflicts of interest. Finally, they can help design solutions that work, a preferred outcome for many citizens. Of course, outcomes are not necessarily equally successful from the point of view of different interests, but the sense that expertise could help deliver effective action is an attractive prospect.

How best to achieve this aim? The beneficial qualities of engaging expertise are not automatically realised in practice. They must be designed into the process of decision-making in a way that minimises concerns about experts overclaiming, hiding their political preferences and crowding out other voices.

Public trust and the pandemic

Public trust as a political resource has been particularly important during the pandemic. Without it the changes to public behaviour necessary to contain and ultimately prevent the spread of infection are slower and harder. People need to trust government enough to support its interventions.

In mid-2020, compared to citizens of Italy, the United Kingdom and the United States, Australia's citizens viewed their government as successful in managing the pandemic (Figure 20.1). The propensity for citizens to lend support to leaders during crises is well documented. In the initial stages of the pandemic's spread, surveys revealed a parallel surge in support for incumbent leaders. Leaders in a large number of countries, including Australia, enjoyed an increase in public confidence.

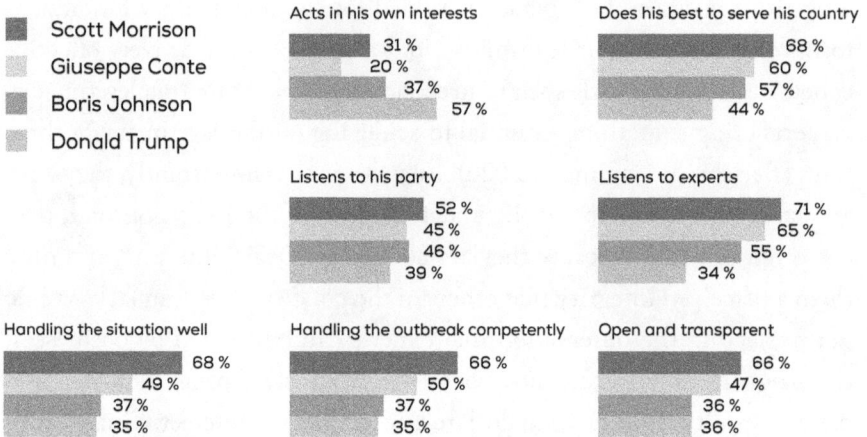

Figure 20.1
Perceptions of political leadership during the COVID-19 crisis, July 2020

SOURCE Adapted from Jennings et al, 2020.

The initial upsurge of support for Prime Minister Morrison is partly explained by what is termed the 'rally-round-the-flag' effect (Hetherington & Nelson, 2003). National leaders benefit from a rush of patriotic fervour to a nation under threat. Australia also benefitted from effective governance.

However, Morrison's high approval rating began to dissolve as the Australian public became disenchanted with the slow rollout of the federal government's vaccine program. The situation became further complicated by mixed government messaging over the relative risks associated with AstraZeneca for vulnerable groups, which rapidly punctured public trust in government. People continue to judge the competence and outcomes of the government's actions in a crisis. If the government is perceived as unable or unwilling to adequately respond to a threat, then public support will fade. It was therefore expected that public trust would increase once the government had got to grips with the vaccine rollout, but this did not prove to be the case. Public trust continued to wane (see figure 20.2), suggesting a return to a longer-term pattern of distrust in Australia's political class.

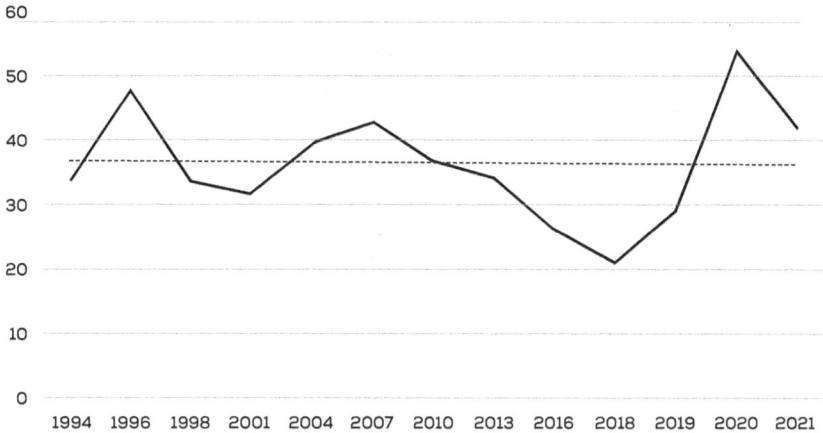

Figure 20.2
Trust in people in government, 1994 to 2021

SOURCES Australian Election Study (1994–2019)
and Democracy 2025 (2016, 2018, 2020 and 2021).

But what of public trust in experts? Prior to the pandemic there was strong evidence, particularly in the United States and the United Kingdom, of anti-intellectualism – the generalised distrust of intellectuals and experts. International evidence shows that anti-intellectualism is connected to populism, a worldview that sees political conflict as primarily between ordinary citizens and a privileged societal elite. However, populism has not been widely embraced in Australia. This is largely because Australia evaded the economic and social dislocation caused by the Global Financial Crisis, and partly because Australia's major political parties absorbed certain populist agendas into the mainstream. For example, elements in both major parties have at times tended towards anti-immigration views and climate scepticism. The Wellcome Global Monitor ran a survey in 2018 on trust in science and scientists in over 140 countries, which also included a question on trust in national government. Australia ranks just

85th out of 134 countries for its level of political trust, but 14th out of 144 for trust in scientists, suggesting that in relative terms it has a high level of trust in experts. Australians have continued to exhibit this throughout the pandemic.

Co-author of this chapter, Mark Evans, and Ipsos Public Affairs conducted a survey to determine the level of trust placed in a range of information sources about COVID-19. Respondents rated the extent to which they agreed or disagreed with each source's ability to provide honest and objective information about COVID-19 (Figure 20.3):

Column %	TOTAL	Builders (born 1925–45) n=282	Baby boomers (born 1945–64) n=284	Generation X (born 1965–79) n=303	Millennials (born 1980–94) n=210	Generation Z (born 1995–2003) n=105
Social media	15%	14%	11%	15%	19%	14%
Television media	40%	45%	45%	39%	36%	36%
Radio media	39%	41%	44%	41%	34%	37%
Newspaper media	38%	40%	41%	39%	36%	34%
Scientists and experts	79%	80%	80%	79%	79%	78%

Figure 20.3
Trust in media or science and experts to provide honest and objective information about COVID-19 (November 2021)

To what extent do you agree or disagree with the following statements?

NOTE Each statement was asked in the following way: I trust [media or science] to provide honest and objective information about COVID-19. Percentages reported are percentage of respondents agreeing or strongly agreeing.

Sample: n=1184, weighted by age, gender, location.

SOURCE Evans and Ipsos Public Affairs, 2021

Unsurprisingly, scientists and experts were significantly more likely to be trusted to provide honest and objective information (79 per cent net agree) compared to television (40 per cent), radio (39 per cent), newspaper (38 per cent) and social media (15 per cent) sources. In short, public trust in scientists and experts continued to increase during the pandemic despite declining levels of public trust in people in government.

Experts and COVID-19 management in Australia

The pre-eminent scholar on the role of expertise, Peter Self (1977) notes that 'no amount of expert evidence will [as a rule] point logically and unambiguously to a given conclusion'. During the pandemic, the leaders of almost every country were forced to rely on their health experts to advise them on the sudden threat.

In Australia, both federal and state governments were at pains to stress that policy prescriptions were evidence-based, driven by expert advice. Morrison adopted the mantra of protecting 'lives and livelihoods', and wanted a balance between the two, which often led to his believing some jurisdictions were being too restrictive, at a high cost to the economy.

Decision Making

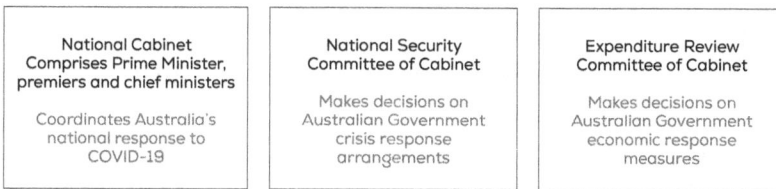

National Cabinet Comprises Prime Minister, premiers and chief ministers	National Security Committee of Cabinet	Expenditure Review Committee of Cabinet
Coordinates Australia's national response to COVID-19	Makes decisions on Australian Government crisis response arrangements	Makes decisions on Australian Government economic response measures

Policy Advice and Coordination

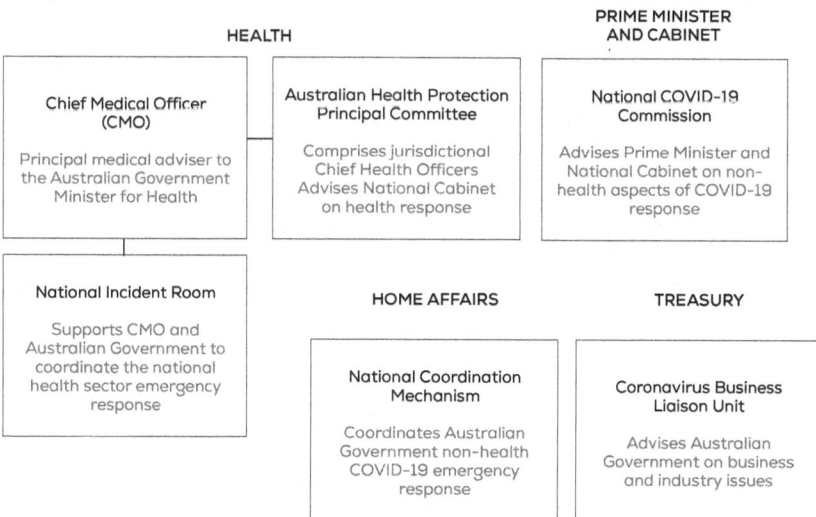

HEALTH

PRIME MINISTER AND CABINET

Chief Medical Officer (CMO)	Australian Health Protection Principal Committee	National COVID-19 Commission
Principal medical adviser to the Australian Government Minister for Health	Comprises jurisdictional Chief Health Officers Advises National Cabinet on health response	Advises Prime Minister and National Cabinet on non-health aspects of COVID-19 response

National Incident Room	HOME AFFAIRS	TREASURY
Supports CMO and Australian Government to coordinate the national health sector emergency response	National Coordination Mechanism — Coordinates Australian Government non-health COVID-19 emergency response	Coronavirus Business Liaison Unit — Advises Australian Government on business and industry issues

Figure 20.4
COVID-19 governance in Australia.

SOURCE Australian National Audit Office, 2020

The counter-argument was that health outcomes would drive, positively or negatively, the economic outcomes.

While the health advice was pivotal to crafting policy responses, Australian leaders, federal and state, also used the presence of their health officials at news conferences to buttress their political authority. Professor Brendan Murphy, Commonwealth Chief Medical Officer in the early months of the pandemic, quickly became a nationally recognised figure.

A range of expertise has been necessary to combat the virus, but given the few absolute scientific truths about the pandemic, policy and process expertise have been pre-eminent, and scientific expertise has been harvested from tried and trusted experts within the government's epistemic community, the Australian Health Protection Principal Committee (AHPPC) – the primary national health advisory body, which draws on knowledge from wider sources through the creation of specialist subgroups such as the Infection Control Expert Group. Figure 20.4 shows where the AHPPC sat within the context of COVID-19 governance at the Commonwealth Government level.

In response to the COVID-19 pandemic, new institutional structures such as the National Cabinet and the National COVID-19 Commission were established. Coordination mechanisms were also set up. Morrison's disillusionment with the ad-hoc nature of the vaccine rollout by the Department of Health led him to bring in the military expertise of Lieutenant General John Frewen to oversee it.

The contest of ideas and its intersection with politics

Evidence is not a sufficient criterion for policy action in a liberal democracy, as it is nearly always contested, and the nature of the contestation often reflects competing social values (Self, 1977; Fenna & Botterill, 2019). In Australia, much of the contest between federal and state governments was not based upon the material nature of the health advice but on the balance between health and economic imperatives. While this chapter focuses on health expertise, economic experts were also crucial. The Morrison Government pursued a comprehensive fiscal stimulus, accepting the advice of Treasury, which argued for a massive injection of funds.

The story of the health 'experts' is more complex than might at first appear. The definition of a health 'expert' was contested because multiple specialties and skills are relevant. Compounding this issue, the information landscape of a sudden pandemic is dynamic and unpredictable, resulting in experts having to accelerate the slow, deliberate processes of research. Individual experts, and whole fields of science, sometimes argued about appropriate responses. Differences emerged among those 'in the tent' of officialdom, as well as between insiders and some outsiders in academia.

As more information and data emerged, experts around the country espoused a range of views. Arguments about how the virus was transmitted – mostly via 'droplets', or with a significant aerosol component – led to an intense debate about the efficacy of masks. Murphy initially recommended against mandating widespread use of face masks due to doubt about their usefulness in the absence of much community transmission, and because of the need to boost the local supply, given that most masks were imported. The head of the Infection Control Expert Group (ICEG), Lyn Gilbert, was sceptical about masks. But Raina MacIntyre, head of the University of New South Wales's Biosecurity Program, and many health professionals were outspoken, especially in urging the use of safer types of masks for health professionals. In August 2020, a group of doctors wrote to health minister Greg Hunt, with a stinging attack on Gilbert and ICEG.

One notable split in expert advice at the pandemic's beginning was on border closures. In February 2020, Australia's borders were closed to people travelling from China (apart from Australian returnees); by March the border was completely closed to all non-residents. The closures came from Murphy's advice, after he examined the epidemiological evidence from China; this was opposed to advice from the World Health Organization, which recommended against shutting borders.

It was a bold step by the Morrison Government, given the importance to the economy of Chinese students and tourists, and Morrison put the decision squarely on the health advice. 'Up until today it has not been the advice of the Chief Health Officer, and our medical experts that this has been necessary', Morrison said. But the advice had changed.

Murphy also commissioned the modelling of scenarios for the future course of the virus from Melbourne's Doherty Institute. Experts from that institute, and elsewhere from inside and outside officialdom, were invited into the broad orbit of the AHPPC, which included federal and state health officers, and would advise the National Cabinet when it was formed in March 2020 to bring together federal, state and territory leaders.

A central imperative was managing the politics of fear. Key decisions (on state borders, the toughness of restrictions imposed, the nature of the quarantine system) involved assessing how much risk to take. It quickly became clear that the Australian public was risk-averse. In April, an Essential poll found 88 per cent were concerned 'about the threat of Coronavirus in Australia'. The fear factor was reinforced by reports of the horrific situation abroad. Morrison and the NSW Government were willing to tolerate a higher level of risk than most states. Voters welcomed the most risk-averse strategies, despite their high economic and social costs.

The official national policy was to 'suppress' the virus – stopping community transmission – rather than 'eliminate' it. Yet some experts argued for elimination. On the AHPPC, Murphy and his deputy (later successor) Paul Kelly, mindful of Morrison's stand and the position of National Cabinet (one of living with the virus), guided the language away from 'elimination'. As community transmissions fell to around zero in various jurisdictions, the mindset of some leaders and their publics was clearly beyond suppression. The language shifted to 'active suppression', defined as no community transmission. This was 'elimination' on any ordinary measure.

Throughout 2020, there were differences between the federal government and some states over what they considered appropriate responses. Leaders would usually justify these divergences by referencing their own health experts. Victoria's Premier Daniel Andrews, speaking in October, said: 'the whole way through this, we have been guided by our public health experts and their advice'. Queensland's Annastacia Palaszczuk said: 'We think it's important to listen to the health experts. Their advice keeps Queensland safe'.

The perception that politicians were looking to the health experts undoubtedly boosted public confidence, and was key in the high level of compliance with restrictions, especially in the extended Victorian lockdowns. But for both the politicians and the experts in officialdom, it was a two-edged sword. The Morrison Government was critical of what it considered some states' overreactions, especially their border closures and Victoria's long lockdowns. But later it backed off criticisms because the states' actions were popular with their own constituencies. Even when flaws in its hotel quarantine and contact-tracing arrangements shut down Victoria, Premier Daniel Andrews retained a surprisingly high level of support.

The experts found themselves operating in an environment where not only was the ground constantly shifting but the proper responses were contested. Some counterparts abroad advocated radically different approaches. In Sweden, Anders Tegnell, the chief epidemiologist at the Public Health Agency, drove a 'light touch' policy of minimal restrictions, which resulted in an initial high death toll. The early goal of 'herd immunity', with its prospective huge death toll, was never a serious option for Australia.

Australian health officials found their advice criticised by some in academia. As the pandemic escalated in March 2020, the federal government commissioned the Group of Eight Universities to convene experts for their options. It came up with two views. The clearly dominant one advocated going hard with a 'comprehensive, simultaneous ban' on all gatherings across the country; the second was for a more 'proportionate response'. Murphy indicated he did not favour the majority view. Another paper circulating at the time, authored by MacIntyre and others, argued for 'a short, sharp lockdown'.

Within the AHPPC, the operating mode was consensus and that was mostly the outcome. But Victorian Chief Health Officer Brett Sutton was a dissenting voice on the need, early on, for a tougher lockdown. The Victorian Government got its way; the restrictions Morrison announced on 22 March 2020 were stricter than the prime minister's preference.

What the AHPPC did not deal with was also notable. It eschewed the question of state border closures, on the grounds this was an area of state responsibility, but equally because consensus would never be reached. The states, which were driving much of the response, went their own way on borders, citing their local advisers. On the key question of schools, the federal government and Murphy believed in keeping them open, but the states took their own, more conservative, decisions.

The health officers inevitably found themselves becoming political figures. The public identified with them, sometimes to an extraordinary degree. Sutton became a cult figure, with merchandise named after him. But they also increasingly became targets. Queensland's Jeannette Young, who under state legislation had extensive direct power over decisions such as border exemptions, came under immense pressure as the Queensland election approached, and the federal government highlighted decisions not to provide exemptions for mercy cases.

Sutton, especially, was in the sights of hard-right critics – he was labelled 'Bambi Eyes' by the Institute of Public Affairs' Gideon Rozner; these critics argued the Victorian Government was reacting excessively with lockdowns and ignoring the costs. Western Australian Chief Health Officer Andrew Robertson was caught in the middle of the debate over the state's hard border policy. After it was suggested he had contradicted the claims his premier, Mark McGowan, had made about the health advice, Robertson issued a statement highlighting changing information and saying his advice had been 'consistent about maintaining current border controls since border restrictions were implemented', merely raising 'possible future options if the epidemiology and national control measures were to change'.

The presence of health officials, federal and state, at leaders' regular news conferences introduced a new, real-time bureaucratic accountability. They had to defend their advice, and in some cases answer for controversial decisions and weaknesses in a state's system.

The legacy of COVID-19 policy

Health experts became used to politically managing community fear during the COVID-19 pandemic, as well as providing the foundation for the policy responses. The Morrison Government built on Australians' high levels of trust in experts, to share and absorb the risk of failure.

The determination of insider and outsider expert status depends on the quality and objectivity of the scientific evidence on offer, the reputation of the expert in the epistemic community and the ability of the expert to translate the evidence in a meaningful way for policy. In the case of COVID-19, it was the status of the expert and the content of their expertise rather than their institutional affiliation that accounted for their influence. There was also an element of 'who knows whom'; some identified a Melbourne circle, which Sydney experts believed had privileged access.

Contestation between health experts was inevitable given that no one has all the answers, but two broad communities of health experts featured strongly – one that followed the international evidence in the worst-hit countries such as the United States and the United Kingdom (the outsiders), and one that was responsive to the national context (the insiders).

We asked our informants whether COVID-19 would lead to a new marriage between politicians and experts, or default to business as usual. Most thought health experts crucial to the relative success of the Morrison Government's management of the pandemic and saw significant gains in fostering stronger trust systems between the public service, insider health experts and political actors; and in augmenting a new dawn for government strategic communications with departments playing a more visible role. However, few were optimistic that it would last into the future. Technocracy is a challenge to representative democracy and dependent on political will.

No political system is likely to be perfectly designed for dealing with pandemics, but the Australian political system has proved more resilient than most. Yet we need to do more to adapt our practices to cope with what unfortunately is likely to be a common and repeated experience of this century: the impact of unexpected, threatening and troublesome events.

We need to prepare democracy for the reality of a regular experience of crisis. There are plainly coping mechanisms that work to some degree. Governments lean on leadership and executive decision-making more than in 'normal' times, but the more representative and reflective branches of government have an enormous role in lesson-learning. The anxiety created by a crisis may lead citizens to place rather too much trust in leaders and to rally to their support. Yet the evidence is that support is never unconditional and rather is contingent on the leader acting effectively. Experts may become more prominent in decision-making in a crisis as their specialist knowledge is seen as the key to unlocking understanding and solutions but, again, there are checks and balances at play.

In learning from the COVID-19 crisis, it will be essential to ensure the principles and practices of democracy are maintained, as well as drawing more specific lessons about whether actions were taken in a timely, appropriate and effective manner. Instances of democratic backsliding will need to be addressed, such as the erosion of civil liberties due to the withdrawal of certain individual rights during lockdown, increased state surveillance through the use of smartphone location tracking and the monitoring of social media. The issue for democracies is not just what worked in terms of beating the virus, but also what maintained the values of democracy and the adaptive practices that made a difference.

References

Australian National Audit Office. *Auditor-General Report No.20 2020–21: Management of the Australian Public Service's Workforce Response to COVID-19*, Commonwealth of Australia, 2020.

Bertsou, Eri and Daniele Caramani. *The Technocratic Challenge to Democracy*, Routledge/Taylor and Francis, 2020.

Edis, Taner. 'A revolt against expertise: Pseudoscience, right-wing populism, and post-truth politics', *Disputatio*, 9(13), 2020, pp. 1–29.

Evans, Mark and Michelle Grattan, 'Health expertise and COVID-19 – managing the fear factor', *Australian Quarterly*, 92(2), 2021, pp. 20–28.

Evans, Mark and Ipsos Public Affairs, *Guardians of our Civic Culture: What museums could and should do*, Council of Australasian Museum Directors, 2021, <https://www.democracy2025.gov.au/resources.html>.

Fenna, Alan and Linda Botterill. *Interrogating Public Policy Theory: A Political Values Perspective*, Edward Elgar, 2019.

Hetherington, Marc J and Michael Nelson. 'Anatomy of a rally effect: George W. Bush and the war on terrorism', *Political Science and Politics* 36(1), 2003, pp. 37–42.

Jennings, Will, Viktor Valgardsson, Gerry Stoker, Dan Devine, Jen Gaskell and Mark Evans. *Democracy 2025 Report No 8: Political Trust and the COVID-19 Crisis – Pushing Populism to the Backburner? A study of public opinion in Australia, Italy, the UK and the USA*, Canberra, IGPA/MoAD/Trustgov, 2020, <www.democracy2025.gov.au/resources.html>.

Lightbody, Ruth and Jennifer J Roberts. 'Experts: The politics of evidence and expertise in democratic innovation', in Stephen Elstub and Oliver Escobar (eds), *Handbook of Democratic Innovation and Governance*, Edward Elgar, 2019, pp. 225–40.

MacIntyre, C. Raina, Louisa Jorm, Richard Nunes-Vaz and Timothy Churches. *The Case for a Short, Sharp Lockdown in Australia*, Integrated Systems for Epidemic Response, 2020, <cdn.theconversation.com/static_files/files/978/COVID-Australia_Lockdown_%281%29.pdf?1585710115>.

March, James and Johan Olsen. *Democratic Governance*, Free Press, 1995.

Merkel, Wolfgang. 'Who governs in deep crises? The case of Germany', Democratic Theory, 7(2), 2020, pp. 1–11.

Self, Peter. *Administrative Theories and Politics*, George Allen & Unwin, 1977.

Shergold, Peter, Jillian Broadbent, Isobel Marshall and Peter Varghese. *Fault Lines: An independent review into Australia's response to COVID-19*, John and Myriam Wylie Foundation, Minderoo Foundation, Paul Ramsay Foundation, 2022, <assets.website-files.com/62b998c0c9af9f65bba26051/6350438b7df8c77439846e97_FAULT-LINES-1.pdf>.

21

A DEEP DIVE INTO 'TEAL' TERRITORY:
A WENTWORTH CASE STUDY

Michelle Grattan and Jane Seaborn

The 2022 election made history in both the number of crossbenchers it delivered to the House of Representatives – 16 – and the substantial and distinctive subgroup of six 'teals' among them.

Crossbenchers have been an intermittent presence in the lower house, but on occasion of critical importance. Two independents brought down the conservative government in 1941, installing John Curtin as Australia's wartime prime minister. Crossbenchers enabled Labor's Julia Gillard to remain in power after the 2010 election. In late 2018, the Morrison Government fell into minority, giving crossbenchers a brief taste of power. Kerryn Phelps, the independent who had won Wentworth after Malcolm Turnbull's resignation from parliament following his loss of the prime ministership, successfully drove legislation to facilitate medical transfers of asylum seekers from Manus Island and Nauru.

Coming up to the 2022 election, the House crossbench numbered seven: Andrew Wilkie, Helen Haines, Rebekha Sharkie (Centre Alliance), Zali Steggall, Craig Kelly (who had defected from the Liberals), Adam Bandt (Greens) and Bob Katter (Katter's Australian Party). Steggall had defeated former prime minister Tony Abbott in Warringah in 2019. While her win was particularly due to Abbott having become very unpopular in his seat for several reasons, the role of the climate issue in her victory was also a harbinger of 2022.

The times suited the 2022 surge of the teals (so dubbed because of the campaign colour some used). Many voters were deeply disillusioned with the major parties, and with the state of politics generally. The Morrison

Government had failed to respond at all adequately to the challenge of climate change. There was a model for 'community independents', especially in the Victorian regional seat of Indi. Cathy McGowan won this in 2013 on the back of a 'Voices for Indi' movement, and then Haines won it in 2019, when McGowan retired. In the 2019–22 parliament, Haines and Steggall had been to the fore on what would be the core 'teal' issues at the election. Steggall produced a draft Bill on climate change; Haines released one for an integrity commission.

Importantly, there was a large available pot of money from Climate 200 to fund candidates for the 2022 election. Climate 200 was set up before the 2019 election, founded by Simon Holmes à Court. It declared of itself that it was 'not a party. It does not start campaigns, select candidates, speak for candidates, dictate policies, or have members. We simply give strong community campaigns a leg up with funding and support'. Its executive director, Byron Fay, described the organisation as Holmes à Court's 'attempt to leverage philanthropy into politics'.

In the 2022 campaign, Climate 200 raised $13 million and supported 23 candidates, 11 of whom were successful (including four of the re-elected crossbenchers). Among those who received funding was David Pocock, who wrested an ACT Senate seat from the Liberals' Zed Seselja – the first time since the territories received Senate representation in 1975 that a Liberal did not hold one of the two ACT upper house seats. Climate 200 also helped candidates with advice and data, commissioned research and assisted with communications. The funding and aid were invaluable to the teals, although they also raised substantial amounts of money off their own bats, much of it from small donors.

The teals also benefitted from advice from McGowan, who travelled extensively, mentoring and encouraging. In February 2021, McGowan ran an online convention billed for 'candidates planning to run as independents, community members keen to support a community leader to run, and others with a commitment to help Australian politics reach its potential'. Some 300 people signed up from about 78 electorates. The convention discussed community engagement, finding a candidate and campaigning. Already, 'voices' groups were established in various electorates, and this was an opportunity to make contacts and share experiences. Steggall, with her high profile and climate focus, was an important role model for what could be achieved in city seats.

It should be noted that there were different drivers of the various 'voices' groups. While in 2022 national issues were to the forefront, in Indi in 2013 stronger local representation and the replacement of a very unpopular Liberal member were central. One strand in the 'voices' push was locals' desire for agency: turning previously safe seats into contested ones meant they received, actually or potentially, more attention from the major parties.

Critics, especially the Morrison Government in the campaign, tried to paint the independents as a de facto party and 'fake', which was not accurate. But many of them could be seen as forming a loose web, or network, for sharing common experiences, advice and funding.

The teals effectively turned the 2022 contest into two elections. Their battles with the Liberals were distinct from the more usual Coalition–Labor contests. The serious teal contests were in seats Labor could not win. Some benefited from Labor running dead or 'strategic' voting by Labor supporters who switched to a teal challenger deemed to have a better chance of winning. Indeed, the Australian Election Study's results 'counter the narrative of Teal voters as disaffected Liberals'. It found that, 'Based on their recalled vote in the 2019 election, a majority of Teal supporters in 2022 were tactical voters intent on unseating the incumbent Liberal … 31 per cent of Teal voters had supported Labor in 2019 and a further 24 per cent had supported the Greens. Just 18 percent said they had voted for the Coalition' (Cameron et al, 2022).

The teals gained from the Liberal Party's pivot to concentrate its appeal to outer suburban voters ('aspirationals', 'tradies', 'quiet Australians'), rather than the inner suburban voters who had usually supported the Liberals. Furthermore, Scott Morrison was a leader with little appeal for these traditional Liberal voters.

The teal candidates were predominantly professional women, chosen by community processes. They ran on a core trifecta of issues – climate, integrity and greater equality for women – but also tapped into voters' disillusionment with politics and how it was conducted. None of those teals who won had been employed as political staffers, the stepping stone for so many major party candidates. But two (Allegra Spender and Kate Chaney) came from very well-known Liberal families. In a time when people were increasingly alienated from the major parties, the teals attracted extraordinary levels of volunteer support, enabling their campaigns to achieve high visibility and make direct contact with large numbers of voters. Many people, it seemed, could be attracted to political engagement if they liked the way politics was done.

The teals introduced a particular element of unpredictability into the election, because they had to climb such big hurdles to win, gaining a substantial first-preference vote and pushing down the Liberal vote to get into at least second place so they could be assisted by preferences.

Teals won the following house seats from the Liberals: North Sydney (Kylea Tink), Mackellar (Sophie Scamps) and Wentworth (Spender) in New South Wales, Goldstein (Zoe Daniel) and Kooyong (Monique Ryan) in Victoria, and Curtin (Chaney) in Western Australia. Their victories decimated the ranks of Liberal moderates. But in the new House of Representatives, the teals are limited to exerting influence, rather than possessing the power they would have had if the house had been 'hung'.[1] The spectacular success of the teals was a product of immediate and longer-term factors. One element was the benefit of abundant funds. In the Victorian election later in 2022, where circumstances were different and donation caps in place, teal candidates fell short of victories.

The battle for Wentworth

The rise of independents in the Australian political pantheon over the past three decades has coincided with a decline in citizen trust, which has been the subject of longitudinal analysis by the University of Canberra. The NSW federal electorate of Wentworth was chosen by the university's Centre for Change Governance for a deep dive at the 2022 election. The seat held obvious prospects for high-profile teal independent Allegra Spender to break through, thanks to the combination of its marginal status, the profile of its voters and its recent volatile electoral history.

In this well-heeled, well-educated and politically aware area with an established inclination towards social progressiveness, action on climate change and political integrity, at the centre of the 'teal' campaigns were issues that would resonate. Kerryn Phelps' brief occupancy indicated Wentworth voters were open to voting independent, especially if protest was on their minds.

Wentworth, a federation seat situated in Sydney's affluent eastern suburbs, was at the 2022 election the second smallest electorate in the country by geographical footprint (38 square kilometres). Preparing for the 2022 battle, candidates had only the 2016 Census to inform them – with the post-election release of the 2021 Census, we have more up-to-date information.

Based on the 2021 Census, Wentworth had a gender split of 47.9 per cent male and 52.1 per cent female residents, and a median age of 38 years. Of its families, 40.8 per cent were couples with children, 46.2 per cent couples without children and 11.5 per cent were one-parent families – 20.6 per cent of single parents were male.

The most frequent response on religion was 'no religion', at 40.6 per cent, and then Catholic, at 19 per cent. The seat includes a large Jewish community, with 13.5 per cent nominating Judaism. Some 53.6 per cent of the Wentworth population held a bachelor degree or above, and the most common occupations were professionals (43.1 per cent) and managers (23 per cent).

Since the Second World War, Wentworth had been held by four federal ministers and a prime minister. Dave Sharma, a former diplomat, wrested it from Phelps with 47.4 per cent of the primary vote in 2019. Sharma was one of the moderates in the Liberal parliamentary party and had crossed the floor during the debate over religious discrimination legislation. Spender came from a high-profile Liberal family. Her father served in federal parliament; her grandfather, Percy Spender, was a federal minister and later ambassador to the United States, and a key figure in the forging of the ANZUS treaty.

Our research started with quantitative polling conducted in the period 19–21 March 2022, before the election was called formally, followed by three rounds of qualitative research. The research was conducted by Landscape Research, with results published in reports on *The Conversation* website, from which the summary in this chapter draws.[2]

The initial poll of 1036 Wentworth voters indicated a close and potentially open contest, and highlighted the challenges facing the two leading candidates who would fight out the result. The Liberal primary vote sat at 42 per cent, while Spender was polling 27 per cent. Sharma would need a higher primary vote to survive. Spender was set to come in second – as she had to for any prospect of victory. Labor was polling 14 per cent, the Greens 9 per cent. When voters were asked to choose between Sharma and Spender on a two-candidate-preferred (TCP) basis, Sharma was on 49 per cent, Spender 46 per cent, and 5 per cent of voters could not say. After the 'don't knows' were eliminated, Sharma remained marginally ahead of Spender 51–49 per cent. Nearly three-quarters of voters said they had already decided how they would vote.

Two months out from election day this benchmark polling showed that more of the electorate viewed Sharma favourably than Spender. At that time, he was much better known, which resulted in fewer 'neutral' or 'never heard of the candidate' responses than Spender. A higher proportion of voters also rated him unfavourably than rated Spender unfavourably. It was clear at this stage that Spender's big challenge was to get herself better recognised and better understood.

As far as issues went, climate change was always the frontrunner in this electorate. When voters were asked which issue (from a list of six) would have the most influence on their vote, the result was: climate change and the environment, 28 per cent; jobs and economic management, 20 per cent; integrity in politics, 14 per cent; national security and defence, 14 per cent; cost of living pressures, 12 per cent; and health and COVID management, 4 per cent.

The polling revealed that prime minister Scott Morrison presented as a serious problem for Sharma; of these voters, a majority (55 per cent) had an unfavourable view of Morrison, and almost half (46 per cent) rated the Morrison Government's performance as poor. Morrison had a net favourable–unfavourable score of –25. On the other hand, Albanese's net favourability was just –7 and only 37 per cent had an unfavourable view of him, markedly less than of Morrison.

The qualitative work with 'soft' voters – people who had not made up their minds about who to vote for or were considering changing their vote – was carried out in three tranches: at the start, middle and end of the campaign. This enabled us to track their thinking as the campaign unfolded. It commenced with focus groups on 11–12 April, immediately after Morrison called the election, followed by the mid-campaign sessions on 27–28 April. The last focus groups were held on 11–12 May, 9–10 days out from the election. Fifteen voters (across two focus groups) took part, with only one substitution in the cohort made after the first round. While this qualitative research was in no way designed to predict the election outcome, it was able to provide snapshots of the thinking of these voters, and the staged approach throughout the campaign delivered key insights along the way on their views as they changed or hardened, on their journey towards determining their final vote.

In the first round of focus group discussions, voters were highly vocal about Morrison, revealing why 55 per cent of the electorate had an unfavourable view of him; they spontaneously criticised him, in general and on specific issues, including about his perceived attitudes towards women. Some older voters would have liked Josh Frydenberg to be leading. The treasurer campaigned in the seat, while Morrison kept his distance because of his unpopularity. While this seat had demonstrated a solid rump of support of around 11 per cent for Labor's Tim Murray in his previous two candidatures (2018 by-election and 2019 general election), these soft voters were not enthusiastic about Albanese (a stumble over numbers as the campaign started was fresh in mind and mentioned unprompted).

Albanese was viewed as a career politician, not as 'stuck up' as previous Labor leader Bill Shorten, but lacking in policy, and concerns lingered around his ties to unions. As with Morrison on his perceived attitudes towards women, Albanese came in for criticism around his response to allegations of Labor bullying of Kimberley Kitching, a Labor senator who had very recently died, with female voters expressing disappointment over the way he had handled the issue. Ultimately, those views had little impact on Labor's vote, with Murray again achieving just shy of 11 per cent of first preferences in 2022.

Spender was not yet well known, other than high-level name recognition, but had appeal on the basis she was seen as 'Liberal-lite', having desirable Liberal credentials and values while addressing more progressive topical policy issues and without the Morrison baggage. Views about Sharma were mixed, ranging from 'bland' to being regarded as a good local member, but ultimately Morrison was the albatross around his neck. As one voter put it: 'If it was just a matter of voting for Sharma, I would; but, unfortunately, he comes attached to Scott Morrison'.

When we checked in next with our soft voters, mid-campaign (27–28 April), we found that views had firmed around Spender but she was polarising voters. A key event a few days prior to our mid-campaign research was the televised live *Sky News* People's Forum debate between Sharma and Spender in front of an audience of undecided voters who got to ask questions of the candidates. Given that it was live streamed, many of our participants elected to tune in to get a serious look at the two frontrunners. That exposure hardened views around Spender, for both better and worse. For some, she 'never slipped up and was talking with passion' and offered 'out of the box solutions while Dave Sharma isn't'. Others found her claims of true independence questionable given her affiliation as a teal and that her campaign funding was at least in part paid for by Simon Holmes à Court's Climate 200 group. Spender's repeated refusal to declare whom she would support to form government in the event of a hung parliament also weighed heavily on some. Only a few of our soft voters had changed their opinion about Sharma over the course of the campaign, and for them it was mostly to a less favourable view.

At the start of the campaign, the TCP vote had split more or less evenly between the two main candidates: eight leaning towards Spender and seven leaning towards Sharma. The same overall split remained mid-campaign, but notably there had been some swapping of allegiance by individual voters. There were also signs electors were anticipating a Spender win. Asked about the likely outcome if a poll had been held then, nine believed Spender would win, three thought Sharma would and three were unsure.

In the final round of focus groups with the soft voters, on 11–12 May, eight of the 15 participants had still not definitely locked into their vote. Of the seven who were 'very certain', six were voting for Spender (the other one supporting the Liberal Democrat candidate and leaning towards Sharma for their second preference). The previous weeks had helped Spender. On a first-preference basis she received nine votes to Sharma's three, while he picked up another three on a TCP basis. There was a strong feeling, as the election entered its final days, that Spender had run a better, more visible, campaign than Sharma. Talk of a hung parliament, with Spender refusing to say whom she would support, continued to raise concerns among some but, overall, Spender had gained momentum and there was a mood for change.

In the washup after the election, 14 members of our research panel responded to our exit poll and shared their votes. First-preference results: Spender eight votes, Sharma three, Daniel Lewkovitz (Liberal Democrats) two, Tim Murray (Labor) one. On a TCP basis the result was Spender eight, Sharma six. Ultimately, Spender (whose campaign cost more than $2 million) won the seat with a 4.2 per cent margin on a TCP basis. Sharma's primary vote had dropped from 47.4 per cent in 2019 to 40.5 per cent.

The voters of Wentworth had sent a powerful message to the Liberal Party. It turned out to be the same message that voters from a batch of electorates were sending.

References

Cameron, Sarah, Ian McAllister, Simon Jackman and Jill Sheppard. *The 2022 Australian Federal Election: Results from the Australian Election Study*, ANU, 2022.

22

SCOTT MORRISON'S CRISIS LEADERSHIP

Brendan McCaffrie

The 2019–22 parliamentary term was overshadowed by crises. For prime ministers, major crises such as natural disasters, terrorist attacks and pandemics represent both stern tests of their capabilities and vast opportunities to show themselves as effective leaders who care about their citizens in a time of need. Competent management of a crisis frequently translates to electoral success for incumbents, as citizens tend to judge performance on a major crisis as a hugely important factor in determining their vote. Leaders' effectiveness on such important issues can often trump other flaws, such as ethical failings (Ciulla & Forsyth, 2011).

Between the onset of the COVID-19 pandemic and the end of the 2019–22 federal parliamentary term, incumbent governments won five of the six state and territory elections held, with rare swings towards incumbents in Western Australia and Queensland. However, despite Australia doing a comparatively good job at minimising COVID-19 deaths and infections, particularly in the earlier parts of the pandemic period, Prime Minister Scott Morrison was relatively subdued in claiming credit for this during the 2022 election campaign. Morrison's election launch speech did not contain the words 'Covid', 'COVID-19' or 'coronavirus'. It referred to the 'pandemic' nine times, almost always celebrating the government's economic response rather than its health response (Morrison, 2022). In part, Morrison's government was seen as less instrumental in keeping individuals safe than state governments had been. In part, perceived blunders, particularly over the vaccine rollout, meant that discussing COVID-19 was less-than-solid electoral ground for

Morrison. It is fair to say that Morrison's record on COVID-19, and other crises during the term, was mixed.

The two biggest crises of the term were the 2019–20 Black Summer bushfires and the COVID-19 pandemic. These crises presented Morrison with particular challenges in three key aspects of public crisis leadership (Boin et al, 2005):[1] *sense-making* – diagnosing and understanding the situation as it evolves; *meaning-making* – providing persuasive accounts of what is happening and why, as well as what is being done about it; and *coordination* – establishing effective collaboration among existing actors.

Morrison learned from key blunders in coordination and meaning-making in the bushfire crisis to provide a better initial response to the COVID-19 pandemic, but later in the pandemic he again lapsed into apparent inaction, allowing others such as the state premiers to take control of the definition of events. Ultimately, this meant that Morrison fell short in his meaning-making. Additionally, his combative communications style frequently undermined his efforts at both meaning-making and coordination, leaving him diminished in political terms by crises from which other leaders may have benefitted.

Black Summer bushfires

Sense-making and meaning-making

In terms of sense-making, and the related meaning-making challenge during the Black Summer bushfires, Morrison appeared slow to understand the gravity of the crisis, and slow to act meaningfully to help affected citizens. A public perception that the Morrison Government was not taking sufficient action made it difficult for Morrison to authoritatively define the issues as they occurred.

The prime minister was criticised for not making adequate preparations for the bushfire season, including in resourcing, despite warnings from former Fire & Rescue NSW Commissioner Greg Mullins and other emergency leaders that the long drought and anticipated hot summer would lead to a need for increased funding (Noyes, 2019). Mullins' requests for a meeting with the prime minister in April 2019 were referred to the Minister for Energy and Emissions Reduction Angus Taylor, and received a response in September to schedule a meeting in October, long after the bushfires were underway (Davies, 2020).

The re-elected Morrison Government's initial priority was to deliver a budget surplus, and its early months were focused on reducing spending. This focus continued as the bushfire crisis hit. Although disaster payments for citizens were activated relatively swiftly, the Commonwealth was reluctant to make further funds available for firefighting. In January 2020, after months of fire devastation and criticism, Morrison announced $2 billion of federal funding for bushfire recovery, and finally made clear that this was a more important priority than the surplus (Martin, 2020). However, a perception of government inaction had already taken hold.

The sense-making and meaning-making challenges were interlinked during the Black Summer bushfires, as public debate focused on whether the fires were in part a result of climate change, stoking existing division on the issue within the Coalition. In November 2019, Morrison preferred to avoid talking about the link between climate change and the bushfires, seeking to blunt journalists' questions by saying, 'My only thoughts today are with those who have lost their lives and their families, the firefighters who are fighting the fires [and] the response effort that has to be delivered' (Morrison, quoted in Fox, 2019). Other politicians saw his reticence as an opportunity to engage in intemperate debate, and Morrison lost the opportunity to control the definition of the issue. Greens Senator Jordan Steele-John criticised the government's lack of climate action, calling the two major parties 'no better than arsonists', and Deputy Prime Minister Michael McCormack angrily retorted against 'raving inner-city lunatics'. With the climate debate now front and centre, Morrison claimed politicians should not debate the issue while the emergency response was underway (Crowe & Koslowski, 2019). Arguably, this was more about taking the heat out of an issue on which his Coalition parties did not agree, but without a particularly positive story to tell about his government's operational achievements against the fires, this deflection failed to assuage critics.

Eventually, Morrison was forced to admit that climate change was an important factor in the bushfires, although his claims that he had acknowledged this 'all year' felt disingenuous to many (*Canberra Times*, 2019). Another apparent backdown came when, after repeatedly insisting that fire services had all the resources they needed, Morrison announced an additional $11 million for aerial firefighting capacity (Coughlan & McCulloch, 2019).

The strongest impression that Morrison was not active enough in responding to the fires came when he took a December holiday to Hawai'i with his family while the fires raged and while Sydney, Canberra and other towns and cities along the east coast were blanketed in hazardous, thick smoke. Arguably, it would not have been a problem if Morrison and his office had not attempted to conceal the trip, with the Prime Minister's Office insisting that journalists were 'incorrect' for suggesting that Morrison was in Hawai'i (Crowe, 2019). His explanation in a 2GB radio interview that 'I don't hold a hose, mate, and I don't sit in a control room', pointed to a reality that there was little that Morrison could do about the fires, but this is not a reality that most political leaders would admit. Certainly, it showed a lack of understanding of the symbolic role played by leaders during crises, and the hose comment was used against him repeatedly during the election campaign.

Coordination

The fires also represented a missed opportunity for Morrison to enhance his leadership standing by leading coordination efforts. Spending months noting, accurately, that fighting fires was a state and territory responsibility was novel for a national leader in a time of crisis. Typically, prime ministers are eager to assume responsibilities beyond their remit, and to use Commonwealth funds to leave citizens with the impression that the prime minister deserves the credit for all action. Morrison could also have better utilised the Commonwealth's responsibility to help manage cross-border challenges in natural disasters and by deploying the military.

In the wake of the bushfires, a Royal Commission into National Natural Disaster Arrangements was called. It found a need for a range of improvements in national governance for natural disasters (see Dare and Schirmer, chapter 18 in this volume). This included: providing a simpler trigger for a national disaster declaration, allow the Commonwealth to mobilise national agencies in response to disasters, a national fleet of aerial firefighting resources, and greater capacity for on-the-ground communications between emergency responders from different jurisdictions. The Royal Commission also led to the creation of the National Recovery and Resilience Agency (originally the National Bushfire Recovery Agency). Many of these reforms would have been impossible for Morrison to implement during the crisis; however, the need for greater forethought with regard to resources also hampered the coordination effort, and as the rapid formation of a National Cabinet and other coordination mechanisms for medical advice during the pandemic showed, the Commonwealth is capable of rapidly upscaling its coordination efforts when the political will exists.

Arguably, where Morrison failed in terms of the bushfire response was not about misunderstanding what was happening, how severe it was or why it was happening, but rather misunderstanding what the Australian public expected of him and his government. Australians expect their prime minister to be active in coordinating and responding to the crisis and they are unlikely to be interested in arguments that fires are a state responsibility. After repeatedly rebuffing opportunities to be more active in managing the crisis, Morrison also lost his authority to define the crisis and to take credit for successes, while being vulnerable to blame for a range of shortcomings, whether they were of his making or not.

COVID-19 pandemic

Having spent the months of the bushfire crisis on the defensive, Morrison was immediately presented with an opportunity to show a better version of crisis leadership, and at least for a time, could be said to have done that.

Sense-making

Morrison and his government began their sense-making challenge effectively, understanding the COVID-19 crisis largely by listening to the experts, particularly in terms of the health advice. This differed from the bushfire response, when a range of firefighting experts complained about being ignored. During the pandemic, Morrison was always eager to remind Australians that he was 'following the health advice'.

Australia was at an advantage compared to many countries, in that infections had spread widely in other parts of the world before the virus had made a significant impact in Australia. This gave medical experts time to assess what was happening before recommending action. Australia was also fortunate to have a border it could close, initially to China, and later to all non-residents, and to have the expert and political will to put that controversial but effective measure in place.

Morrison and his government were fast to recognise the severity and depth of the crisis, and therefore were able to quickly abandon any thoughts of delivering a surplus. They did this in the full understanding that they could explain why the surplus was no longer the government's key priority. Arguably, the same prioritisation could have come much earlier in the bushfire response. It meant that Morrison was freed up to focus on delivering outcomes, rather than on reducing spending. Morrison's sense-making in both crises involved a balance between the operational, financial and economic aspects of the crisis response. His understanding of the pandemic gave more importance to the economic side of the crisis than many, including most state and territory leaders, who prioritised the health side. Again, this had consequences for people's perceptions of Morrison's leadership.

Meaning-making

In the early weeks of the COVID-19 pandemic, Morrison's response was occasionally puzzling. In March 2020, Morrison announced a ban on gatherings of 500 or more to take effect in a week but planned to attend a rugby league match between that announcement and the ban taking effect. Ultimately, Morrison chose not to attend, but the mixed messaging caused unnecessary confusion. In part, this reflected Morrison's attempts to calm a clearly panicked Australian public as it attempted to come to terms with a new reality and did peculiar things like purchasing absurd quantities of toilet paper and other household items from supermarkets.

Reassurance was the focus as Morrison delivered a direct, televised address to the nation on 12 March 2020, in which he stated, 'I want to assure you and your family tonight that while Australia cannot and is not immune from this virus, we are well prepared and are well equipped to deal with it'.

Morrison was also eager to balance the health aspect of the crisis with its economic aspect in his attempts to define the meaning of events. The $2.4 billion health plan announced on 11 March 2020, in an effort to boost Australia's medical capacity to respond, was paired with the 12 March 2020 announcement of a $17.6 billion economic support package, supplemented ten days later with a second $66 billion economic support package, including the coronavirus supplement, which increased JobSeeker payments to unemployed people. Similarly, the 12 March 2020 televised address largely sought to downplay the virus's health effects. While acknowledging the risk to vulnerable Australians, Morrison stated, '… for most Australians in good health who contract the virus, they will experience a mild illness'. He spent more time addressing the economic side of the virus's effects than the health side. Morrison's reassurance was reasonably effective, largely because in the weeks that followed, as stricter health measures came into effect, case numbers declined to a trickle and his reassuring tone accorded with events.

Morrison also did a good job of conveying information in the early stages of the pandemic. Many Australians will remember their basic understanding of what was happening being shaped by the frequent press conferences delivered jointly by the prime minister and a range of others, often Chief Medical Officer Brendan Murphy in the early stages, Treasurer Josh Frydenberg and Health Minister Greg Hunt. The basic information they imparted included pleas for people to reconsider travel, and information about restrictions on social gatherings, handwashing regimens and case numbers (Bernard et al, 2021). Morrison and others, including the state premiers, made persuasive arguments for a range of restrictions and changes to people's lives, which the public largely accepted, as evidenced by increasing trust in government through the early stages of the pandemic (Jennings et al, 2020).

Morrison's meaning-making was assisted by the fact that the Labor

Opposition largely chose to support the government's approach, particularly in the early phase of the pandemic. This led to occasional criticism of Labor leader Anthony Albanese for failing to seize opportunities to differentiate the opposition (Kelly, 2020), and speculation that Labor frontbenchers such as Tanya Plibersek were positioning themselves to contest the leadership (Murphy & Karp, 2021). Public disagreements were more common between Morrison and various state premiers, particularly those who took hardline approaches to closing their state borders and to imposing lockdowns when their local cases rose. As the pandemic wore on, greater differences emerged between the government and opposition, particularly on the handling of vaccines.

On vaccines, Morrison began to again look inactive, as he had in the bushfire crisis. By appearing to fall behind the events he lost authority to control their meaning. In large part, this owed to changing circumstances within the country. Many of the comparator countries that were initially faster to vaccinate their populations were also suffering far greater case numbers and fatalities than Australia. However, as Australian cases rose in 2021, the delays in making vaccinations available and the confusing advice about the safety of the AstraZeneca vaccines left Morrison open to serious criticism (see Duckett, chapter 7 in this volume). Perceived inactivity was highlighted by Morrison's repeated defence of the rollout, that 'it's not a race'; a phrase he later regretted (Crowe, 2021).

Morrison was also criticised for his government's vaccine-procurement strategy, which had invested in only two potential vaccines, while other countries had invested more widely. When Pfizer initially sought a meeting to discuss vaccine availability for Australia, Health Minister Greg Hunt sent a public servant in his stead, a revelation that implied to the public that vaccines had been deprioritised (Martin, 2021). Arguably, Morrison was slower to react than some national leaders because comparatively low case numbers meant vaccines were deemed less urgent in Australia than elsewhere. However, the prime minister's desire to see Australian businesses operating in a normal manner, and an end to lockdowns, suggested a need to ensure the most rapid vaccination drive possible. Morrison's perceived inaction on vaccinations diminished his ability to control the meaning of events, and as with the 'I don't hold a hose' comment, the 'it's not a race' line became emblematic of a prime minister who had been overtaken by events, rather than mastering them.

Coordination

It is notable that as with the bushfires, many of the federal responsibilities for dealing with a health crisis fell to the states and territories, not the federal government, but Morrison was far more active in responding to the crisis directly, and in seeking to play the role of the coordinating leader. The creation of a National Cabinet provided a forum for national decision-making involving the state and territory heads of government and the prime minister. Preceding chapters have provided differing takes on the National Cabinet, with Fenna (chapter 5) praising the fact that it had ensured the sharing of information, while Duckett (chapter 7) focused on the negative effects of the lack of consensus among states and territories. State and territory differences were sometimes borne of different balances among health and economic strategies, and sometimes borne of different political pressures within states. The states and territories facing elections tended to be stricter in applying health measures than those that were not. Coordinating the various states and territories to an extent that saw a uniform approach could never have been easy, but arguably some of Morrison's actions and rhetoric exacerbated federal tensions, rather than assuaging them.

As the crisis developed, it became clear that the prime minister's sense-making led to a balance between economic and health aspects of the crisis that differed from many state and territory approaches. The states – with the exception of New South Wales, whose approach Morrison praised – prioritised health to a far greater extent, leading to public differences of opinion between Morrison and various state premiers as state borders closed to residents of other states. On some occasions these were more understandable than others: when Victoria was dealing with hundreds of daily cases and other states had few or none, closing the border to Victoria was a sensible way to reduce the spread of the disease. In other cases, movement was restricted despite few cases on either side of a border.

Morrison tended to side with those who advocated for more open borders, more open economies and freer movement. Again, this put him on the side of perceived inaction against the health crisis compared to many state counterparts. And while few enjoyed lockdowns and border closures, when the justification is an attempt to save lives, most people are willing to be persuaded. In the second half of 2021, as Victoria, New South Wales and the Australian Capital Territory were in lockdown, the Morrison Government sought to pressure Queensland and Western Australia into opening their borders, prompting angry replies from the states' Labor premiers. Morrison largely ignored similar policies when they were pursued by Liberal governments in Tasmania and South Australia (Grattan, 2021). Morrison's divisive partisan attacks were the antithesis of coordinated action. His support for Clive Palmer in his High Court action against Western Australia for its border closure was perhaps Morrison's most significant misstep, as voters in that state proved decisive in rejecting the Coalition Government.

Morrison's crisis leadership in context

It would be overly reductive to say that Morrison's crisis leadership was the reason he and the Coalition lost the 2022 election. However, it was one reason they lost, and the conclusion that Morrison himself was one of the Coalition's key weaknesses is unavoidable. Analysing the Australian Election Study, Ian McAllister found that Morrison had been the most unpopular Liberal leader at any election since the study began in 1987, and that while views on how well his government had handled the pandemic were mixed, 'negative perceptions about the pandemic were channelled through Morrison's leadership and were a major drag on the Coalition vote' (McAllister, quoted in Karp, 2022).

Morrison's leadership was criticised from many angles. He became emblematic of the Coalition's difficulties with Australian women, through his clumsy remarks on issues of gender equality and sexual violence against women, detailed by Rowe (chapter 12). Similarly, Morrison had become emblematic of the failure to act adequately on climate change (Sinclair and Mummery, chapter 19), and on an integrity commission (Watson, chapter 17). As Morrison himself admitted during the 2022 election campaign, his style could alienate people, because he was 'a bit of a bulldozer'. His approach to questioning from journalists was often combative, as was his approach to those on the other side of politics. The long crises offered an opportunity to rise above the political fray, and he managed it briefly, before his instincts to attack those who disagreed with him resurfaced. At times it worked, but it left him on the wrong side of the debate for too many voters, who largely preferred a stronger health response.

For all of the other problems, it is likely that had Morrison been more widely seen as effective against the crises that dominated the term, particularly against COVID-19, many of his other failings would have been forgiven by enough people that he might have won the election. Most would credit Morrison with considerable success on economic aspects of the response to the pandemic, as well as the early part of the health response. Ultimately, however, Morrison left the impression that he did less in the face of crises than some leaders might: first, by leaving the states and territories to manage the bushfires, and second by appearing to move slowly on later aspects of the pandemic, such as the vaccine rollout. Appearing inactive at key times left the impression that others, like state premiers, were the architects of Australia's successes in crisis management, and that Morrison had fallen short on the most important test of his term.

References

Bernard, Natalie Reyes, Adbul Basit, Ernesta Sofija, Hai Phung, Jessica Lee, Shannon Rutherford, Bernadette Sebar, Neil Harris, Dung Phung, and Nicola Wiseman. 'Analysis of crisis communication by the Prime Minister of Australia during the COVID-19 pandemic', *International Journal of Disaster Risk Reduction*, 62, 102375, 2021.

Boin, Arjen, Paul 't Hart, Eric Stern, and Bengt Sundelius. *The Politics of Crisis Management: Public leadership under pressure*, Cambridge University Press, 2005.

Canberra Times. 'Prime Minister's change of position welcome', 13 December 2019, <www.canberratimes.com.au/story/6540725/prime-ministers-change-of-position-welcome>.

Ciulla, Joanne B and Donelson R Forsyth. 'Leadership ethics', in Alan Bryman, David Collinson, Keith Grint, Brad Jackson and Mary Uhl-Bien (eds), *The SAGE Handbook of Leadership*, Sage Publications, 2011.

Coughlan, Matt and Daniel McCulloch. 'PM responds to pressure over NSW bushfires', *Australian Associated Press*, 11 December 2019.

Crowe, David. 'Two leadership blunders in the otherwise trivial affair of the PM's holiday', *Sydney Morning Herald*, 20 December 2019, <www.smh.com.au/politics/federal/two-leadership-blunders-in-the-otherwise-trivial-affair-of-the-pm-s-holiday-20191220-p53lsm.html>.

Crowe, David and Max Koslowski. '"Take it down a few notches": Morrison urges calm as fire blame game escalates', *The Age*, 12 November 2019, <www.smh.com.au/politics/federal/take-it-down-a-few-notches-morrison-urges-calm-as-fire-blame-game-escalates-20191112-p539zb.html>.

Crowe, David. 'Morrison regrets "not a race" remark, promises to make up lost ground', *Sydney Morning Herald*, 21 July 2021, <www.smh.com.au/politics/federal/morrison-regrets-not-a-race-remark-promises-to-make-up-lost-ground-20210721-p58bq3.html>.

Davies, Anne. 'Australian bushfires: How the Morrison Government failed to heed warnings of catastrophe', *Guardian*, 3 June 2020, <www.theguardian.com/australia-news/2020/jun/03/australian-bushfires-fois-shed-new-light-on-why-morrison-government-was-ill-prepared>.

Fox, Aine. 'Aust at risk warns NSW mayor who lost home', *Australian Associated Press*, 9 November 2019.

Grattan, Michelle. 'The transition to living with "endemic" COVID could be rough', *The Conversation*, 2 September 2021, <theconversation.com/grattan-on-friday-the-transition-to-living-with-endemic-covid-could-be-rough-167218>.

Jennings, Will, Viktor Valgardsson, Gerry Stoker, Dan Devine, Jen Gaskell and Mark Evans. 'Political Trust and the COVID-19 Crisis', *Democracy 2025*, 2020, <www.democracy2025.gov.au/documents/Final%20Pushing%20populism%20to%20the%20backburner.pdf>.

Karp, Paul. 'Scott Morrison and Barnaby Joyce were most unpopular leaders at election since 1987, study shows', *Guardian*, 24 June 2022, <www.theguardian.com/australia-news/2022/jun/24/scott-morrison-and-barnaby-joyce-were-most-unpopular-leaders-at-election-since-1987-study-shows>.

Kelly, Sean. 'Politics doesn't wait: Could Anthony Albanese be missing his chance?' *Sydney Morning Herald*, 16 August 2020, <www.smh.com.au/national/politics-doesn-t-wait-could-anthony-albanese-be-missing-his-chance-20200816-p55m4p.html>.

Martin, Sarah. 'Coalition promises $2bn for bushfire recovery as it walks back from budget surplus pledge', *Guardian*, 6 January 2020, <www.theguardian.com/australia-news/2020/jan/06/coalition-pledges-2bn-for-bushfire-recovery-as-it-walks-back-from-budget-surplus-pledge>.

— 'Scott Morrison insists "every effort" was made to get vaccines, despite Greg Hunt missing Pfizer meeting', *Guardian*, 9 September 2021, <www.theguardian.com/australia-news/2021/sep/09/scott-morrison-insists-every-effort-was-made-to-get-vaccines-despite-greg-hunt-missing-pfizer-meeting>.

Morrison, Scott. Election Speech, Brisbane, 15 May 2022, <electionspeeches.moadoph.gov.au/speeches/2022-scott-morrison>.

Murphy, Katharine and Paul Karp. 'Joel Fitzgibbon calls for changes to Labor's leader selection rules as Albanese finalises reshuffle', *Guardian*, 28 January 2021, <www.theguardian.com/australia-news/2021/jan/28/anthony-albanese-to-bump-mark-butler-out-of-the-climate-portfolio-in-weekend-reshuffle>.

Noyes, Jenny. '"We saw it coming": Former NSW fire chief says government was warned on bushfires', *Sydney Morning Herald*, 14 November 2019, <www.smh.com.au/politics/federal/we-saw-it-coming-former-fire-commissioner-says-government-was-warned-on-bushfires-20191114-p53agj.html>.

AUTHORS

Tully Barnett
Tully Barnett is an Associate Professor in Creative Industries and Director of Assemblage Centre for Creative Arts at Flinders University.

Lain Dare
Lain Dare is a Professor at the University of Canberra's Centre for Environmental Governance.

Emma Dawson
Emma Dawson is the Executive Director of the think tank Per Capita. She has worked as a social policy researcher at both Monash University and the University of Melbourne.

Stephen Duckett
Stephen Duckett is an Honorary Professor at the University of Melbourne and is a former Secretary of the federal Health Department.

Mark Evans
Mark Evans is Deputy Vice-Chancellor (Research) at Charles Sturt University, and the Director of Democracy 2025.

Alan Fenna
Alan Fenna is a Professor at Curtin University, where he researches areas of Australian government and politics, public policy, and comparative federalism.

Stan Grant
Stan Grant is the Vice Chancellor's Chair of Australian/Indigenous Belonging at Charles Sturt University, and a journalist with the ABC.

Michelle Grattan
Michelle Grattan is a Professorial Fellow at the University of Canberra and chief political correspondent at *The Conversation*.

Richard Holden
Richard Holden is Professor of Economics at the University of NSW, and co-author of *From Free to Fair Markets: Liberalism after Covid-19*.

Renée Leon
Renée Leon is the Vice Chancellor of Charles Sturt University and was formerly Secretary of the Department of Human Services and the Department of Employment.

Brendan McCaffrie
Brendan McCaffrie is a Senior Lecturer in the School of Politics, Economics and Society at the University of Canberra.

Julian Meyrick
Julian Meyrick is Professor of Creative Arts at Griffith University, Literary Adviser for the Queensland Theatre and General Editor of Currency House's New Platform Papers series.

Karen Middleton
Karen Middleton is the Chief Political Correspondent for the *Saturday Paper* and author of *Albanese: Telling It Straight*.

Jo Mummery
Jo Mummery is a former Senior Executive with Commonwealth Departments responsible for climate change, and an Adjunct at the Centre for Environmental Governance at the University of Canberra.

Katharine Murphy
Katharine Murphy is Political Editor for the *Guardian Australia* and is author of the *Quarterly* essay *The End of Certainty: Scott Morrison and Pandemic Politics*.

Andrew Norton

Andrew Norton is Professor in the Practice of Higher Education Policy at the Centre for Social Research and Methods at the Australian National University. Previously, he was the Higher Education Program Director at the Grattan Institute from 2011 to 2019. In 2013–14 he was the co-author of a government-commissioned review of the demand-driven student funding system.

Justin O'Connor

Justin O'Connor is a Professor of Cultural Economy at UniSA.

Brenton Prosser

Brenton Prosser is Professor of Public Policy and Leadership, and Director of the Public Partnerships and Impact Hub at UNSW Canberra. He is also the Director of the John Howard Prime Ministerial Library, which is located in Old Parliament House, Canberra.

Matthew Ricketson

Matthew Ricketson is Professor of Communications at Deakin University and co-authored *Who Needs the ABC?: Why taking it for granted is no longer an option.*

Pia Rowe

Pia Rowe is a Senior Research Fellow at the University of Canberra.

Jacki Schirmer

Jacki Schirmer is a Professor for both the Health Research Institute and the Centre for Environmental Governance at the University of Canberra.

Julianne Schultz

Julianne Schultz is a Professor of Media and Culture at Griffith University. She is the author *The Idea of Australia: A search for the soul of the nation* and *Reviving the Fourth Estate: Democracy, accountability and the media.*

Jane Seaborn

Jane Seaborn is the Director of Landscape Research and Communications – a social and market research firm which has a focus on strategic communications.

Darren Sinclair

Darren Sinclair is a Professor and the Director of the Centre for Environmental Governance at the University of Canberra.

Tony Walker

Tony Walker is a Vice-Chancellor's Fellow at La Trobe University, Fellow of the Australian Institute of International Affairs, and a member of both the *The Conversation*'s Board and its Editorial Board.

Chris Wallace

Chris Wallace is a Professor in the University of Canberra's School of Politics, Economics and Society in the Faculty of Business, Government and Law and is author of *How to Win an Election* and *Political Lives: Australian prime ministers and their biographers*.

Geoffrey Watson

Geoffrey Watson is on the Board of Directors for the Centre for Public Integrity. He has appeared as counsel assisting in inquiries investigating corruption allegations.

NOTES

1   The Morrison Government 2019–2022

1   Former staffer Bruce Lehrmann was charged with sexual intercourse without consent. He pleaded not guilty. His 2022 trial was aborted after a juror did their own research, flouting the judge's explicit instructions. A second trial was expected but the ACT Director of Public Prosecutions decided not to proceed after expert medical advice warned of a 'significant and unacceptable risk' to Higgins's life.

4   The Australian Public Service under Morrison

1   As at March 2022.

2   The author was one of the secretaries whose department was abolished and whose appointment was terminated.

3   ASL represents the number of full-time equivalent positions.

4   In 2015–16, the total administered expenditure was forecast to be $434.5 billion. In 2019–20, the first Budget of the Morrison Government, and the last before the COVID-19 pandemic, the total administered expenditure was forecast to be $500.9 billion.

5   The Morrison Government and Australian federalism

1   The two big reforms of those earlier governments had been the Howard Government's introduction of the Goods and Services Tax (GST) commencing 1 July 2000 and the Rudd Government's reform of special-purpose payments to the states, both of which addressed state grievances. The total net proceeds of the GST are hypothecated to the states by the *A New Tax System (Commonwealth–State Financial Arrangements) Act* 1999, passed pursuant to the *Intergovernmental Agreement on the Reform of Commonwealth–State Financial Relations* of that year. Meanwhile, the *Federal Financial Relations Act* 2009 rationalised a large number of specific purpose payments into a handful of block grants (Fenna & Anderson, 2012).

2   The Grants Commission is a Commonwealth Government statutory agency advising the Commonwealth Treasury. Here, 'direct' means that it is achieved by shifting funds directly from one state or territory to another: while the GST revenues are the fruit of a Commonwealth tax, by virtue of their hypothecation they are state and territory funds.

3   Exacerbating the problem was how fluctuations in revenue resulted in the three-year rolling calculation used by the Commonwealth Grants Commission and was bound at some points to penalise the state for windfalls it had received (and typically spent) in previous years.

4   *Treasury Laws Amendment (Making Sure Every State and Territory Gets Their Fair Share of GST) Act.*

5   The 2021–22 budget surplus of $5.7 billion was only kept below the previous year's record surplus of $5.8 billion by declining over $1 billion worth of dividends from state government business enterprises that year (Treasury, 2022, p. 32).

6   The Liberal Party is, of course, not monolithic on the issue.

7   The absence of a carbon tax and the reluctance to commit to significant emissions reductions were the main manifestations of this position.

8   The prime minister wrote to the premier of Western Australian to this effect on 1 August 2020, as case numbers were reaching their peak. Victoria took the unprecedented step of declaring a 'state of disaster' the following day.

9   *Palmer & Anor v. The State of Western Australia & Anor* HCA 5 (6 December 2020). The High Court's first move was to refer the case to the Federal Court to determine the factual matters on which the argument turned: whether the border closures were 'reasonably necessary' and whether there was no 'equally effective' alternative. On 25 August, the Federal Court brought down its finding that they were an appropriate measure, and on that basis the High Court then upheld them as a valid exception to the requirements of section 92.

10   The 47th had been 9 August 2019.

11   *Patrick and Secretary, Department of Prime Minister and Cabinet (Freedom of Information)*, AATA 2719 [2021].

12   COAG Legislation Amendment Bill 2021. See also the Senate Finance and Public Administration Legislation Committee report on the Bill, October 2021.

13   The new arrangement made provision for a COAG-like annual meeting of the first ministers, the treasurers and the president of the Australian Local Government Association – the 'National Federation Reform Council' – and implemented another shake-up of the ministerial council system, this time with an emphasis on imbuing those bodies with the 'agile' character of National Cabinet (see Conran, Peter. *Review of COAG Councils and Ministerial Reforms: Report to National Cabinet*, Commonwealth of Australia, 2020).

11   Higher education

1   Significant numbers of casual staff lost work too, but an accurate number is not available.

17   The battle for a federal integrity commission

1   The 'Greiner affair' was a reference to the resignation of the New South Wales Premier, Nick Greiner, following a finding of corrupt conduct by the state's ICAC. That finding was set aside in a split decision of the NSW Court of Appeal. It is incorrectly cited, as though it reflects an excessive use of power by the NSW ICAC; in truth it is a highly technical decision relating to statutory construction over which the judges and experts have disagreed.

20   Experts and democracy in Australia

1   This chapter is adapted from an article that originally appeared in the April–June 2021 edition of *AQ: Australian Quarterly*.

21   A deep dive into 'teal' territory

1   For a comprehensive account of the community independents movement, see Brook Turner, *Independents' Day: The inside story of the community independents and volunteers who changed Australian politics forever*, Allen & Unwin, 2022; and Simon Holmes à Court, *The Big Teal: In the national interest*, Monash University Publishing, 2022.

2   Statistical research for the first of these reports was also conducted by Max Halupka, University of Canberra.

22 Scott Morrison's crisis leadership

1   Boin et al (2005) also include a range of other public crisis leadership challenges (decision-making, delimitation, consolidation, accountability, learning, remembering), which are out of scope for this chapter.

INDEX

Other titles in the Australian Commonwealth Administration series

Kouzmin, Alexander, John R Nethercote and Roger Wettenhall (eds).
Australian Commonwealth Administration 1983: Essays in Review,
School of Administrative Studies, Canberra College of Advanced
Education in association with ACT Division, Royal Australian
Institute of Public Administration, Canberra, 1984.

Nethercote, John R, Alexander Kouzmin and Roger Wettenhall (eds).
Australian Commonwealth Administration 1984: Essays in Review, School
of Administrative Studies, Canberra College of Advanced Education
in association with ACT Division, Royal Australian Institute of Public
Administration, Canberra, 1986.

Wettenhall, Roger and John R Nethercote (eds). *Hawke's Second
Government: Australian Commonwealth Administration 1984–1987*,
School of Management, Canberra College of Advanced Education, and
ACT Division, Royal Australian Institute of Public Administration,
Canberra, 1988.

Halligan, John and Roger Wettenhall (eds). *Hawke's Third Government:
Australian Commonwealth Administration 1987–1990*, School of
Management, Canberra College of Advanced Education, and ACT
Division, Royal Australian Institute of Public Administration, Canberra,
1992.

Stewart, Jenny (ed). *From Hawke to Keating: Australian Commonwealth
Administration 1990–1993*, Centre for Research in Public Sector
Management, University of Canberra, and Royal Institute of Public
Administration Australia, Canberra, 1995.

Singleton, Gwynneth (ed). *The Second Keating Government: Australian
Commonwealth Administration 1993–1996*, Centre for Research in
Public Sector Management, University of Canberra, and Royal Institute
of Public Administration Australia, Canberra, 1997.

Singleton, Gwynneth (ed). The *Howard Government: Australian Commonwealth Administration 1996–1998*, UNSW Press, Sydney, 2000.

Aulich, Chris and Roger Wettenhall (eds). *Howard's Second and Third Governments: Australian Commonwealth Administration 1998–2004*, UNSW Press, Sydney, 2005.

Aulich, Chris and Roger Wettenhall (eds). *Howard's Fourth Government: Australian Commonwealth Administration 2004–2007*, UNSW Press, Sydney, 2008.

Aulich, Chris and Mark Evans (eds). *The Rudd Government: Australian Commonwealth Administration 2007–2010*, ANU e-Press, Canberra, 2010.

Aulich, Chris (ed). *The Gillard Governments: Australian Commonwealth Administration 2010–2013*, Melbourne University Press, Melbourne, 2014.

Aulich, Chris (ed). *From Abbott to Turnbull: a New Direction?*, Echo Books, Geelong West, 2016.

Evans, Mark, Michelle Grattan, and Brendan McCaffrie (ed.). *From Turnbull to Morrison: The Trust Divide*, Melbourne University Press, Carlton, 2019.

www.ingramcontent.com/pod-product-compliance
Lightning Source LLC
Chambersburg PA
CBHW021211270326
41929CB00038B/1304

9 781742 237886